TEEN
TORMENT

TEEN TORMENT

Overcoming Verbal Abuse
at Home and at School

PATRICIA EVANS
Author of *The Verbally Abusive Relationship*

Adams Media Corporation
Avon, Massachusetts

Published by Adams Media Corporation
57 Littlefield Street, Avon, MA 02322
www.adamsmedia.com

ISBN: 1-58062-845-1
Printed in Canada.

J I H G F E D C B A

Library of Congress Cataloging-in-Publication Data
Evans, Patricia.
Teen torment / by Patricia Evans.
p.   cm.
Includes bibliographical references.
ISBN 1-58062-845-1
1. Youth and violence. 2. Verbal self-defense. 3. Invective.
4. Criticism, Personal. 5. Psychological abuse. 6. Aggressiveness in
adolescence. 7. Self-esteem. 8. Teenagers--Conduct of life. I. Title.
HQ799.2.V56 E9 2003
303.6'0835--dc21
2002014292

This publication is designed to provide accurate and authoritative information
with regard to the subject matter covered. It is sold with the understanding that
the publisher is not engaged in rendering legal, accounting, or other professional advice. If legal advice or other expert assistance is required, the services
of a competent professional person should be sought.
—From a *Declaration of Principles* jointly adopted by a Committee of the
American Bar Association and a Committee of Publishers and Associations

Many of the designations used by manufacturers and sellers to distinguish
their products are claimed as trademarks. Where those designations appear in
this book and Adams Media was aware of a trademark claim, the designations
have been printed with initial capital letters.

This book is available at quantity discounts for bulk purchases.
For information, call 1-800-872-5627.

Contents

PART TWO: WHERE VERBAL ABUSE SHOWS UP/85

PART THREE: WHAT CAN WE DO ABOUT IT?/161

Acknowledgments

Thanks to my publisher, Adams Media, and its great staff, who helped to bring this book into print. Particularly, I appreciate the support of my editor, Tracy Quinn McLennan, who made it happen; Kate McBride, Managing Editor; and Laura MacLaughlin, Copy Chief, who pulled it together; as well as Carrie Lewis McGraw, Publicity Director, who patiently waited for it as she made plans to launch it.

Many people contributed to this book with ideas, information, time, and energy. My gratitude and thanks to Linda Catron, who, as a great friend, read copy and listened endlessly. I am indebted to Rick Lewis, Training Coordinator, Safe Schools, FL, who contributed his expertise in bringing about win/win outcomes, as well as his empathy for and understanding of teens. Thanks to Dindy Fuller, Betsy Sweetland, and Debbie Brown for their insights into the teen world.

A special thank-you also to Chuck Barney, TV critic for the *Contra Costa Times* newspaper, who gave me his time and perspective in a very helpful interview about TV media. Also, thanks to writer Sharon Salyer with *The Herald* in Everett, WA, who knows about teens and teen violence and shared her thoughts.

Introduction

THIS BOOK IS FOR EVERYONE: PARENTS, TEACHERS, TEENS, and, of course, anyone who once was a teen!

If you are a teen, it is likely some of you are helping your parents navigate the Internet or are convincing them that you need a computer to do your homework. Whether this is true of you or not, I believe that you will find this book easy to read and not at all as complex as some of the work you have already done. If you find it helpful or want to give me your input, please let me know. Just click on "contact" at *www.VerbalAbuse.com*.

If you are a parent, grandparent, teacher, relative, friend of a teen, or are just around teens now and then, I hope you will find the suggestions and perspectives you find here an adjunct to your support of the teens in your life. This book may also shed new light on your own younger years. Possibly, you will have an even deeper appreciation of your own resilience, fortitude, and strength, having survived the challenges of those years without this book.

I believe that, if you so choose, together we can stop verbal abuse in its tracks and overcome the code of silence around verbal abuse. We can, at least in the near future, reverse the momentum of an ever-increasing problem. One word at a time, one school at a time, one teen at a time, this can be done.

The problem of verbal abuse is endemic in our schools, just as it is in our culture. Thousands of my readers ask me what to do about it, especially after they come to the realization that verbal abuse is a lot more than name-calling. The problem of verbal abuse (people defining people) has accelerated over time. In some cases, it has led to such violence in schools that it has come to the attention of the media. Millions of adults, both teachers and parents, either don't know exactly what it is, or, knowing that it's abuse, don't know what to do about it. The mental anguish of the child—taunted, disparaged, criticized, tormented, and ostracized—is immeasurable.

Countless children, teens, and adults endure mental anguish and emotional pain while having no name for their experience and few tools to deal with it. Many people are discouraged from objecting to verbal abuse and are even trained to perceive themselves as weak or flawed if they feel the emotional pain that verbal abuse engenders. In fact, mentally wrestling with this impossible concept—how to "not feel" painful assaults—is one of the causes of their mental anguish.

I have talked with thousands of people who found themselves, at one time or another, baffled or brainwashed by verbal abuse. They did not know just what verbal abuse was, or why they often felt hurt by what they were told, or how to deal with it. As if in one voice, they said, "Why wasn't I taught this sooner? This should be taught in every school." Their heartfelt longing for clarity and an end to the acceptance of verbal abuse encouraged me. In fact, I would not have written *Teen Torment* if these people had not so often said, "I wish someone had told me that when I was a teen."

Although some readers may say, "I survived verbal abuse in my own childhood, and I'm doing fine," I hope that they will ask themselves, "Where would I be if it hadn't happened to me? What potential might I have realized? Did I become a better person for having had to survive it? Might the experience of verbal abuse in my own youth have impacted my relationships today?"

Although people subjected to verbal abuse can recover, the confusion, pain, and loss are beyond measuring. Childhood anguish can, however, count for something: It can be transformed into the passion and determination needed to take a stand against verbal abuse and for awareness and life. This stance can be put to good use, to bring awareness, to save countless others from the relentless erosion of their self-perception, their personal reality, their minds.

It is so important to identify verbal abuse and confront it for what it is, that this book is entirely devoted to teaching parents, teachers, teens, and anyone who was a teen, how to see what verbal abuse really is, to understand why it happens, and to confront it appropriately. If you are a teen reading this book, I suggest that you use it for discussion with your friends and parents. It is meant to be a guide that will serve you the rest of your life.

Verbal abuse impacts people's spirits like radiation impacts their bodies. It can be unseen, insidious, destructive, enervating, and, because it creates enormous stress, one way or another, it can be a killer. Battering the spirit, verbal abuse attempts to destroy the dreams, potential, and even the reality of its victims.

The cases and schools in this book are all real, though, with the exception of public news events, the names and details are changed. Throughout this book, I will refer to the person who indulges in verbal abuse as the "abuser" or "perpetrator." This is not meant to define or label the person as not a "person." Instead, it is used to describe, in shorthand, "the person who indulges in verbal abuse in specific verbally abusive interactions or in general." I will refer to the recipient of the verbal abuse, or the person or persons to whom it is aimed, as the "target" or "victim." This is not meant to define the person as accepting of the abuse or as less than a person. Overall, in this book, to "define someone" is to tell them what they are, think, feel, and so forth.

Part One

About Verbal Abuse

PART ONE PRESENTS THE PROBLEM OF VERBAL ABUSE AMONG TEENS. It shows how little understood it is, considering the enormous consequences of verbal abuse to developing minds and emotional lives. We see that defining others in numerous ways assaults rationality and freedom, and may lead to violence against self or others.

Chapters in Part I explain what verbal abuse is and why it is rejecting of our individuality. We find out why it is not okay and explore the teen world in which it thrives, as well as its impact on the millions of people it assaults.

Chapter I

What Is Verbal Abuse?

IF YOU HAVE EVER HEARD SOMETHING SAID TO YOU OR ABOUT YOU that, if believed, would lead you to assume that you are less than you are, different from whom you know yourself to be, or even not who you are, you have heard verbal abuse. If you have heard, "You're too sensitive," you've heard verbal abuse.

When verbal abuse occurs in school or among teens, it is commonly called *dissing*. When physical assault or intrusion accompanies verbal abuse, or is directed toward a child by an older teen or an adult, it is called *bullying*. When verbal abuse occurs over a period of time (more than a sudden outburst), it is called *harassment*.

BOBBY'S STORY

Bobby, age fifteen, stood frozen—immobilized as a deer caught in the headlights of an oncoming car. All color had drained from his face. He was staring at his mother.

Bobby was in shock, but he hadn't just witnessed some great catastrophe or heard some serious bad news. He was in his own home, in his room—a safe place. Bobby was impacted by truth. His mother had just told him something that changed his life forever.

While Bobby was struck dumb, his younger brother, Danny, who had been playing a computer game nearby, also heard the same news, but he handled it differently. He blew off what he heard, rolled his eyes, and said, "Yeah, sure, Mom, like you expect me to believe that. You've got to be kidding!"

Their mother, Susan, wasn't kidding. In recent months, she had come out of a kind of daze, one she had been in since childhood. And, she'd just shared her latest discovery with her sons. "Guess what, guys," she'd said. "Most dads, probably at least 80 percent, don't call their sons "stupid" and "idiot," don't wake them in the morning with shouting and ridicule, like, 'Wake up, dummy!'"

Susan had come to the realization that what went on in her household was not normal. Just to be sure, she had surveyed dozens of soccer moms, car-pool moms, neighbor moms, and moms who volunteered with her at her sons' schools.

"Does your husband call your kids 'stupid,' or 'idiot,' or 'wimp,' just about every day? At baseball games, does he say, 'You throw like a girl!' to your son?" she had asked.

All the moms had responded in pretty much the same way: "Uh, no . . . why?" But almost before they could finish their question, she explained that she was taking a survey about verbal abuse.

At some level, of course, they were getting the message that verbal abuse was happening in Susan's home. And they

4

could hardly believe it. Susan's husband was very, very high up on the socioeconomic ladder of success, and he seemed so nice.

Most parents, like those Susan surveyed, would likely answer no to her question. Most people do not indulge in name-calling. Most people are not that overt. Even parents who are unaware of some of their children's needs or are, in some ways, insensitive to them know that calling children names just isn't the thing to do. They learned this from their families and communities. Susan was not so fortunate.

I'll refer to Bobby's story again because it exemplifies many cases where I have suggested that my client conduct her own research to gain clarity about verbal abuse.

THE PATTERNS OF VERBAL ABUSE

Verbal abuse often shows up in a pattern of behavior in which a teen, for instance, attempts to undermine, or dominate, or intimidate another teen by using verbal methods, or even by deliberately withholding an appropriate response.

Although verbal abuse now permeates our culture, it is often a multigenerational pattern that is passed down from parent to child and first shows up at the beginning of adolescence or even earlier.

When teens indulge in verbal abuse, they define the target not only with words, but also with a defining attitude. Usually this is an attitude of superiority. For example, a teen might try to put down someone while projecting disdain, or while conveying an air of authority over him or her.

Verbal abuse is usually launched at someone when they least expect it. The shock sometimes leaves the target speechless. Sometimes, too, it can be so subtle that it is difficult to know how to respond.

Have You Experienced Verbal Abuse?

Verbal abuse is a lot more than name-calling. Let us look at some of the ways that people experience it, keeping in mind that a person is not necessarily a "verbal abuser" because he or she indulges in a rare harsh word that is followed by an apology.

Knowing what is abusive is the first step toward eliminating it as a behavior that harms people. Here are some of the ways you might have experienced verbal abuse.

Have you ever been:

- Taunted with repeated mean comments?
- Ostracized or snubbed by anyone?
- Ignored with the silent treatment?
- Accused with "You _____" statements?
- Blamed, especially by the person abusing you?
- Diminished as if you or what you do is worthless?
- Defined, especially by a name someone calls you?
- Put down in a pretend joke?
- Silenced by shocking words?
- Ordered around without being asked or agreeing to take orders?
- Belittled as if you were stupid or a baby?
- Threatened with loss or harm?
- Criticized for how you look?
- Cut with sarcasm?
- Ridiculed?

Clearly, there are many ways that teens and adults define people. We've looked at most of them. Some are very obvious, like name-calling and taunting, and some are subtler, like giving someone the silent treatment or pretending a putdown is a joke.

If, in childhood, you heard one of your parents verbally abuse your other parent or both parents verbally abuse each other, the event may have impacted you as if you, too, were abused. Although you may not know how you were affected, it is possible your sense of trust in the future and in other people was diminished. According to a study at the University of Maryland in 1998, hearing verbal aggression between parents is more traumatic to children than observing physical abuse. Possibly this is so, because when someone defines someone they are attempting to mess with their mind and to eliminate or erase the real person. Witnessing this is very painful.

Name-calling is obviously defining. A name defines you as something different from a person. Less obviously, other kinds of verbal abuse define you because they define your thoughts, feelings, motives, and so forth. Here are a few examples.

How Verbal Abuse Defines You

The following examples show how verbal abuse defines you by *lying* to you. Verbal abuse tells you:

Who you are: "You're the teacher's pet."
What you are: "You're a wimp."
How you are: "You're too sensitive."
What you are trying to do: "You're just trying to be right."
What you think: "You think you're so smart."
What you say: "Now you're saying I don't care."
What you want: "You want everything your way."
How you feel: "You've got nothing to cry about."
How you experience pain: "You're not hurt."
What your motives are: "You're just trying to get attention."
What your future will be: "You'll never amount to anything."
What to do: "Just get over it."

Verbal abuse also defines and denigrates your humanity
when it:

- *Ridicules you:* "Has the cat got your tongue?"
- *Mimics you:* "Ooh, 'im just can't 'member his 'omework."
- *Infantilizes you:* "First you pick up the pencil, then you hold it in your hand, then you put the point on the paper."
- *Disparages you:* "When I see you, I see trailer trash."
- *Discounts you:* "No one cares what you think."

Verbal abuse is in the silence that looks through you as if you don't exist. Withholding an appropriate response is as hurtful as an abusive one, and so is a category of verbal abuse.

WHAT IS HEALTHY AND WHAT IS NOT

If someone hears verbal abuse often enough, they may think it is normal. This is especially true of teens who might have heard verbal abuse in early childhood as well as in the media. They may not have had enough life experience with nonabusive people to compare and evaluate abusive and nonabusive behaviors. In other words, they do not know what is normal, healthy behavior and what is not.

In Bobby's Story, Bobby and Danny didn't know what abuse was. Bobby was shocked to realize that this behavior wasn't okay, or at least wasn't the norm. If he hadn't been wounded by the names his father called him, I don't believe the news would have stunned him. Danny, the younger boy, didn't believe it and didn't want to, possibly because he felt he *was* a "dummy," or, even worse, maybe his dad was lying and being mean.

Sometimes teens and even preteens hear or indulge in verbal abuse so often at school that they think it is just a normal way of talking. When later they try to form a boyfriend-girlfriend relationship, or when they get a job, they find out that the relationship or the job does not work out. They have trouble getting along with others; they have many fights; they find themselves caught up in a situation where they feel increasingly wounded; they escape the pain of verbal abuse with drugs, alcohol, or compulsive behaviors; or they develop eating disorders. *All along, they haven't recognized that their sense of self was distorted by what they were told about themselves.*

Teens don't expect to end up with any of these problems. Nor do they expect to be confused about their talents and abilities, or to be caught up in a relationship that suddenly becomes abusive. No one does! But, without a clear understanding of what verbal abuse is, millions of people do find themselves in one or more of these situations.

COMMUNICATIONS NOT TAUGHT IN SCHOOL

One reason Bobby's and Danny's father, James, called his children names, I learned, was that no one had pointed out to him that his verbally abusive behaviors were unacceptable. And, although he was highly educated, he had not even acquired the basics of interpersonal communications, much less parenting skills.

James was like most people who indulge in verbal abuse. He did not know why he put his sons down, nor did he know the impact of his words. He had not been taught how to communicate truthfully and clearly, not in the schools he had attended, and certainly not at home. And he never thought about the fact that every time he called his sons names, he was, of course, lying to them.

Although students and teachers are communicating all day long, most schools don't teach students the most basic differences between acceptable and unacceptable comments, intrusive and nonintrusive remarks, sensible and senseless statements, and what is actually "pretend" talk versus real talk. Education about the harmful effects of verbal abuse, the irrationality of it, what it reveals about the person indulging in it, is sadly lacking. There is only an occasional glimmer of light on the subject.

If the issue of verbal abuse, and why people indulge in it, were discussed in an informative and helpful way in schools as well as in homes, teens and the world as a whole would benefit enormously.

On the other hand, when teens and others indulge in verbal abuse, if no one calls them on it or pays attention to it, they gain tacit agreement from bystanders, as well as dominance over a target.

LINDY'S STORY

Sixteen-year-old Lindy, just home from school, came running into her house, calling, "Mom, Mom. Oh, there you are. Guess what, Mom. I know what Jane is doing. It's in this book; it's called verbal abuse."

Lindy's textbook from her high school health class had just one small paragraph referring to verbal abuse. But it was enough for Lindy to not only give a name to her classmate Jane's behavior, but also, with the term "abuse," to realize this meant Jane's behavior was wrong. So, it was not Lindy's fault that Jane often put her down in very sarcastic ways. Lindy did not have some basic flaw. Lindy did not have to explain herself to Jane, because Jane had mistreated her. Soon Lindy realized that this is what abuse means. What Jane did was not okay, despite the fact that many people saw it, pretended it was not happening, or acted like it was nothing. It was something. It was abuse and it was hurtful.

Pretending can be fun. You might remember having a good time playing pretend. But, pretending is only fun when both people agree on the game. Playing pretend with a friend might have been like this. Your friend said, "Let's pretend you're the bad guy!" Sometimes you might have said, "Okay." Other times your friend might have wanted you to pretend to be the bad guy, and, since you didn't want to, you'd say, "No, I don't want to pretend to be the bad guy today." In verbal abuse, the pretending is one-way and done entirely without your permission.

VERBAL ABUSE IS PRETEND TALK

Generally speaking, verbal abuse attempts to erase your perceptions and replace them with pretend ones. It is easy to see how this takes place when we think of name-calling. When a person is called stupid, verbal abuse attempts to erase his or her self-perception and to replace it with something "made up."

People may define you in many ways. But, when they do, they are always pretending that you are not who you are, or that you are not the self that you know yourself to be. Making up things about you and pretending that they are true is a kind of crazy talk. When little children indulge in it—"you're a garbage head"—one might laugh, but when peers or authority figures do it, it hurts because these people are rejecting the real you. Even refusing to respond to you is a kind of verbal abuse.

Verbal abuse is a lot more than name-calling. It is also a way of pretending. When people indulge in verbal abuse and direct their words at you, or even withhold appropriate responses, they are pretending. We'll look now at some examples of verbally abusive statements, seeing how they are "pretend talk." People who indulge in verbal abuse may pretend in any of the following ways.

- They may walk away while you are in a conversation with them, pretending that you are nonexistent. On campus, teens frequently form cliques, groups that pretend that other people and groups don't exist.

- They may tell you what you think, pretending to know *your* very own thoughts; for example, "You think you're so smart." Even older teens may pretend to know what someone is thinking.

- They may tell you about your perceptions, pretending to know what you hear; for example, "You're not listening." This pretending is most prevalent among teachers and parents who may really want to know why a teen doesn't understand or respond. No one can really know if another person is listening. One can only ask ("Are you listening?") or state a complaint ("It doesn't look like you're listening—are you?"), or make a request ("Will you please look at me while I'm talking?"), or clarify ("Do you understand what I'm saying?").

- They may tell you about your intentions, pretending to know your motives; for example, "You're just trying to start a fight." This kind of pretending is often used in boyfriend-girlfriend relationships when one party doesn't want to discuss something the other party has asked or complained about.

- They may tell you what you say, pretending that you said what you didn't say, "Now you're saying I'm . . . " Teens, who don't want to ask what someone means or to hear what someone has to say, will often pretend that someone has said something they didn't say.

They may tell you about your future, pretending to know your potentials and abilities; for example, "You'll never add up to anything." Parents who try to control teens through assigning guilt might say something like, "You'll be the death of me yet."

IS INTERRUPTING PRETENDING?

If someone asks you if you would please be quiet or please let him or her finish, they're usually asking for a specific reason: to finish talking, or to hear something, or to let someone sleep. Most people feel okay about meeting this kind of request.

However, no one wants to be interrupted when they are talking. If someone almost always interrupts you without nicely requesting a chance to speak, they are likely pretending, either that you weren't talking, or that you don't exist, or that what you say is worthless, or that you said something completely different from what you said. Other than that, they may have heard a pause and interpreted it to mean that you were finished speaking. A simple, "I'm not finished," allows you to go on.

There is one general rule about interrupting. It is okay to interrupt abuse. People don't feel okay about letting someone define them or pretend something about them. Interrupting people who are verbally abusing you is not abusive. A good goal is: Interrupt verbal abuse.

DIVERTING

Some teens and some adults use diverting when they don't want to answer a question. Diverting is a form of verbal abuse that can be stopped by not responding to it and by interrupting the flow of conversation to ask the question again. Asking the question again is not abusive.

Here is an example of diverting.

JACK DIVERTS JILL

Jack is sixteen years old and Jill is fifteen. They've gone on dates for about six months. A weekend is coming up.

Jill nicely asks, "Do you have any plans for tomorrow?"

Jack, sounding irritated, says, "What do you mean, plans? Do I have to have plans?"

"Well, no, I thought it might be fun to go on a bike ride and take a picnic," says Jill, explaining herself.

"Well, why didn't you just say so?" says Jack.

"I did, just now," Jill says.

Jack is angry and says, "Now you're trying to start a fight."

"But, I'm not," Jill says.

Jack says, "Would you just quit arguing? We'll go biking if that's what you want!"

Jill and Jack did go on the bike ride, but Jill felt really lousy for a while. She was trying to be nice when she suggested the bike ride. Jack just got mad, and she couldn't get through to him. She was confused.

Can you see how easy it would be to try to explain yourself, like Jill did? If you respond by explaining to someone who makes up something about you, they get the message that it's perfectly okay to make something up to divert you. Jack pretended like he didn't know what "plans" meant when he said, "What do you mean, plans?" and he pretended that Jill expected, or wanted, him to have plans, when he angrily said, "Do I have to have plans?"

Jill answered Jack as if he was rational, like he was not pretending. She acted as if being diverted is okay. But it's not. If she had repeated her question, "Do you have any plans for tomorrow?" until she got an answer, Jack might eventually have answered her. Instead, she was diverted and sucked into Jack's pretend world. She was diverted into explaining.

Later, we'll see why Jack diverted Jill and why he would even want to divert her and avoid answering her question. This book will explain the pretend world that Jack was in and how, when people make up things about you, they are, in a certain respect, in a separate world—and they don't know it. Since they don't realize it, we might say they are under a spell. We'll see why people pretend all kinds of things and look at the fears that drive them.

The spell is like a powerful illusion that leads a person to believe things about another person that are not real. When generations of people pass behaviors on to other generations without explanation, especially when these behaviors don't work or hurt others, it's as if people are under a spell cast by an evil wizard a long time ago. No one can remember the wizard or why the spell was cast, but they just go on without questioning it.

I would like to emphasize that it is very easy to be sucked into a pretend world like Jack's. If the "Jack and Jill" scenario seems complicated, please read it over a few times.

Jack in this story isn't necessarily a bad person. He simply lives in a pretend world that is so real to him that he makes up things. People who behave as Jack did are exceptionally confusing to teens. They are often older or in a position of authority, so most teens think they are rational and, like Jill, they try to respond with reasonable explanations.

Teens and others who attempt to define you may persist when you object or they may become angry if you won't be quiet and accept their definition of you. They may also blame you for their anger, and in a strange way really believe you made them angry.

People who flagrantly assess you, your motives, and your potential in limiting ways are often so limited themselves that they can't even recognize fine qualities! Adults who look back on their teen years (or even some current relationships) have generally found this to be the case.

GANGING UP AGAINST
Teens who habitually indulge in verbal abuse often try to get other people to join with them in pretending something about another

person or a group of people. Teens experience this when two or three kids gang up against them, label them, verbally abuse them, or ostracize them.

It is important to understand how dangerous ganging up against others is. Two of the worst, most horrifying and notorious, cases of people pretending to know something about others and getting people to join them are that of Hitler and Bin Laden. Hitler defined the men, women, and children of Jewish and certain other heritages as not really people, as faulted and not worthy of being on planet Earth. Bin Laden and his terrorist network have defined the people of America and certain other nationalities similarly. Both Hitler and Bin Laden got people to bond with them against other people, and even got people to kill people whom they (Hitler and Bin Laden) defined.

VERBAL ABUSE THREATENS FREEDOM

When teens indulge in verbal abuse by threatening you, or by ordering you around, they clearly attempt to take away your freedom. They may even say that they have a right to order you rather than ask you. They cannot ask you, because they do not want to recognize you as a real person and an equal. Older teens sometimes order younger teens, "Get out of my way" or, "Shut up." Or bigger teens order around smaller teens, backing up their orders with physical threat because of their larger size.

Verbal abuse can also threaten freedom in another way. If kids who indulge in verbal abuse can influence you to doubt yourself and to think that you are not valuable, you may not make good decisions for yourself; for instance, you might limit your goals because you can't see yourself as able and worthy.

Shockingly, a bright, tall, and handsome thirteen-year-old boy told me that because one of his ears was formed differently, he had been ridiculed his whole school life. "My torment began in kindergarten," he said. "What did kids say?" I asked. "They called me a freak and an alien, from then on, all through school," he said. There were no counselors or teachers to work with his classmates to help them overcome their fear of difference. And there still aren't.

Very often it is the most unique child, the one with unique gifts, that is singled out for abuse simply because he or she is different. To be punished for the way you were born is a terrible thing.

As children grow into early adolescence, they are already making up how things are. If they begin in fear of difference, they can end up creating a separate world. It is because of their fears and the pretend world they make, that they try to erase the real world and real people's perceptions by telling them what they are. They may become so used to making up what is and what isn't, that if you object, they may tell you that what just happened did not happen—that what you just heard wasn't said. That is denial.

DENIAL IS ABUSIVE

When someone denies what they have just said, or the impact of their statements, they are automatically denying truth, as well as the other person's experience. Denial is verbally abusive. Denials define others because they are full of accusation and blame. Let's look at some examples of blaming denial.

- You're making it up.
- You're making trouble.
- You did it.
- You're talking back.
- You're just trying to get out of it.
- You're making a big deal out of nothing.
- You're looking for trouble.
- You're crazy.

- That never happened.
- I never said that.

When you bring up something that bothers you about what you have heard, even when the person you are talking to isn't sure he or she said it, it is not okay for him or her to simply deny your perceptions or to deny that the incident occurred.

There can be misunderstandings in normal conversation. If you tell someone that something he or she said bothers you, he or she may respond by:

A. Denying the incident.
B. Apologizing for the incident.
C. Asking you about the incident.

A is not okay! *B* is a common and healthy response. So, too, is *C.* Very often people say things that they don't recall a moment later, or they say something that they think is funny, but you, the listener, thinks is hurtful. Asking is a healthy way to resolve the issue. For instance, "What bothered you about that?" or "How did it sound? Maybe it came out wrong."

VERBAL ABUSERS ARE UNDER A SPELL

When people chronically indulge in verbal abuse, when they are pretending and are in a pretend world, they seem unable or unwilling to speak truthfully. In fact, it can be said that they are under a spell that is both toxic and contagious. This "spell" stops real communication about real events and real people. People who have to deal with spellbound people can't seem to get through to them. The spell removes awareness. It intrudes where it is not wanted. The spell stops people from noticing how they *really feel*. It stops people from expressing their true selves. Sometimes it only descends when certain people are around the spellbound person. Usually the verbal abuser only targets certain people.

Although there will be more about the pretend world and the spell in coming chapters, it deserves a bit of discussion here. What we've seen so far is that, people who indulge in verbal abuse have created a pretend world in their own minds. But it is important to know that *they may not seem to be spellbound around people they want to impress.*

SAYING IT IS SO, MAKES IT SO

In terms of kids who indulge in verbal abuse, the pretend world seems so real to them that they make up who and what people are and seem to believe their illusions. To them, *saying it's so, makes it so.* They feel secure in their pretend world. That is why I describe them as being under a spell or spellbound. Leaving their pretend world would, in a sense, leave them adrift, disconnected from everything. It is like the pretend world is the only world they know.

For more information about the spell, how people become spellbound, and why spellbound people become controlling, please read my book, *Controlling People.*[1]

Here is an example of how the spell works. If someone—I'll call him Lee—stepped in front of me while I was standing in line, I might say, "Hey, what are you doing? I was here." But if I were under a spell in some fantasy or pretend world where no one ever stepped in front of me, I might irrationally make up who and what Lee is, and pretend to know his motives without asking. I might say something like, "Hey! You dork. You're looking for a fight." In other words, I might be influenced by the spell to pretend that Lee is not a person and that I know his intentions. By pretending that Lee is something other than who he is, and telling him what he is and what he is trying to do, I would be acting spellbound, and I would be indulging in verbal abuse.

Pretending to erase the real Lee—by telling him what he is (a dork) and what he is trying to do (his motives)—would be abusive.

Lee might say, "Hey, where'd you come from? Don't be calling me names." If I answered, "I was here, and you took my place," I would be telling the truth and being real. Lee could respond, in a real way, "I didn't see you. Here's your place. And don't call me names." If I responded with an apology, "I'm sorry I called you that," I would have fended off the spell. But, if I told him the opposite of his experience, "You *did too* try to get in front of me," I would be pretending to know his motives. I would be talking in an irrational way. I would be acting spellbound.

THE PRETEND WORLD

People may say things in anger before they know if there is anything to be angry about. After all, in their pretend world, their people never make a mistake. Their pretend world is perfect. People are more likely to become spellbound and to create a pretend world if they grow up around people who cross their boundaries a lot. People who cross other people's boundaries are people who act as if they live within others, know their experience, and can tell them what they are. If I grew up around such spellbound people, I might immediately think the worst of Lee and think nothing of pretending to know why he stood where he did. I might assume he intended to take my place. People most often indulge in verbal abuse when their vision of how things should be and how certain people should be, is disturbed. This disturbance is what shows that they are spellbound.

If Lee had said, "Well I'm here now and you can't make me move; I don't care what you say," I would need to respond in a completely different way. Lee would have taken my physical space in the line. Chapter V discusses this kind of actual transgression.

Almost everyone can recall a time when he or she just felt angry and got into an argument and "lost it." We may say things that are not true of someone, and we end up feeling very uncomfortable about it. Saying harsh things leaves everyone disturbed. It is not a situation most people are comfortable with, so they try to stay cool and be civil in their dealings with others. If they've been abusive, most people try to resolve the problem by apologizing.

Learning to apologize and not make assumptions can keep the spell of verbal abuse away and can protect us from making up a pretend world. Asking first, "Did you know this was my place in line?" can keep the spell from descending at all.

EXPLAINING DOESN'T WORK

Many people grew up thinking that if what someone was saying to them was not name-calling or swearing, it was not verbal abuse. Many people thought that if a parent, older person, authority figure, or person who was supposed to love them, defined them in some negative way, then maybe it was true. Maybe they *were* too sensitive, maybe they weren't listening, maybe their opinions were wrong, maybe they shouldn't even have opinions. On the other hand, many other people knew that what they were told about themselves wasn't true. They knew they weren't, for instance, too sensitive, or looking for trouble, but *they believed that they could and should convince the person who defined them that what he or she said wasn't true. This rarely, if ever, is possible.*

VERBAL ABUSE IS NONSENSE

People who indulge in verbal abuse want to keep *real* people out of their pretend world. They want to turn real people into pretend people. *They feel they have succeeded if they can get the real person to try to explain him- or herself.* If the real person tries to explain and argue against what the abuser is saying, the real person is acting as if the abuser's world *is* the real world, instead of a pretend one. It is a "win" for the abuser because he or she has gotten someone to take his or her pretend world seriously.

It is better to say, "Nonsense!" to verbal abuse (since it is nonsense) than to try to deal with the abuser in a logical way. In other words, explaining why something said to you is wrong doesn't keep the verbal abuser from abusing you. When people indulge in verbal abuse, they are not being logical. They are being irrational. Verbal abuse is all pretend talk.

Another reason not to try to explain yourself (for example, "I'm not stupid, I've got a high IQ score"), is that abusers love to win against all explanations and arguments. They love to "prove" that real people are wrong. *In the abuser's pretend world, no one who is different can be right, because only the abuser can be right!* In the pretend world, if you are different, you *have* to be wrong! And, if you don't say or do exactly what the abuser thinks you should say or do in his or her perfect pretend world, you are wrong!

AS IF YOU WERE NOT YOU

When people are caught up in a pretend world, verbal abuse may take over their lives. They may indulge in verbal abuse on a regular basis. Their "pretend world" is usually so real to them that they cannot or will not let the real world, truth, in. That is why they tell people who they are and how they should be, and get angry when other people do not act like they want them to act. And, most especially in the teen years, habitual verbal abusers particularly abuse people who are different. Since they have made up a pretend world that includes them, they do not want to see anyone who looks different. It is as if they feel that they have made themselves up best and so anyone who is different is not equal and should not exist, at least not happily. This is why verbal abuse defines people as *not who they are.*

Thinking about it, we know that no one lives inside another person, so no one knows our inner world. But when someone tells us who we are or how we feel, or anything else about our inner world, our identity, how we do what we do, or how successful we'll be, most of us feel as if we want to set them straight, correct them, or give them an explanation. In other words, we want to talk to them as if they were in the real world with us. But they are in a pretend world.

The verbally abusive comments discussed above can be magnified in their intensity and impact by the abuser's tone of voice and gestures such as eye rolling, head shaking, smirking, or mimicking. Additionally, the level of the abuser's anger or coldness contributes to the abusive nature of the comments.

Chapter II

Why Verbal Abuse Isn't Okay

IF ASKED ABOUT VERBAL ABUSE, I BELIEVE THAT MOST PEOPLE WOULD say it is not okay, but, if it is obviously not okay, why do so many people ignore it, condone it, laugh at it as if it is clever, or indulge in it? Why don't families discuss it with their children, asking if they have heard it at school, if it has happened to them, to their friends, or to other teens? Why isn't it an occasional topic in all classrooms?

Verbal abuse isn't okay because it devalues people, is an inadequate and even infantile way of attempting to make others be the way one pretends they should be, and is indulged in for many negative reasons; for instance, perpetrators want to appear superior, important, and dominant over others. They want to look smarter, funnier, stronger, and give the impression of being "over" the other person.

As we have seen, verbal abuse attempts to convince people that they, or their inner reality—their feelings, perceptions, intentions, intuitions, motives, and even their experiences—are not real or are not worthy. In essence, verbal abuse moves against truth, attempting to shape reality into the perpetrators' versions of how it should be, or how they want it to be, or how they believe it is. Just knowing this, we may slow the insidious proliferation of verbal abuse in our culture. Who wants to be caught in a spell that influences him or her to live in an irrational pretend world, separate from the real world, always confronted by *real* people who won't be part of the pretend world?

The knowledge of what verbal abuse is and that it is not okay may lessen its impact on many individuals. It may even lower the numbers of today's teens—tomorrow's adults—who are either subject to it or indulging in it.

DENIAL ASSAULTS YOUR MIND

Recall the earlier example of Lee stepping in front of me and my calling him a dork. When Lee objected, if I had denied Lee's experience by saying, "Well, you *are* a dork. I'll call you what I want. *You're just trying to get out of it,*" then I would be acting irrationally.

Saying, "You're just trying to get out of it," is the kind of verbal abuse that not only attempts to erase the other person's perceptions but also communicates the weird message, *I know your motives because I am "in you," checking out your intentions and making up your reality.*

Teens who hear this kind of talk feel as if someone *is* trying to erase their minds, a weird feeling indeed. This kind of abuse sets up teens for hurtful, destructive, crazy-making relationships. They could become the target of an abuser, especially if they think it's not cool to confront verbal abuse, or if they are afraid to speak up. It is even more harmful if they have already heard a lot of verbal abuse at home, and, like Bobby and Danny, they don't even know what it is or that it's not okay. If they have learned to close off their feelings, and so have lost awareness, they may themselves become confirmed verbal abusers.

WHAT MAKES VERBAL ABUSE ABUSIVE

When people deny your perceptions, or make up who and what you are, they are acting as if they can erase your inner experience or knowledge of yourself, and replace it with whatever they have made up about you. They are pretending to know something about you that isn't true. That is why this behavior is abusive. For instance, they may pretend to know if you are listening, or if you are trying to start a fight.

Usually when people are pretending, they don't seem to know it. Sometimes they do know but they think it is funny. And even then, they don't seem to know how cruel their behavior is.

Sometimes when teens experience this behavior, it feels scary because abusers don't seem to know what is real, and they can't seem to hear real people. Actually, abusers have entered a pretend world where the real you doesn't exist. If you depend on them for understanding, security, or even love, you may feel traumatized by realizing that the kind of world they are in locks you out. Generally, people who indulge in verbal abuse don't want to leave their pretend world for anything.

Very often, when people are taken totally by surprise because they have learned that someone has done some terrible deed and they never saw it coming, nor imagined the person would do such a thing, it is because they never realized that the person they thought they knew, and understood, was, in fact, not in the real world with them. The person was living in a pretend world, making up people as he or she went along.

People who enter such a world are out of touch with themselves. It is as if they are half asleep. All their attempts to erase another person's perceptions or to taunt or harass them are verbally abusive.

AAP REPORT

Chronic verbal abuse is described as psychological maltreatment, and certainly, it is. The American Academy of Pediatrics (AAP), in a recent report,[2] discusses the fact that the psychological consequences of such maltreatment of children can last longer in some cases than physical abuse. Its prevalence is difficult to document and it can result in many emotional, social, and physical problems.

This AAP report also sites a survey indicating that 50 percent of teenagers surveyed experience severe aggression in the family. Included in the examples mentioned is "calling the child dumb or such other belittling names."[3]

Adults who experience chronic verbal abuse in *their* relationships,[4] report similar emotional, social, and physical problems. Verbal abuse distorts truth so much that people subject to it either lose themselves trying to deal with it, as if it were rational behavior, or they become so damaged by it that they enter the pretend world of the abuser, making up reality as they go. Overall, verbal abuse is not okay, because by distorting the truth, it attempts to change individual reality and consequently limit personal freedom. For these reasons, it is important that we implement the kind of education that will diminish it.

Clearly, no one lives within anyone and no one knows another person's inner reality, but teens who perpetrate verbal abuse on a regular basis seem to have no clear idea of the futility of such attempts to tell another person who or what they are. And few seem able to stop them.

Since defining others *is* irrational, it cannot be accepted as okay, or ignored by parents and teachers. If it is ignored, children can begin to think that someone, besides themselves, is the authority on their inner reality.

The only way anyone can know about you—or anyone else—is by asking you what you think, mean, want, feel, et cetera. Without this understanding, children may accept someone's definition of them, or of another person, as fact. They may even accept someone's definition of a whole gender or race.

Most adults involved with teens want the same things for them, to see that they grow up to live satisfying, independent, and productive lives. Verbal abuse runs counter to this goal. It is not okay because it has a tremendous impact on people. It moves against awareness and reality itself. And if that were not sufficient reason to be alert to it, we cannot forget that verbal abuse supports a pretend world where whole nations have been caught in the spell.

The following chart describes the difference between the real world and a pretend world. I recommend that it be used in homes and classrooms for discussion.

What Is Real	What Is Pretend
People come in different shapes and sizes.	People who do not look like the pretender wants them to look are unacceptable.
People are all different colors.	Only people who look like the pretender are acceptable.
People have different gifts and talents.	Only the pretender's gifts and talents are recognized.
People are held accountable.	People who are smart enough don't suffer consequences.
People win through discipline and effort.	People win any way they can.
People face difficulties.	People get what they want or they get mad.

(continued on next page)

What Is Real	What Is Pretend
People grieve their losses.	People feel no pain.
People's inner nature and character are what is important.	People's image and the way they appear are most important.
Everyone has his or her own view.	There is only one right view.
Sometimes people need assistance.	People should be able to handle problems by themselves.
Past events can't be changed.	Saying an event was different or did not happen makes it so.
Survival depends on understanding mutuality and win/win resolution.	Survival depends on your winning and others losing and getting people to help you get rid of the losers.

Let's look now at some of the ways that teens, and even some adults, fear the real world and real people. Here are some examples.

Afraid to live in the real world, the teen who is caught up in a pretend world will put down people who are different in order to preserve the pretend world and to get others to enter it as if it were real, so he or she will not be alone in it.

Similarly, the teen who is caught up in a pretend world will, if a boy, put down girls to preserve his superior pretend world and to get others to enter it so he will not be alone in it.

Likewise, the teen who is caught up in a pretend world will, if a girl, believe it's okay to verbally abuse her boyfriend to preserve her superior pretend world and to get others to enter it so she will not be alone in it.

Any teens who are caught up in a pretend world will, of course, put down and ridicule people who show their feelings to preserve their pain-free pretend world and to get others to enter it so they will not be alone in it.

WHEN NAME-CALLING IS JOKING

Some teens, as well as some adults, have *very connected and close relationships with established customs such as greetings that tease but don't provoke.* An example of such an exchange would be something like this:

> "Hey skinny, what-da-ya-know?"
> "Not much. What about you, dingbat?"
> "I made the team, my position."
> "Hey, alright, gimme five."

People who know each other well sometimes enjoy such an interchange. *It comes as no surprise to either person.* It's their thing. They have agreed to nicknames that they think are funny or cool, and they feel a kinship, and some comfort, in a long-established ritual.

In some cultures and ethnic groups, teens look at verbal abuse as some hip thing, something new, something to be admired like quick wit.

People who have not established a custom wherein they exchange defining comments as jokes are not likely to be pleased by being called "dingbat" or "skinny." Teens are developing a sense of who they are and are particularly assaulted by other people's definitions of them.

Thus far, we have seen that verbal abuse is not okay for many reasons. In review, here are a few.

- Verbal abuse is all about a pretend world.
- Verbal abuse denigrates and diminishes human beings.
- Verbal abuse invades a person's inner world and self-definition.
- Verbal abuse is kept hidden and seldom discussed.
- Verbal abuse may seem normal to some teens and adults.

- Verbal abuse coerces people to protect the perpetrator.
- Verbal abuse assaults freedom.

VERBAL ABUSE SUPPORTS OTHER ABUSES

Very often, if a spellbound person's entire approach to, and attitude toward, a real person is one of shaping them into a pretend person (possibly to join them in their pretend world), they may resort to other abuses to reach their objective. This is obvious when we consider how some people will resort to violence when someone won't be the way they want him or her to be. Or, if not violence, many parents will coerce and threaten their children. For example, "I'll pay for college, but only if you go here or become that." In their need to bring to life their pretend children (tough, smart, beautiful, athletic, whatever), some parents are completely unaware of their real children.

VELA'S STORY

Petite, sturdy, and dynamic, Vela, a true country girl, enjoyed an idyllic childhood growing up on a ranch, with wealth and every advantage. At thirteen, she was already shining as a gifted athlete—a champion high-speed skier and a daring and skilled rider. Her room was filled with ribbons and trophies. She loved speed, adventure, and the challenge of calculated risks. But as she reached adolescence, her extraordinary achievements no longer seemed to count to her family. Her parents couldn't see their real daughter anymore. Their idea of an adolescent girl was *not* a "tomboy" who liked adventure. To her parents, Vela, the adolescent, was to become a feminine, delicate girl—a ballerina. This was the pretend daughter who had taken Vela's place.

"You'll like being a ballerina," her mother said.

Thus, the abuse began.

Vela was yanked from the life she knew and found herself in a freezing room in a pink tutu for ballet class, where the teacher slapped the students with her cane.

Her mother would say, "Look at the ballerinas. Why aren't you like that? You should look like the beautiful ballerinas, with your hair pulled back, with long legs, and dark hair."

Rejecting the true nature of their real child, her parents embraced instead the dream child they had always wanted.

The real Vela was being erased in hours of ballet practice aimed at perfecting minuscule and restricted movements. This was her fate, instead of the big, broad strokes of racing and riding.

"But, Mom," Vela would say, "It's just not what I like spending time doing. I don't like ballet."

"Yes, you do, you just haven't given it a chance," said her mother, believing she could shape her daughter's style and interests.

Her father grew angrier and angrier as Vela remained who she was. Her mother was more persistent: "Why can't you be the way you should be?"

But she couldn't. Everything about ballet and being a ballerina was exactly the *opposite* of who she was.

The point, of course, is that a child can suffer when parents who believe that they are doing what is best for their child, also believe in a *pretend world with a pretend child.*

Parents who try to shape a child into a dream child, cannot but indulge in defining the child. And, of course, defining people is what verbal abuse is. Verbal abuse is a tool used to create and maintain pretend people and pretend worlds. It is designed to shape a separate reality from the one that exists in the heart and soul of nature.

In the next chapter, we will see how verbal abuse has infiltrated and has even, in some places, gotten a strong foothold in the teen culture.

Chapter III

The Teen World

THERE ARE MANY WONDERFUL TEENS WHO ARE MANAGING WELL despite the alarming prevalence of verbal abuse in the teen world. However, the spread of verbal abuse among teens has become an epidemic. There is every indication that the incidence of verbal abuse has increased in intensity and frequency at an alarming rate in the last twenty years.

As I talked to teens, teachers, and administrators around the country, I was shocked and saddened by the realization that, the values that I cherish are the opposite of those many teens hold dear. The primary goals of these teens are to feel nothing; to win, no matter what; to demonstrate strength and superiority over others; to dominate and diminish those who are less able or smaller; and to ridicule the weakest.

Even though there are many teens too intelligent, empathetic, and aware to indulge in verbal abuse or to subscribe to values that reek of tyranny and hate, verbal abuse is a real and growing problem among teens. It claims victims and shatters lives. We will look at the teen world to gain some insight into it. And we will find out what teens and those who have survived their teen years have to say about it.

The teen's world is different from the child's and different from the adult's. It is a place of transition with its own rules, values, music, and slang. Every school is different. Each is a mini-culture with variations in dress code, groups, diversity, academic ratings, and customs.

The teen's world reflects the adult's world, only it is more intense, dramatic, extreme, and less restrained than the broader society in which we all live. Young, middle, and late teens are in different stages of development. As they mature, they usually learn to see people from a broader perspective. They develop inner restraints to emotional and angry reactions to hurts and slights. They also learn that their feelings will change and that a bad feeling now will not necessarily translate into a bad feeling tomorrow. However, as transitory as pain often is, for some it seems to last forever. That teens should have to suffer because verbal abuse is normalized, is wrong.

INTERVIEW WITH A YOUNG WOMAN

A young woman, not much passed her teens, shared her perspective on the teen world with me. I found her to be exceptionally aware and articulate. Her candid revelation echoed what many teens had told me.

How would you describe the teenager's world?

"The teen world is about being one up. The crazy world of one-upmanship is so validated on TV; there is the sense that this is the way it should be. In the teen world, verbal abuse doesn't exist as a real thing. When people put you down, as they are "supposed to," if it bothers you, there is something wrong with you. The world is built on this one-up, one-down idea."

Do teens who think this way feel good about verbally abusing someone?

"Yes, putting people down is what you are supposed to do. They think that if you are strong enough, you could stand it. No one wants to admit that anyone has feelings. The problem, according to teens, lies in the victims. They are weak, pathetic, and losers. They need to learn not to feel. If you look good, then you are okay. You're not selected to endure much abuse. There are no major problems."

Is looking good like a pass that gets you through your teen years?

"Appearances are everything. In some ways, appearances are all there is. Looking good, having the right, current, cool clothes, means you are okay and well adjusted. If you're awkward or shy, you are not okay; if you can't meet their standard, it means you haven't 'made it.'"

It sounds like an empty existence. Would you say so?

"We know it's not true happiness. Kids feel the pressure at school and see it on TV, and if parents buy into just appearances, if parents believe only in looking good on the outside, how can teens develop inside? If the putdowns go on at home, and they must face them in school, they have no refuge from a verbally abusive world. No place they can go. If there are no real communications, no real values, there is no way teens can transition to a happy life."

Do teachers help the victims and perpetrators of verbal abuse?

"Some teachers want to think it is normal. Some teachers don't want to deal with bullies because they are afraid of them.

"If a person can become impervious to his feelings, he has passed the test. Once he becomes impenetrable and unfeeling, he will then be valued and admired. He can then go forth into college and eventually probably be head of some company. That is called success."

Do you think any of these so-called successes ever develop into real, caring, contributing people?

"The ones who made it before me, are striving and striving and pushing, but I wonder, for what? They can't admit that they are empty and unfulfilled. If they did, it would mean they are weak, pathetic, and losers. It's the opposite of truth and of reality."

How did you, personally, manage those teen years?

"I was born lucky; although I had no home life or support, I was born to be beautiful. I would have been cremated in high school if I hadn't been beautiful, because I had no self-confidence and no security at home."

By "cremated," do you mean if you hadn't looked like a model, you would have been a major target of verbal abuse, especially without family support?

"Yes, but I was blessed with good looks and athletic ability, which I believe allowed me to make it in school. I have no doubt that without these, I would have been the object of much verbal abuse and control.

"I put all my energy into looking, being, achieving, *everything*. Now I wish I had stayed friends with the nerds; then I'd be friends with interesting people who actually were real and actually achieve things."

We need only turn on a TV, watch a movie, or listen to conversations around us to know that verbal abuse permeates both teen and adult culture. It is a societal issue.

TEEN DEVELOPMENTAL TASKS

During their teens, young people have at least three major developmental tasks. They are built-in natural drives. The first is to develop independence, that is, self-reliance. In their teen years, they learn to make good decisions, to seek advice, to take care of themselves, and to become responsible adults. If verbal abuse has reduced their self-esteem to an all-time low, they may not feel they can take care of themselves at all.

The second is to develop a strong sense of who they are, their talents, abilities, likes, dislikes, interests, and so on. This is their identity and it develops, in part, out of their emotional intelligence and intuitive knowledge. They try many things; take a variety of classes and so forth; and notice how they feel about themselves, what they like and don't like, what they do with ease, and what seems to go against their grain. With emotional awareness and honest feedback, they see where they are in relation to others, and they build their identity from within. If nothing goes awry, they develop a confident and realistic sense of themselves. However, if they are verbally abused for being who they are, it will be much more difficult.

The third major developmental goal is to find, or move toward, their future work and place in the world. As they become more self-reliant and more certain of their identity, they can assess the potential in possible careers. Just as they cannot know if they have the intelligence to, say, become a doctor, without knowing their abilities in science in relation to others, they can't be sure of their best career without having some idea of how they come across in relation to others. If the feedback is clouded by verbal abuse, the outcome can be a disaster.

CONSTRUCTING THE TEEN WORLD

Until about ten years of age, the child's world is his or her immediate family and extended family. These are the people the child is close to and sees frequently. Eventually, the young person's social nucleus moves from family to school.

In their preteens and teens, young people develop a bond to the world outside of their home. Their world is comprised of their peers. Later, as they reach adulthood, it becomes the broader world of work, organizations, institutions, and so forth. To teens, "The World" is a teen world.

Belonging and acceptance in a group is very important to many teens, because it is their developmental goal to belong in a world outside the home. Unfortunately, they do not realize that the world some teens have constructed is entirely superficial, based on surface appearances. And even if they do sense this, where can they go for belonging and acceptance?

In their search for their place in this expanding world, for what suits them and for connection and friendship, teens turn primarily to their peers. They are the inhabitants of this new world. Teens' need for acceptance has expanded from their family to the small community of classmates, team members, and the teens they get to know in activity clubs, teen organizations, sports, and other groups.

This is how they break away from their parents. It is a process that helps them to move into the greater world. Their teen world is a new world, and they want and need to be part of it. In time, as they mature, they will move beyond this into a broader community.

Because they are moving beyond the immediate influence of family into a larger world, they enter the teen world with a need to be different from adults, to look different, to talk differently, and, especially, to be different from their parents.

Because they have an inner developmental drive to form an identity and to gain acceptance outside of their homes, teens automatically merge into the teen world in their school and neighborhood. This world is based on the most obvious external characteristics of others. It is like an ever-evolving newly constructed pretend world. Most commonly, each person's value is based on appearances, and it is a world of perfection.

At the very time that they need acceptance from their peers, many teens will face rejection. Why? Because they are different. Not just different from their parents—after all, that is acceptable—but because they are different from the ideal held in the minds of teens. If they don't have the characteristics their peers most aspire to, they are automatically labeled and segregated. Thus, they become the victims of verbal abuse—at best, called names like "nerd"; at worst, targeted by abusers. Verbal abusers go after the unprotected, the ones who don't have friends standing by, and the ones who don't belong to an "in" group.

A high school junior said that in his school, if kids were studious, quiet, didn't party a lot, and didn't have many friends, they were called geeks. If kids didn't try to fit in, or never fit in, then they weren't safe. "The more friends you have, the safer," he said. "If a kid seems isolated, he's a target."

Repeatedly, teens told me, "You can't survive if you're a loner, if you don't have a group." When verbal abusers become relentless and aggressively pursue their target, they are called bullies. I believe that a person who is at this extreme is a sadist in the making—or has already become involved in sadistic behavior. Perhaps such a young person feels so vulnerable, the power to dominate gives the pleasure of security.

If this is so, one can see that the extreme abuser doesn't want to stop. The hook is the pleasure of security in an insecure environment, a way to make the pretend world be their world. And it is not difficult to see that such abusers believe that "might makes right" and that power over others is the only power there is. In a pretend world, one would have to have a lot of power just to maintain it—to shut up those people who won't agree with you and follow your lead.

In the teen world, teens achieve exclusivity by forming highly defined groups. A teen who is new to a school may be confused as he or she tries to figure it all out. "Maybe if I date a or b, I'll be in the popular group," thinks one teen.

LABELS

Each group has a label, and there are subgroups within groups. Once a teen is labeled, that label may stick for life, or at least for the duration of the teen years. And once labeled, a teen is expected to fulfill the expectations of his or her category and is excluded from other groups. Then each group puts down the groups that it is not in. There is always the worry of inadvertently appearing to be like the teens in a different group. Or doing something nonconforming that pushes one out of his or her group and into another one. Many teens have voiced these concerns. As a fifteen-year-old boy said, "If I talk seriously, I may be labeled a nerd. If I don't make the team, I may be labeled a loser. I'm working out all summer so I'll be strong enough to fight back, whatever it takes."

If a boy looks big, tall, strong, and plays sports, he is valued as a jock. Jocks are usually a subcategory of the popular group. Girls who are especially attractive, thin, tall, and socially sophisticated are also members of the valued popular group.

Teens who have an interest in learning, in science, or in computers are called nerds. Nerds are not part of the perfect pretend world, so they are put down. Another boy confides that in school, he talks like he is dumb so he will not be thought of as a nerd.

I asked him what he could tell me about them. "Nerds are smart but don't have many friends and don't get in on parties and stuff," he said.

"I don't talk about anything serious," he said. "If I did, people would walk away, think I was somehow alien. The only place I can be myself is when I'm with kids in an advanced placement class."

If he spoke about something "real," that is, something that was not superficial, he would not be part of the pretend world.

If you make a mistake, will you be excluded? Will you survive? teens wonder. The TV show *Survivor* tells them no. Exclusivity is poured into the minds of teens in media and interactive video, where anyone in the way of one's path is always rejected or annihilated. Exclusivity is a manifestation of the spell.

In a self-defeating way, the transitional teen world of divided and labeled groups promotes the very fear teens are trying to escape: the fear of being excluded.

When verbal abuse prevails in the teen world, a boy who is not tall, handsome, strong, and athletic will be ridiculed and treated as an outcast among his peers, the very people from whom he needs acceptance. If a girl is not pretty, slim, and sophisticated, she also may be an outcast.

Teens, and in some cases preteens, who have the characteristics their peers aspire to, will be seen as the popular kids. Although they may not always notice how they are seen, they are usually not targeted for verbal abuse.

Other teens may feel just fine as the "nerds." But some teens are bound to be on the outskirts of all groups. These teens may be both victims and abusers. Some teen loners put down classmates in an attempt to put themselves up. Some try to get others to bond with them against a target, so they won't feel so "on the outskirts" of the teen world. A gang is organized in this way, with teens bonded together against others. In this group, however small, they feel that they belong and have a connection.

There are some teens, it is only fair to say, who have so much support at home, they simply pursue their interests. If not terrorized, they get through without many friends, lonely but resolved to endure.

A young teen told me that she once entered a new school and was asked if she would take a test that all the kids were about to take. She said, "I made the mistake of saying that I like tests." She did this, she said, to sound nice and obedient to the teacher's wishes; however, some of her classmates heard her. This sounded different from what they were used to. Difference is a big threat to the pretend world of teens, so they immediately made her the object of abuse, telling her, "You're trying to be a teacher's pet."

This episode reveals an interesting phenomenon. Anything positive, like intelligence, or an interest in science, is subject to ridicule in the teen world. But, teens universally agree that being an accomplished athlete is admirable.

Only a couple of generations ago, anyone who was able to get a high test score and seemed smart was admired in school. Now, there is a fear of showing intelligence.

An eighteen-year-old girl told me that, in her early teens, "If you didn't fit in at school, you were ostracized." She felt the shame of being an outsider. "It was like a cult. You had to talk and be like everyone else or you were an outcast. My self-esteem was so low, it didn't even exist," she said.

"If a guy has a musical interest and plays in the school band, he's 'one of the band fags,'" says one sixteen-year-old boy, speaking of his school's culture.

In some schools, dying your hair and dressing differently are a message, a thirteen-year-old boy told me. "The message is, 'don't say anything to me. Leave me alone.'"

The categories that teens are placed in, or place themselves in, must often be endured for the duration of their high school years. Teens who are in schools where their groups are highly defined, have very limited social interaction with teens in other groups. Some teens want to break out into a different category; for instance, a teen who is labeled a nerd wants to take up a sport. Will he be accepted? he wonders. A young girl wanted to be in an advanced class but dreaded being called a nerd. Should she move forward and face verbal abuse and its rejection or stay in her current class and not realize her potential?

Some teens, who refuse to be placed in a category, call themselves the "normals." In some schools, each group has their own territory where they hang out. Each group occupies a certain part of the campus during lunch and between classes. Beyond the categorization by surface characteristics, in many schools, students group by class, freshman to senior. What is interesting is the intensity with which they exclude others. No one trespasses on the other's territory.

A seventeen-year-old girl says, "I just started at this school after my family moved here. I was standing on the grass looking around when I was shoved from behind and a guy yelled at me, 'This is senior territory, get off our grass.' I told him I *am* a senior. Then he apologized and later was friendly."

In the determination and establishment of insiders and outsiders, valued and devalued, idealized and dehumanized, winners and losers, I believe it all sounds like training for war.

There are some definite differences between younger and older teens. More teens indulge in verbal abuse in early adolescence. In late adolescence, young people have more self-control and more assertion skills. However, confirmed verbal abusers and bullies focus as they get older. They are more selective. If a teen is still indulging in verbal abuse and aggressive behavior by sixteen, he or she is more dangerous than at thirteen.

ACCEPTING VERBAL ABUSE

Because verbal abuse has become so prevalent, many teens are desensitized to it, not even recognizing verbal abuse as abuse. When they feel wounded by a verbal assault, they believe something is wrong with them. Or they believe that throwing verbal barbs is a way of showing how smart and clever they are.

Since teens want acceptance in the new world outside of their homes, they are anxious to be accepted by their peers, and anxious that they might be judged inadequate. They want to be masters of everything, to have all desirable teen traits, to be accepted.

Completely unaware of the way they have been manipulated to accept verbal abuse and another person's dominance of them, they actually believe that objecting to being hit with words is a sign of weakness. This is so especially in male culture. Weakness is abhorred because it is, to their minds, a cause for not only rejection, but also outright ostracism.

Not knowing the truth about weakness, in fact, being trained to accept the opposite of the truth, some teens pretend that they have no feelings until the day comes that they have so buried them, they don't know what they feel, except anger, despair, and confusion.

Chapter IV

The Code of Silence

TEENS HAVE AN UNWRITTEN, DON'T-ASK–DON'T-TELL CODE of silence around verbal abuse, bullying, and even threats of violence. They are communicating on the Internet, keeping their problems to themselves, staying anonymous, and remaining silent around adults.

WHAT IS BEHIND THE CODE OF SILENCE?

Understanding how important the pretend world is to spellbound teens helps us to see how the code of silence has taken control of young people, preventing them from getting the support they need when they are targeted by an abuser. Recall the parents who defined their real daughter, wanting to turn her into their *pretend* daughter, a ballerina. They had good intentions, and they just wanted her to be someone else. But they couldn't hear her or see her, at least not the real person. No matter what she told them, she couldn't get through. Their pretend world was absolutely real to them.

When people believe their pretend world is *real,* as did Vela's parents, they will do almost anything to keep it going—to make it real. They don't even have to think about it. They automatically close off input from the outside. They don't see defining people as being abusive, because they think that the person they are defining is, in fact, what they say they are, or at least should be, and deserves their anger for not being as he or she should be. Clearly they believe that objecting to verbal abuse, or to being defined, is a sign of weakness, while tolerating verbal abuse, their definitions of you, is a sign of strength. This nonsensical idea is a fundamental tenant of teen culture, some game-show culture, and some adult culture.

People who seek power over other people have instilled in victims the idea that taking a stand against verbal abuse and threats is a sign of weakness. Many victims have come to believe their abusers. Furthermore, since teens naturally need to move into a transitional world different from their parents' world, their need to keep themselves separate from their parents further influences them to maintain a code of silence around their own abuse.

As long as spellbound people feel right about having pretend children, friends, and so forth, they automatically feel right about defining (verbally abusing) real people. So, of course, they will promote any idea that will stop all protests. A very effective way to do this is to thoughtlessly create a culture that leads teens into believing that *their need to be strong cannot be met unless they accept verbal abuse.* Similarly, being able to take a hit in football and keep playing, despite the pain, is a sign of strength and toughness. And, like war, continuing to fight despite being wounded is considered "heroic." For some, adhering to this belief, can, ultimately, be the destruction of their self-concept and the loss of their self.

The big weapon abusers use is name-calling. Verbal abusers call people who stand up to verbal abuse, *weak*. And teens accept this.

> *Whoa! That's like, "You can call me anything, just don't call me weak, because then I'll believe you. I do believe that you live within me, playing God and can tell me what I am or what I will be."*

If you are a teen and believe that, I wonder if some older person, some parent, brother, authority figure, coach, or teacher got you to believe it.

I wonder if you were too young to know that the person who instilled this belief in you was abusing you. That person was lying to you, just like Bobby's and Danny's father was lying to them. Recall how shocked they were. Danny couldn't take it in. He blew it off. He though he had a normal, healthy dad. He was too young to know his father was lying to him. But Bobby, his older brother, *knew.*

When people fall under the influence of a spellbound person and start to believe in the pretend world, they, too, are under the spell. Being spellbound is like saying to a sadist, "Go ahead and stick pins in me. I won't tell anyone. I won't say that what you're doing is not okay, if only you'll not call me weak."

Spellbound teens want desperately to believe in their pretend world. Other teens, spellbound or not, want to believe in the code of silence, because it is part of their teen world. But if you're a teen who's been under the influence of the spell, and you actually have the courage to face the pain that someone has been lying to you about what is weak and what is strong, if you know that no one can define you, then you can break the code of silence. When you do, you'll break the spell at the same time!

NAME-CALLING PERPETUATES THE CODE OF SILENCE

Spellbound people have tricked some teens, who want to be strong. They think that if they put up with verbal abuse, they will be strong, and if they don't, they will be weak. Nothing is farther from the truth. Additionally, they think that someone has to tell them how they are. "If you do this, you are weak. If you do that you are strong."

Unfortunately, no one has taught these teens that revealing abuse, wherever it occurs, is essential to our freedom. They fear that if they do reveal verbal abuse and call it what it is, if they tell a teacher or parent when someone is verbally abusive to them or bullies them or threatens them, they will be any or all of the following:

- A whiner
- A complainer
- A loser
- A wimp
- A victim
- A crybaby
- A nitpicker
- A snitch
- A cheater
- A rat fink
- A betrayer
- A coward

When they reach adulthood, they believe that to talk about verbal abuse in a relationship is "airing the dirty laundry." This is a saying that pretty much sums up the list above. It is an accusatory comment that perpetuates abusive relationships. Actually, talking about verbal abuse, and pointing out where it has a grip on someone, is a way to get rid of it. Isn't telling the truth a way to show courage?

On the other hand, isn't calling people names to get them to do what you want a cowardly kind of behavior? Would standing up to verbal abuse and breaking the spell be a heroic and helpful thing to do? Would it be mature and self-reliant to go to parents, counselors, teachers, peer groups, or administrators for advice and assistance in resolving an abuse problem?

If you are a teen who has remained silent in the face of abuse, please ask yourself if your silence perpetuated or ended it?

If you decide to stand up to verbal abuse, it must be done in a safe way that attacks the abuse, not the perpetrator. See Chapter XI, "Stopping Verbal Abuse," for details on how to take a stand against it.

The name-calling list on the previous page shows the lengths spellbound people will go to to move against life, the human spirit, and consciousness itself. The names, like "wimp" and "loser" and "snitch," that abusers call spell-breakers, are made up by spellbound people. They are designed to perpetuate verbal abuse and to silence spell-breakers. People who try to gain power over you have to silence you to maintain control of you.

Do you recall how spellbound people are so unaware that they seem to be half asleep, as if in a dream state, making up all kinds of things about real people, denigrating or mocking them? They clearly don't want to let go of their pretend worlds. In a pretend world, they are the rulers and they pretend that everyone who isn't like them is a lesser human being. So, of course, they feel more secure if they can make up a rule or code that protects them from having to be accountable for their behavior—a rule that keeps them from having to give up their pretend world.

THREATS ENFORCE THE CODE OF SILENCE

Many teens are afraid of verbal abusers because they threaten violence against anyone courageous enough to break the code of silence. Even though verbal abuse doesn't necessarily create violence, it does precede it. Teens have to take these threats seriously. However, a general guide is that the more adults there are who know about the abuser, the less power the abuser has. And, the more teens understand how cowardly abusive behavior is, the less inclined teens will be to act abusively.

Teens want to be independent, handle their own problems, be accepted by their peers, and, to sum it up, be successful teens. All these good aspirations can work against them when they are confronted with verbal abuse and harassment if they try to deal with them on their own.

The code of silence is maintained not only with name-calling, threats of violence, and harassment, but also by *victims* of verbal abuse who support it by their silence. Teens keep the code of silence for many other reasons. The following list presents some and can be used for discussion between teens and their parents or in the classroom. Anyone can add to the list.

Teenagers hesitate to take a stand against abuse, and maintain a code of silence around verbal abuse and threats, for the following reasons:

- They fear retaliation, much as a battered wife is afraid of more battering if she tells.
- They believe everyone will laugh at them for objecting to it because they believe the lie, "words will never hurt you."
- They want to appear so universally accepted that no one knows they're being harassed or ostracized.
- They are afraid that they'll lose control, slug the abuser, and end up looking like the person who is abusive.
- They want to pretend it didn't happen because they feel ashamed that an abuser has picked them out to abuse.
- They are not sure if what they're hearing is abusive enough to talk about.
- They believe that it's not cool to take a stand against verbal abuse.
- They don't want to look weak.
- They believe that the verbal abuse may have some truth in it, so they can't say anything.

- They are confused by the abuser's denial: that it didn't happen or that they're taking it wrong.
- They want to handle problems by themselves.
- They hope it will stop if they ignore it and don't say anything.
- They don't have any idea of what is the best way to deal with it.
- They believe it will be futile to speak up.
- They don't know whom to talk to.
- They have false beliefs about being a target.
- They have already tried to talk to teachers, parents, or administrators who:
  - Don't think it's important enough to do anything about.
  - Don't believe it.
  - Don't have any idea what to do about it.
  - Hope it will go away.
  - Think it is a learning experience.
  - Think you have to deal with it yourself.
  - Think your suffering is your comeuppance.
  - Think it is your Karma.
  - Say, as did one teacher, "Don't be a snitch."

TEENS ARE BETRAYED BY PLATITUDES

The statement, "Sticks and stones may break your bones, but words will never hurt you," is abusive because it tells you what you feel. And, it dismisses verbal abuse, which terrorizes, ostracizes, punishes, wounds, defames, and traumatizes real people. It is a handy phrase for anyone who wishes to denigrate human beings with impunity. It is also a handy phrase for those who try to placate someone, but it denies human experience.

Platitudes often automatically pour from the mouths of very well-meaning folks. Unfortunately, they are ineffective at best and blaming at worst. By glazing over verbal abuse with platitudes that subtly lay the responsibility for abuse on the person who suffers from it, adults betray teens just as they were betrayed in their own youth. If teens don't learn the truth at home, *school may be their last chance.* These platitudes can be topics for classroom discussion. What meanings do they convey?

A child, turning to an adult for protection, support, and understanding, may hear any of the following—hopefully not in your home or school.

PLATITUDES

Boys will be boys.
Those girls are just cliquish.
That's just the way your coach talks.
Don't let it bother you.
They're just that way.
Consider the source.
She was just having a bad day.
They don't really mean it.
Toughen up.
Don't be thin-skinned.
Forget it.
You'll feel better in the morning.
Don't let what people say bother you.
Quit whining.
Take it with a grain of salt.
Are you going to believe everything you hear?
Can't you take a joke?
Talking about it won't make it better.
Why should you care about what s/he said?

What did you do to provoke it?
You're just trying to get attention.
Don't be so sensitive.
Don't worry about it.
I don't want to hear your complaints.
It takes two.
You've got to give as good as you get.
Don't let them get to you.
Don't pay attention to it.
Think about something else.
Put it behind you.
They're just trying to get to you.
You must have done something to them.
Grin and bear it.
Words can't really hurt you.

These platitudes tell teens almost anything but the truth: "That was verbal abuse. What they, he, or she just said isn't okay." Platitudes may be voiced in an attempt to placate or quiet the target of verbal abuse—to help them not to feel hurt, or to tell them to fight back, but platitudes don't address the fact that they leave the target of verbal abuse feeling inadequate.

TEENS INTERPRET PLATITUDES

A platitude suggests to the person who objects to the abuse that he or she is somehow to blame for feeling its impact. Teens get the message that they are wrong if they are affected, that, in some way, they are to blame for their pain. This affects the core of their self-concept. Their sense of themselves is damaged. They feel that they are intrinsically lacking because verbal abuse hurts, shocks, or traumatizes them.

Feeling wounded by cutting remarks, a teen might think that's just the way people are, they didn't mean it, or maybe if I were different, it wouldn't have happened. Clearly teens take in platitudes and, trying to make sense of their pain, decide that they are made wrong, with too much sensitivity, or that they should not let it bother them for countless reasons. No one has told them that what they heard was abusive, that the person who said it was, at least for the moment, trying to establish a pretend world where saying it's so, makes it so.

There is a price to be paid for telling children that the verbal abuse they experience is "nothing." Saying something like this, instead of acknowledging the impact of the abuse, gives the victims the message that it is okay.

Platitudes don't address the problem and don't tell the truth about verbal abuse. Instead, they create confusion and pain in the very people they are meant to placate. And since they don't address the abuse as abuse, accepting the unacceptable becomes the norm. Once an abuse is normalized, it seems okay to indulge in it. The rationale is: It's okay to say these things because everyone else does.

Another message that platitudes instill, is that there is no use saying anything. This realization reinforces the code of silence. Teen culture is created this way. Looking to adults, even when they claim not to trust adults, teens take their cues from their parents and other adults.

We've looked at many reasons why some teens, and even some adults, might not want to take a stand against verbal abuse, and why some teens feel reluctant to say anything to the person who is verbally abusive toward them, even reluctant to ask for advice. We see also that some teens have fallen under the influence of the code of silence. But there is one more reason why teens don't often speak out against verbal abuse. It is that sometimes the impact of verbal abuse is so stunning, they are left speechless.

Chapter V

Verbal Abuse
Precedes Violence

TEENS MAY TURN THEIR ANGUISH OUTWARD INTO A RAGE THAT victimizes others with abuse and violence. Although verbal abuse does not always lead to violence, it does always precede it. Usually a teen who becomes violent has been abused somewhere, and usually a teen who perpetrates violence expresses his or her anger in revealing remarks before the violence erupts. Such was the case in incidents of campus killings that have rocked the country. The shooters were troubled youth. All had indulged in verbal abuse. All had felt bullied or picked on, and all had access to weapons.

With only anger and hate, unable to survive in a world where appearance is all, a few teens have exploded outwardly. This is when violence can erupt, as happened in Littleton, Colorado; Santee and El Cajon, California; West Paducah, Kentucky; Springfield, Oregon; and Jonesboro, Arkansas.

Number two on a checklist of what shooters do, developed by the National School Safety Center: Resorted to name-calling, cursing, or abusive language. And yet, as we will learn in the Chapter XIII, "For Teachers," some schools have no policy about verbal abuse. In some schools, a student can call anyone anything, as long as it is not construed to be sexual harassment, a hate crime, or a threat of bodily harm. People who don't want to hear abuse have no perceivable rights.

It would seem that one could shout, curse, and put people down in a free country where free speech is allowed, but doesn't it go against human rights to force people to be in a place where verbal abuse terrifies and traumatizes them?

Children realize the pain of verbal abuse. As we will see later, a middle school girl says it bruises inside, and a young boy, wanting to know what to do, asks if we should tell the president.

COLUMBINE

Violence broke out at Columbine High School in Littleton, Colorado, on April 20, 1999. A teacher and twelve students were killed, along with the two perpetrators. Dozens of students were injured.

The *Rocky Mountain News* reported that a student at Columbine said that the perpetrators of the deadly rampage were called "faggots," teased, and referred to as "psychos" and "freaks." Later, people claimed that some students were so abused by other students that they were afraid to go to school. Some of those interviewed thought it was worse than at other schools. "The jock hierarchy was extreme and overbearing. There was lots of competition around clothes," a resident said.

Others felt things were normal at Columbine and were surprised that the perpetrators enacted a massacre that, to students, seemed out of character. Not like the people they knew.

The principal of Columbine High School made it clear in interviews that he knew nothing of any abuses, that no one had told him of any problem of this nature, and that when he knew about problems he handled them. Perhaps students maintained a code of silence.

"Accounts of these tragic incidents repeatedly indicate that in most cases, a troubled youth has demonstrated or has talked to others about problems with bullying and feelings of isolation, anger, depression and frustration."[5]

As I look at what we know of teens and teens who shoot, I see that verbal abuse played a part in the violence. Both the *defining* of people as objects, and the blurry boundary between the real world and the TV/video world are catalysts to violence. It seems that a common denominator of school shootings is being subject to verbal abuse.

Teens who shoot are short-circuited in their developmental goals. As they enter the transitional world of their teenage years, they incorporate into their new world whatever is "out there" that is different. Like all teens, they need their teen world to be different from their parents' world. Clothing designers, music makers, producers of all kinds quickly come up with something new for each teen generation. However, when their developmental goals are short-circuited, teens may choose to meet them in a disastrous way.

THE SHOOTERS

They looked out there at the real world, saw TV and video, and saw *different clothes,* so they incorporated them into their teen world. For instance, if Dad wears trim pants, they wear different clothes: baggy pants.

They looked out there at the real world and heard TV, CDs, and videos, and heard *different music,* so they incorporated it into their teen world. For instance, Dad listens to jazz, so they listen to different music: rap.

They looked out there at the real world and saw TV, videos, and games and saw *different solutions,* so they incorporated them into their teen world. For instance, if Dad works all day for what he wants, they will use different solutions to get what they want.

Goal: Separate from family
Solution: Hide something really big and maintain silence

Goal: Get an identity
Solution: Instant infamy

Goal: Be heard and seen
Solution: Make a big scene

Goal: Stop real-world intrusions
Solution: Remove them

Goal: Ensure a win
Solution: Plan it out

Goal: Silence real voices and hurtful voices
Solution: Kill real people

In this way, they arranged to accomplish all their goals of traditional adolescence *plus* their goal of preserving their pretend world, virtually all at the same time.

The FBI states that there is *no* way to predict an outbreak of violence in schools but points out some of the issues the perpetrators are dealing with, such as depression, anger, and frustration. But most teens do have to deal with these issues at some time. In fact, almost everyone has had transitory depression, rage, even intolerance but has not become violent or indulged in verbal abuse as a long-term coping device.

Most teens experience trauma at some time, feel depressed at some time, feel like dying at some time, feel so frustrated they could explode at some time, feel that they are not being treated fairly at all, feel like they haven't got a real friend in the world, at the moment. Teens, not to mention many adults, at some time feel these emotional upheavals, but if they go on for a long time, then something is wrong. If feelings of abandonment, that no one cares, escalate into a detachment from teachers, students, and school, some counseling is called for. If teens become intolerant, disrespectful, unyielding, and insensitive toward others, they are, no doubt, indulging in verbal abuse and also very likely have been its target.

Recall the student who turned to a teacher for help and heard, "Don't be a snitch." This is a cruel and verbally abusive comment. It is not only verbally abusive name-calling, but it is a betrayal of trust, coming from an authority figure. This power-fully perpetuates the code of silence.

An exception to the statement "verbal abuse precedes vio-lence" is the rare case in which a child expresses violent outbursts sometimes even before kindergarten. Very often in these rare cases, the child has warm, loving parents, is never abused in any way, but still, inexplicably, expresses sudden rages or attacks other children. This may be a treatable neurobiological problem. See Chapter X, "The Teen Who Verbally Abuses."

Talking things over with someone, getting understanding, and finding warmth and safety are ways that we deal with emo-tional upheavals and traumatic events. Learning how to negotiate and to cope with assaults and slights are skills that must be learned. Learning that the impact of verbal abuse is so great that it reverberates through generations, bruises people inside, and rings in the ears of the very young who beg for it to stop, begins the process of stopping it.

Chapter VI

How Verbal Abuse
Impacts Teens

A YOUNG WOMAN, I'LL CALL HER ANN, TOLD ME HOW VERBAL ABUSE impacted her. She wasn't much past her teens. She vividly recalled the most difficult years of her life, experiencing verbal abuse both at school and at home. It was as if she had been born into a world where all of her experiences were wrong.

Verbal abuse told her that her mind was always lying to her, because when she felt one way, she was told she felt another way; when she thought one thing, she was told that she was thinking something else. Because verbal abuse always, in some way, defines a person's inner reality, someone was always in her mind, telling her *what* she was and what she experienced. It was as if, when her body sensed cold, the rest of the world sensed hot, or so she was told. She said,

> *I always knew something was not right. It brings me*
> *great shame and confusion that even with all the under-*
> *standing I have, that I suffered from verbal abuse,*
> *I cannot seem to find the courage to take back my life.*

I am afraid. It is like "not existing" is familiar and living away from that is frightening. When I go to make choices that are good for me, or go against others' expectations, I feel the terror of rage, of being isolated and rejected, of being humiliated and abandoned, of finding no mercy, so I back down.

The battle is no longer external. It is now internal.

When there is no person actively executing control over me, I do it to myself now.

Could anything be more devastating than to have someone constantly attempting to erase your perceptions, only to punish you when you try to gain them back? As a child, what other reality or world would you have? None, if there were no loving people in your life.

Verbal abuse has lurked behind all kinds of violence, from assaults in homes and schools to so-called religious wars where one group defines another as infidels to be destroyed. Looking into the causes of violence in schools, the National Association of Attorneys General conducted an investigation. They listened. They heard teens tell them what went wrong. They published a comprehensive and highly valuable report, "Bruised Inside." This report took its title from the eloquent, clear, and honest statement of a middle school girl who knew the truth. When asked about physical violence, she said, *"There is another kind of violence, and that is violence by talking. It can leave you hurting more than a cut with a knife. It can leave you bruised inside."*[6]

We now know that the insidious cloud of verbal abuse has descended on schools around the nation. Until violence erupted, possibly no one realized how bad it was. It has so profoundly taken a grip in the minds of some teens, that it has, in many instances, disabled them. They felt unable to speak out even when, in some places, they knew of guns on campus and the possibility of disaster. It is likely that even now, they feel unable to break the code of silence.

We saw how insidiously verbal abuse has convinced some teens that they can be defined as weak—that someone's saying it's so, makes it so, as if teens are not self-defining individuals like other human beings.

In some cases where verbal abuse had that much impact, teens were unable to make decisions that might have saved lives. Adhering to the code of silence, they did nothing to reveal planned violence that might have been stopped.

When teens are convinced that saying something is so, makes it so, their minds are controlled, and they end up believing that they must suffer verbal abuse while pretending it's not happening.

When we believe lies that are told to us, that are about us, we lose our freedom. So many people are so used to having people make up who and what they are, that they are like lambs led to the slaughter, never questioning, never saying, "That's pretend talk."

Some parents and other adults may wonder how teens can be so misled that they accept other people's definitions of them, but there are groups today who define people—and are believed by some folks—because they claim to be speaking for God, or they claim to know what God wants for them.

Standing up to a barrage of lies told to us, and about us, is emotionally exhausting. And, when teens suffer verbal abuse alone, while they are told it is nothing, they are bruised inside.

I believe Ann, whose story opens this chapter, is bruised inside. The impact of verbal abuse is so devastating to the mind and emotions of its target, it can hardly be compared to most physical blows. Verbal abuse can scar for life. If teens who are targets of verbal abuse at school were raised in a household where verbal abuse prevailed, they are even more impacted by the abuse. The cost to human life and well-being is immeasurable.

A teacher said, "Despite the impact of verbal abuse on people, many very intelligent people believe words cannot hurt you. How sad. If I hear, 'Sticks and stones can break your bones, but words can never hurt you,' one more time, I think I'll scream."

It is not hard to understand this teacher's frustration.

We know that verbal abuse is rejecting and exclusionary for teens and most other folks. In their struggles to get a grip on their own truth—their own reality—even while others define it, they suffer from confusion, mental anguish, trauma, depression, an inability to focus, physical illness, or, as happens to some, a complete loss of feelings. It very often leaves teens in need of long-term therapeutic treatment.

Another sad outcome of verbal abuse toward teens is the destructive ways they try to deal with it. The pain they experience from rejection and disparagement may be turned toward escape in drugs or alcohol or, at the extreme, escape in suicide.

A school counselor said, "I think if parents realize that verbal abuse can be, and often is, so damaging it results in thoughts of suicide or even carrying out the act, they will be more inclined to not brush it off as a necessary, uncomfortable part of growing up that you just have to get through."

The National Institute for Mental Health reports that suicide was the third leading cause of death among young people fifteen to twenty-four years of age in 1999. The gender ratio for this age group was five males completing the attempt for every one female. More women than men report a history of attempted suicide, with a gender ratio of three to one. "The strongest risk factors for attempted suicide in youth are depression, alcohol or other drug use disorder, and aggressive or disruptive behaviors."[7]

Mental health professionals are generally agreed that the act of suicide by a teen is prompted, at least in part, by emotional pain, and the teen who attempts or succeeds in committing suicide is depressed and despairing. Prior to the suicide or its attempt, the teen may show signs of withdrawal, or may be more angry and hostile than previously. Many teens also give hints of their intention, such as, "No one would care if I lived or died." In many cases, they feel emotionally abandoned.

Since verbal abuse defines teens as "not who they are," it impairs their ability to define themselves. Recall the parents who defined their daughter as a delicate, feminine ballerina, when she was really a tomboy cowgirl, into competition and daring athletics. She spent many years establishing her ability to be self-defining.

The negative impact of verbal abuse on teens cannot be overstated. Verbal abuse traumatizes its victims and this stress can hinder learning, damage emotional intelligence, impair focus, and even impact health, because the unbearable stress of verbal abuse compromises the immune system. Adults, too, who are subject to verbal abuse at home or at work, most commonly suffer these same serious consequences.

Verbal abuse has kept many people caught in a pretend world where only appearances are real. Daily, people tell me of the havoc verbal abuse has wreaked in their lives. A severely verbally abused young teen said, "I wish I could be *anorexic,* but food is my comfort for my depression and anxiety. At least that's how I feel. No one really understands. They never question me. They just judge me."

I believe that teens commonly develop eating disorders from the impact of verbal abuse, which leaves them isolated, living in a teen world that will not accept them. To gain control, they starve themselves. Additional studies showing the relationship between verbal abuse and eating disorders will need to be done. Eating disorders are epidemic in America.

If you suspect your daughter or son has an eating disorder, contact the National Association of Anorexia Nervosa and Associated Disorders (ANAD), listed in Appendix B. If your child shows symptoms, it does not mean that you are verbally abusive to your child. Barbie dolls and the media define a girl's "ideal" shape. Peers are also a big influence. ANAD research estimates that 716,000 students may have eating disorders. Our teens are especially vulnerable to this terrible illness—86 percent of those with the illness report onset by the age of twenty.[8]

Pain and trauma induce some teens to self-medicate with drugs and alcohol. Alcohol abuse is a growing problem among teens. Some teens take risks and join friends in dangerous activities such as binge drinking just to be accepted, to avoid a put-down. Their vulnerability to damaging and even irreversible outcomes, including death, increases as their need for acceptance increases.

Verbal abuse is a major cause of depression and self-doubt. A large part of the self-help industry and therapeutic practices of all kinds are designed to heal and restore self-esteem, self-confidence, and self-trust.

Verbal abuse may be the single largest factor contributing to the high divorce rate in the United States. Hundreds of thousands of women have left relationships because of verbal abuse. Divorce affects countless youngsters, who do not always understand what has caused the rift.

If teens do not feel accepted at home, rejection from even one or two of their peers is magnified a hundredfold. And, to a much greater degree, rejection by a teacher or a coach leaves them feeling deeply unworthy, inadequate, and as if they are intrinsically flawed.

One of the most common outcomes of verbal abuse is that it traumatizes victims. Many teens are traumatized by verbal abuse because it is unexpected, confusing, rejecting, and has an extraordinary impact on the mind and consciousness itself. Of the many thousands of people I have spoken to, they almost universally say, "No one can imagine what it is like, unless they experience it."

It is one thing to have one's spirit broken; it is another to have one's brain broken. This is a way to imagine the impact. Of course, we do know that traumatic stress impacts the brain. A young child we'll read about later says, " . . . it is making my brain hurt . . ."

I believe that teens and many children who suffer from traumatic stress are described as having an attention deficit disorder. A large number of people who describe ongoing verbal abuse at home tell me of one or more children in their household who seem scattered and unable to focus their attention for long. Many are on medication. This finding deserves further research. The AAP lists "learning impairments" as one of the consequences of psychological maltreatment.[9]

One example of learning impairment that I have observed is that the trauma of verbal abuse interferes with children's ability to *choose* to focus. Just as the bombardment of images from TV can impair this ability, so, too, can verbal abuse.

VERBAL ABUSE IMPACTS NORMAL DEVELOPMENT

In a culture that overlooks verbal abuse, teens who are tormented by it face great difficulty accomplishing their developmental tasks: independence, identity, and career goals. If their peers or teachers put them down, or rage at them, they often lose the confidence they need to become independent. A teen says, "I've heard, if you don't believe in yourself no one else will, but how do I believe in myself if no one else does?"

If teens do not have the confidence and sense of self that they will need throughout their life, they will find it even more difficult to discover their best vocation.

One of the most frightening outcomes of long-term verbal abuse is that it disconnects teens from their emotional self.

A fifteen-year-old boy said, "It's not that you get used to verbal abuse. By the time you reach your junior or senior year, you learn how not to feel anything." "Oh, wow," I said, thinking of the implications. Then, without prompting, he said, "But then you don't have empathy for anyone."

One way boys commonly survive being verbally abused is by shutting down their emotional awareness. Many young boys are part of a culture that tells them that they cannot become men if they have feelings. Losing emotional intelligence becomes a goal. Unfortunately, verbal abuse holds the terrible power of defining boys, telling them what they will, and will not, be if they retain their emotional intelligence. Many boys and some girls suffer the dehumanizing and devastating loss of their emotional awareness. Teens are changing and growing rapidly, and since they are in the process of developing their own identities, independence, and plans for the future, verbal abuse can hinder their progress through the crucial stages of adolescent development.

IDENTITY

Many teens and adults take in subtle assaults, not realizing that they are verbally abusive, and, if they hear them often enough, they start believing them. "Maybe I'm not very smart," the verbally abused teen may think. If this happens, they already doubt themselves, feeling inadequate and innately unacceptable. Consequently, they can't quite sort out who they really are, versus who they are told they are.

On the other hand, if they shut down their emotional pain, lose awareness of their feelings, and slow or stop their emotional development, they can't perceive themselves accurately. They don't know what they feel or even what they really like.

They begin looking outside of themselves for their identity. They begin to make it up according to what they think would look good, be cool, get respect. Of course, they end up with a false image.

They might develop a great appearance so that no one really knows what has happened to them. But if they begin to believe that they are nothing but this image, they'll have a tremendous need to be right about everything. They need to be right because they need to feel that they have made up themselves right. They'll also have a tremendous need to put down anyone who is different, for the same reason.

To maintain their image, they might take up sports they don't care about, or take risks to be popular. Their real interests and their real talents may be lost to them. Being an image and maintaining an image are the driving forces behind many abusers' behaviors.

The Lasting Effects of Verbal Abuse on Identity

Many people spend years ridding themselves of the negative image that they have of themselves because of the way they were defined in their teen and even younger years. Many brilliant and kind children were told they were just the opposite.

A woman told me that she wasn't part of any popular high school group and her teachers didn't accept her because she was shy and silent. In actuality, she felt a little out of place because she had been promoted two grades due to her intellect, but that left her two years behind her peers socially.

She finished graduate school, working quietly and reaching a top corporate position, but all along, she felt like an imposter and that she really wasn't very capable. She still felt dumb because her father had told her that she couldn't do anything right, her mother had stood by saying nothing, and teachers had given up asking her to speak up. No one had asked her how she felt.

Comments made to teens from people they want acceptance from affect their core self-concept. Their sense of self is shaped by the way they are reflected, that is, the feedback they get from others. Home and family count most; parents have the greatest impact on their children.

One way to understand how verbal abuse shapes a person's self-perception is to imagine the game where one person is looking for a hidden treasure and the other says, "You're hot" when the seeker is getting close and "You're cold" when the seeker is moving away. If the feedback is dishonest, the seeker will never find the treasure, the true self.

THE INDICATORS OF VERBAL ABUSE

There is a good chance that someone is verbally abused even when you don't see it, if you spot four or five of the following symptoms.

Teens who are verbally abused either at home or at school may:

- Show a noticeable change in behavior
- Become isolated and withdrawn
- Pull away and refuse to talk
- Seem depressed
- Cry easily or often
- Not have close friends
- Have bad dreams
- Complain about going to school
- Cut classes at school
- Refuse to go to school
- Throw up before school
- Seem to daydream a lot
- Have trouble concentrating
- Get much lower grades than usual
- Seem to have lost enthusiasm for everything

- Develop repetitious behavior:
    Playing one kind of game or video repeatedly
    Doing the same thing over and over
- Become self-critical:
    "I'm not any good at anything."
    "I can't do anything right."
- Hurt themselves, cut themselves, and pull their hair
- Act aggressively toward siblings, peers, or parents
- Get angry often
- Lash out at others
- Get in many fights

No single one of these indicators conclusively proves that a teen is being verbally abused. Even with wonderful homes and schools, a teen may have biological, neurological, or developmental problems that have nothing to do with verbal abuse. If your child shows a number of these symptoms, try to find counseling for your child with an experienced licensed therapist who specializes in teens. It is also important to be open and available to him or her, and to ask how he or she feels. It may take some time before a teen will open up about a problem, but being there for him or her is important.

Teens in the United States have lethally vented their rage in and near schools in more than a dozen shootings, with more than two dozen deaths, between 1998 and 2002. Do some teens become violent despite a supportive home and school atmosphere? Were the teens who became the "shooters" included in groups and activities at school? If any were mistreated, did they have someone to talk to? And, I wonder, if there were any warning signs, would anyone have known how to read them or what to do about them?

When teens are put down by peers or people who have some kind of authority over them or who have a familial relationship with them, they feel even more pain than if the abuse came from a total stranger. With their need for acceptance, their shaky identities, their hormonal upheavals, and their unknowable futures, rejection is a blow they can hardly bear.

People who experience this kind of abuse feel as if they have been psychically raped or kicked in the gut. It is as if the offender has stepped into their mind, body, or spirit, looked around, stepped out, and told them what they found there. "Hey, *bitch,* you're looking for trouble."

Common platitudes such as those from our earlier list— "They don't really mean it," "Don't let it bother you"—contain the unspoken message, "There is something wrong with you if you feel hurt."

Imagine being in such a bind. Teens must tolerate the unacceptable and make it seem acceptable, or they must have something wrong with them. The frustration of bearing criticism, and of being ostracized, while not being able to show the impact or get help is intolerable.

VERBAL ABUSE AFFECTS LEARNING

Verbal abuse has a detrimental effect on many teens' ability to learn. When confidence is eroded and emotions are in turmoil, the teenage mind will drift toward sorting out problems and trying to understand. Teens lose vast amounts of energy and time thinking and rehashing upsetting interactions, trying to figure out why they've been put down, why they've been excluded, why they are hurting, and how they are supposed to behave to have it all stop. This is energy and time that would otherwise be focused toward learning, planning, setting goals, and aspiring to new achievements.

An eighteen-year-old girl described her teen years.

My entry into high school was entry into a very pres-tigious school. I was young and unsophisticated, still in jeans, and the girls were into spike heels, long mani-cured nails, and plunging necklines. Being different, nobody accepted me. I was always on the outside looking in.

I spent a lot of time trying to figure out what was expected of me and why I was not accepted. Why didn't I have a bunch of friends; how could I change myself? Was I smart or dumb? My teachers, clearly, had already formed opinions about my abilities, because I didn't have flare, or style, or any kind of polished presentation. They were either ignoring me or trivializing my opinions. I didn't know how others were assessed, so I had no way to gauge my teachers' assessment of me.

In their early teens, when children move beyond home to the new teen world at school, they are often very defenseless, unso-phisticated, and perplexed by the way they are treated. They are still developing. Verbal abuse can affect even their thought patterns.

They may see things in superlatives. A girl said, "I think Joanie is twice as good as me skiing." Her friends said, "No. She's hundreds of times better than you." This is typical of a young teen.

The point is that very young teens can magnify what they hear so that it has an even greater impact than it would, for instance, to an eighteen-year-old.

Teens are particularly vulnerable to verbal abuse because they are still unsure of themselves and the world. It is hard to have confidence in themselves and their own evaluations if they are told they're wrong. They cannot imagine someone would tell them things that have *no* basis in reality. Young teens usually believe that it happens to them because they are, in some way, not as competent or adequate as others. They can't understand how someone who is smart, popular, older, respected by others, or who supposedly cares for them, would define them with utter conviction if there weren't some misunderstanding on their part or some other logical explanation for it, or if it weren't somehow, in some way, true.

VERBAL ABUSE CREATES CONFUSION

The teen who is confused has no way to tell what is really wrong. When a teen has been abused for most personal decisions and expressions, making choices is difficult. And, when they are made, they are not necessarily in the teen's best interests, because he or she will have difficulty foreseeing even easily anticipated outcomes.

This is how verbal abuse destroys a teen's self-perceptions, even pushing him or her toward losing a sense of reality. This outcome can be tempered, if the teen has strong emotional support and good reality feedback.

Being called names is pretty easy to spot as abuse, and most teachers and parents are aware enough to say, "Hey, no name-calling," when they hear it. But statements by adults to young teens such as, "You're to be seen and not heard," are also verbally abusive. They make something up about the child. If you heard something like this as a young teen and you believed it, you would think that you were not equal with people who *are* seen and heard.

Teens, as well as children and adults, cannot help but be confused by verbal abuse when it comes from someone who claims to care about them, or to have their best interests at heart. It is as if they hear, "I care about you," and they also hear, *"who you really are* is not okay with me." The girl whose mother told her she wanted her to be a ballerina comes to mind. The mother spent much time, energy, and money to both support and to change her daughter. The girl was getting a double message: "I care about you. I don't want to accept you as you are."

Rejection

The teen years hold a crucial initiation into society as a whole. What happens to teens during these years impacts the rest of their life. The first moments of understanding themselves in relation to others can take place in a mutually supportive environment or in the context of rigid and artificial structures of "in-groups" and "out-groups"—insiders and outsiders.

At the very time that they need acceptance from their peers, when their development compels them to find a place for themselves in the teen world, beyond the first world of family, some teens will face rejection.

Teens defining teens according to their looks, abilities, and interests may be a long-established custom in some schools, but its effects are magnified to a teen who has tremendous needs to feel included, valued, accepted, and understood. After all, the teen world is the only "real" world to some teens. Peers are now like family away from home, the people who are most important to them for a sense of belonging and acceptance.

One of the most common ways that verbal abuse takes hold of the lives of teens at school is the labeling of people according to how they look or what they do.

Labels are similar to name-calling. Teens, and even preteens, may find themselves suddenly labeled as part of a group. When this happens to teens, they find that they are either in a group that other groups put down or in a group that puts down some other group. Labels attempt to restrict a person from being real. For instance, a very intelligent boy who was a great athlete was called a jock. He thought that was okay, but he didn't want to show that he could talk about anything serious, because he was afraid he would be called a nerd.

Rejection by peer groups is extremely confusing to the unaccepted child. A senior teen girl said, "I spent a lot of energy trying to figure out the social alliances, what was relevant and what was wanted of me, where I fit in and where I was out of step. I could never conform to their rules and expectations. In the end, I focused on my goals. I gave up trying to fit in and fortunately had a couple of good friends to keep me sane."

Being defined by others can be normalized, that is, made to seem okay, because everyone goes along with it. But, the truth is that defining people is abusive. Having to face social ostracism if he or she does not match some external criteria can be crushing to a teen's sense of self.

A middle school girl said, "I am basically an outcast, excluded from many groups."

The groups that exclude this teen and others limit their social interactions to their own group. Their world is small. It is agreed on, and it is extremely conforming. If teens face rejection from their peers, they may struggle to conform, to fit in, and to be accepted.

The intense pain and rejection that a teen may feel at school because peers do not accept him or her is immeasurable. One of the worst punishments a person can experience is ostracism. When a teen is made the brunt of attack by other teens, and doesn't have a close friend or two, the teen feels ostracized from the world, entirely.

A seventeen-year-old boy says, "I was blamed for not being able to better stand their rejections."

Who Is the Teen Target at School?

Teens who indulge in verbal abuse usually target only people who are different from them, people who seem unprotected, or a family member.

A young teen boy said, "You have to have friends; if you don't have friends, they'll get you."

One of the reasons that verbal abuse is so hurtful is that it rejects real people. It tells them that they are something they are not. Teens experience intense rejection when peers, coaches, or teachers verbally abuse them. Rejection for a teen is rejection by the world—the very world where they, as developing people, are designed to seek acceptance.

Recall that teens move from the world of their home family to the peer world and then finally to the greater world. These transitions will not take place, as they should, if one of these worlds does not accept them.

Verbal Abuse Creates Under- and Overachievers

Since verbal abuse so often attacks a teen's core self-image and is extremely rejecting of the real person, teens can lose the self-confidence they might have had at a much younger age. Without self-confidence, they may not set high goals for themselves. Consequently, they may give up before they start and be under-achievers. On the other hand, they may be driven to overachieve and, later in life, drive others as well, becoming demanding and tyrannical in the workplace as well as at home.

Verbal Abuse Impacts Physical Health

Trying to deal with verbal abuse, ignore it, or figure it out is usually the most stressful and painful experience teens have. Over time, the emotional pain and mental anguish can affect not only a teen's emotional well-being and self-image, but eventually affect his or her physical health. Long-term stress impacts the human immune system and makes verbally abused teens prone to many illnesses. The emotional toll can leave them exhausted, and subject to eating disorders, headaches, digestive problems, overall "sickliness," and an inability to resist infections. However, in no way does this mean that any particular illness-prone child has been verbally abused.

How Abusers Can Define You

Like all verbal abuse, labels reject the real person. The following list shows how verbal abuse is always against the real person and how the rejection of your true self takes place when abusers define you or your experience. The person who indulges in these kinds of verbal abuse is called "the abuser" in the interaction, but is not so characterized in other circumstances.

Snubbing-Ignoring:
The Silent Treatment—Rejecting Your Existence

In the midst of your conversation, the abuser walks away without a word. The real you is rejected.

Mind-boggling Denial—Rejecting Your Experience

After being asked, "Why won't you answer?" the abuser says, "I already did," and then remains silent. The abuser takes no responsibility for the failed communication. If there had been an answer, the response would have been something like, "Didn't you hear me? I said . . ." The abuser forces the victim to ask the question over again, to maintain his or her dominance. This abuse rejects your own reality and perceptions.

Opposing, Countering—Rejecting Your View

Hearing, "That was a good mystery book," the abuser says, "You're wrong. Lots of mysteries are better." This is one of the most common forms of verbal abuse, especially when the person indulging in the abuse doesn't want to sound overtly aggressive by, say, calling you a name. Of course, this abuse rejects your perspective.

Denying by Accusation—Rejecting Your Feelings

Hearing, "I felt bad when you said that," the abuser says, "You're too thin-skinned." This abuse is often experienced as a psychic rape because the abuser pretends to be within you and consequently to know how you feel. It rejects your emotional reality and emotional intelligence.

Denial by Lying—Rejecting Your Perceptions

Hearing a question about, or objection to, something said, the abuser says, "I never said that. We never had that conversation." This terrible abuse assaults your mind and so rejects reality as a whole, and your reality particularly, that deeply spellbound people believe they've changed your experience, as if saying it is so, makes it so.

The Putdown "Joke"—Rejecting Your Human Dignity

Watching you eat, the abuser says, "Look at you, oink, oink." This abuse takes the form of rejecting and ridiculing your humanity.

BLOCKING AND OBSTRUCTING—REJECTING YOUR CONTRIBUTION

Hearing a question or statement, the abuser says, "Just drop it! Who asked for your opinion?" This attempts to silence you and, like all defining statements, rejects you as a person with a separate view, as well as your thoughts and feelings.

DIVERTING—REJECTING YOUR GOAL

Hearing a question or statement, the abuser changes the topic. If you need an answer or to give information to a person who won't answer or respond to you, the communication ends until the person is open to hear you. No relationship exists when information cannot be exchanged.

ACCUSING—REJECTING YOUR INTEGRITY AND MOTIVES

When you least expect it, the abuser says, "You cheated to get that grade" or "You never leave well enough alone." This rejection truly has erased and rejected the real you, in the mind of the abuser, because your personhood and integrity are so deeply integrated.

PUTTING YOU DOWN—REJECTING YOUR INTELLIGENCE

When you don't match his or her expectations, the abuser says, "Boy, are you stupid. You can't keep anything straight. Get over here, dummy." The abuser is unable to see you and so defines you as not you, rejecting your intelligence, abilities, and personhood.

Intimidating and Threatening—Rejecting Your Freedom

When he or she cannot control you in other ways, the abuser says, "If you don't do what I want, I won't be your friend." This rejects your freedom to chose to do or act as you see best.

Ordering—Rejecting Your Ability to Choose

When he or she is afraid to ask nicely, the abuser says, "Get rid of this." "You're not wearing that." "Shut that off." "Get in here and clean this up." The abuser rejects your freedom again.

Name-Calling—Rejecting Your Self-Definition

When he or she cannot control you with threats, the verbal abuser says, "You're a wimp." "You're a wuss." This is one of the most blatant rejections of you as a person.

Sarcasm—Rejecting What You Value

When he or she wants to cast doubt on you, or something you've done or valued or achieved, the verbal abuser's comment drips with derision and doubt. This form of verbal abuse is usually a cover-up for jealousy in the abuser, who wants to reject the envied quality or object and its importance to you.

Part Two

Where Verbal Abuse Shows Up

THE PURVEYORS OF VERBAL ABUSE CAN APPEAR ANYWHERE IN A TEEN'S life, particularly in the media, where verbal abuse is normalized in sitcoms, videos, songs, talk shows, and even sports arenas. Verbal abuse also gets a foothold in some homes where one or both parents has turned verbal abuse into a lifestyle. Lastly, we see that in schools, verbal abuse invades the lives of some students, educators, and coaches.

Chapter VII

Verbal Abuse in Media and Sports

THE GENERAL CONSENSUS OF PARENTS, TEACHERS, AND PROFESSIONALS who are trained to counsel children, is that the media contributes to the problem of verbal abuse in teen's lives but is not the underlying cause. However, it is a big contributor. The prevalence of abuse and violence on TV and in videos, as well as in music and interactive games, desensitizes children to the impact of harmful behavior, and shows children how to be abusive.

"The average American child has viewed 200,000 acts of violence on television by the age of eighteen."[10] This means that violence has, to some extent, been normalized in the culture. Although there are people who believe that this has no impact on children, the increasing severity of youth-related violence that does occur and the increasing incidence of verbal abuse in our schools clearly indicate that the media does have an influence on young people.

The National School Safety Center says that a characteristic associated with violent school deaths is that the perpetrator consistently prefers TV shows, movies, or music expressing violent themes and acts.[11]

TELEVISION

If a teen has grown up with healthy values and is so clear about them that he or she wouldn't dream of putting someone down, then obviously a TV show filled with verbal abuse will not induce this teen to indulge in verbal abuse. However, if this were a teen looking for a way to get back at another teen, or if this were a teen with a deep fear of his or her own gender preferences, he or she could take in the abusive media as if it were a training ground for an attack of words or worse.

Television is like a giant market where people sell things. Some things, like the food in a supermarket, are good to take in. Some things, like the poison in bug killers, are not good to take in. Just like a big market, TV carries food and poison. And the seller makes money on both. The profit motive, not people appreciation, is the deciding factor for some shows.

It isn't difficult to select good TV shows, because those shows that support respect, understanding, tolerance, and education are easy to recognize. However, shows that may seem innocuous, or shows that have captured media attention, may seem okay because everyone is watching them. However, they may, in fact, teach exclusionary practices, ridicule "losers," disparage human beings, discriminate against people who are different, and demonstrate ways to be verbally abusive, all the while presenting these toxic behaviors as if they were normal, even to be emulated!

In one of his columns, TV critic Chuck Barney of the *Contra Costa Times* pointed out the "mean-spirited tone that has crept into so much TV fare these days."[12] He generously gave me some of his time to discuss popular TV shows. The mean spirit he spoke of does show up in many shows; it does normalize verbal abuse and desensitize teens and children, and possibly adults. I asked him about verbal abuse in the media.

What is TV like compared to twenty years ago?

"In the American tradition, the host of a game show rooted for the contestants, 'Come on, you can do it. There's still a minute to go.' The struggling contestants heard the audience dropping hints, trying to help. The wrestlers wrestled and, rough as it was, no one got vile with name-calling perversions about you being with your mother or father. In the daytime talk shows, the stories unfolded and people got help."

And now?

"Today, it is different. Conflict sells and offers quick solutions. Throw out the opposition: the weaker, the less prepared, the real people, and keep the toughest and meanest of all in the limelight. It's 'televisual' dodge ball—cutthroat stuff. There is a lot about not losing, and weeding out, and cutting out the 'losers.' Being mean seems to gain a lot of attention. I wonder if being mean might seem an attractive goal to some teens. I wonder if some teens dream of being mean enough to get a lot of attention, not to be cut out, but to be the one cutting out."

What shows portray meanness or an exclusionary style?

"'Reality' shows: They present as reality, ganging up against the underdog, to exclude or eliminate the competition.

- *Survivor*—Eliminates the less able.
- *South Park*—It's aired late, as comedy, an adult show, crude, and satiric. College students will find it very funny. The kid Kenny who died every week and came back to life is killed off for good. But I was more appalled

by the name-calling, profanity, et cetera: 'Your mom's a crack whore.' If kids watch, it's the parent's fault. It's not for any child.

- *The Weakest Link*—It's a syndicated British show where the host taunts and scorns contestants for their lack of knowledge; you are, she says, 'the weakest link.'
- *Dog Eat Dog*—Trash talk prevails. [*Author's note:* I watched this show and I found it sad because a contestant had "taken in" the label she had been given. In this show the players gang up against each other, trying to pick the person who will, they decide, be most likely to fail the challenge. In other words, the players try to pick losers. A young woman misses a test. She's told, "You're a loser." She says, "I'm such a loser." Losers all end up in the dog pound.]
- Daytime shows: Some daytime TV is arranged to bring out a fight. Often teen guests swear at the audiences that boo them. The scorned teen comes back to taunt the scorner, 'Screw you and look at me now.' The scorner says, 'You're still a bitch. And, f*** you.' Even court shows are more feisty and fiery now. They deride the unprepared."

Haven't TV sports also changed over the years?

"It used to be that, if you scored a touchdown or made a basket, you took quiet pride in it and moved on. Now, trash-talking is all the rage. Football players spike the ball in an opponent's face and do a wacky little dance. Basketball players sneer and bark at their defenders when they dunk the ball on them. Wrestling always did have some violence, but it has become a hyped-up show that is filled with blasts of bleeped-out profanity along with sexual soap-opera-type sideshows that look like you've entered a harem. Men say extremely degrading things to women.

A stereotypical 'bimbo' looks good next to the women in these shows. It's not a sport, but they label it entertainment and say, 'If it's entertainment, everything is permissible.' And they act as though they have a right to fight over a woman as if she were their property."

"Kids buy the characters marketed on the shows, in the form of toys and action figures. Everybody makes a buck on a cable show touting 'For 18 years or older.' And they know it isn't so. Not with the advertising to young kids."

After this conversation with Barney, I could see how kids were not embarrassed or ashamed to put down kids or to exclude them, or to deride the underdog. It looks like a normal way to be, on many TV shows. Possibly, producers cater to young audiences with the sensationalism of verbal abuse, because it is the "forbidden fruit" that draws viewers and thus sells advertising.

A lot of TV is designed to disparage people and to make the abuse look good or normal or perfectly acceptable. I watched one of these shows the other day, *American Idol.* I was amazed to see that exclusion and verbal abuse are part of the show. Like walking through fire, the contestants know they may be burned. A judge who happily condemns them with scorching disapproval slams those who don't make it to the final round.

This talent contest normalizes verbal abuse as a test one must endure and as a joke that entertains onlookers. I wonder how teens can help but see it this way.

It is certainly important that parents discuss shows that disparage life, and talk about the power to be selective and to be *for* life, not against it.

I interviewed a fourteen-year-old girl and asked her if she could tell me what watching one of these shows was like for her.

Do you watch the TV show American Idol?
"Oh, yeah, I missed it last night."

What do you think about how the contestants feel when they don't win?
"The judge tries to be mean, putting them down."

How do you think kids feel when they see him do that?
"They see the contestants' expressions. They know they're hurt even when the contestants try not to show it.

"They give their heart and soul. I wouldn't want to be told that. I think the contestants feel they have to go on. Like their friends want them to, but it turns off some kids. When I first heard him, I was shocked. After a while, I got so I wasn't shocked. I was ready for it."

Do you think you weren't shocked after a while because you expected it or you were desensitized?
"Probably desensitized. Like, if you hear some word you know that you're not supposed to say, but you hear it for a while, and after a while, it's not shocking."

I didn't know that this fourteen-year-old girl would know what "desensitized" meant. But, she clearly did. Feeling shock or being stunned by seeing someone hurt is our natural human response to another person's pain. Losing that ability is what is behind educators' and parents' dislike about abuse and violence pouring into homes where children do not have a parent around to monitor their intake or to educate them about making good choices or, at least, to evaluate what they watch so they can understand what is not okay about it.

All parents are urged by educators everywhere to talk to their kids about abuse and violence in the media. There are millions of people who grew up without television or video games. They rarely, if ever, saw verbal abuse and violence. When we compare 200,000 acts of violence on TV alone to zero to two acts of violence that previous generations saw in their whole childhood, common sense tells us that seeing violence, not to mention verbal abuse, has a negative influence on children. However, children can be taught to be very selective about what they watch. Just because it's there, doesn't mean it's good.

The same holds true for the hundreds of thousands of verbally abusive comments that children hear before they are eighteen.

Since verbal abuse usually *precedes violence* in incidents where the perpetrator and target know each other, it is of prime importance that parents and educators do everything possible to teach children that just because they see verbal abuse on TV and in movies, and hear music that includes verbal abuse, doesn't mean it's okay.

VIDEO GAMES

In considering the desensitization of teens and the normalization of verbal abuse, some video games are leading offenders. The video game Doom, for instance, was a favorite of the Columbine shooters. Millions of players can hunt and kill from computers across the world.

Games that destroy people, that, in essence, teach children how to go against life, make verbal abuse seem not so bad. But any way that children learn to hurt increases the ease in which they can inflict extreme pain on peers through verbal abuse and bullying.

The general consensus among teens is that these games don't hurt them, but the general consensus among educators is that they do have a negative impact. Although they may not be the cause of verbal abuse, tactics of domination and power over others show kids how to go about destructive acts. So, these could be the scenarios they contemplate, if they are already pre-disposed by anger, resentment, or hatred to enact them. Even "nice" kids, if life changes and they encounter abusive people, can fall back into their "reserve" education in dominance via fantasy games. These games, as well as TV violence, might be innocuous at one stage of life, but become a tutorial in how to be violent if an extremely difficult or demanding stage of life emerges.

When children involve themselves in interactive violence in video games and on the Internet, violence seems all the more normal, and, of course, there are no consequences. All studies to date indicate that exposure to violence on TV and in games skews the child's world. What is dangerous is that interactive video games reward a person for striking back. If children learn by watching, modeling, and practicing, as we know they do, they learn violence if they are exposed to it and made a part of it.

NEGATIVE MEDIA MESSAGES

A teacher said, "Sixth graders mimic *South Park.* A real Kenneth child was tormented unmercifully. 'Let's kill Kenny,' said the kids." To adults it may be *virtual* reality, but to many children it seems to be *actual* reality.

Because TV brings actual violence from all over the world into our homes, teens can develop a slanted and unrealistic view of the world and the dangers around them.

Another example of the media's ability to influence is its presentation of thinness as an ideal for women. This idea is backed up by words that influence teen girls to be thin. The subtle signs of acceptance and rejection that accompany TV shows, magazines, movies, and advertising all conspire to put the thinnest women in the best roles. This message has not been lost on teen girls.

Although it is not *verbally* abusive to emphasize underweight women as the ideal image, there are no notices to the young that this is part of a pretend world and is only a current fashion. "A study of young elite swimmers revealed that more than 60 percent of average-weight girls and nearly 18 percent of underweight girls were trying to lose weight."[13, 14]

When we think of the pretend world that people who define others create, it becomes extremely important that we teach our children the difference between what is real and what is pretend.

We do know that exposure to media violence correlates to aggressive behavior, that children learn from observing, and that the media creates a "pretend world" that can seem real to children.

We also know that children average about six hours or more a day absorbing media messages including films, video games, music, television programs, and the Internet.

Although we need more research into the prevalence of verbal abuse in media to provide accurate statistics, it is reasonable to assume that the incidence of people put down, diminished, defined, and verbally assaulted is hundreds of times greater than the portrayals of physical violence.

The AAP recommends that parents should ensure that their children are "thoughtful, critical consumers of media. They should set content and time limits on media use, monitor and discuss the media their children consume, and take TVs and video games out of the children's bedrooms."[15]

Violent video games desensitize children. Their empathy for real victims decreases, because they have destroyed many virtual people. Some technology even allows them to put faces on the victims so that they are personal to the teen.

Verbal abuse, the defining of human beings by other human beings, thrives wherever people devalue life and the spirit of life within all living creatures.

Verbal Abuse in Sports

Verbal abuse becomes contagious, spreading from coaches, teammates, and spectators—showing up in sporting arenas and locker rooms. Everyone has observed people who declare actual lies about others as if they were factual: "You're a failure [or dork or wuss]," for example.

More often than not, the sporting arena—gym, playing field, and locker room—are where criticism and name-calling are most often heard. Verbal abuse in sports has long-lasting effects; its prevalence and cultural acceptance are damaging to teens who learn to indulge in it simply because it seems normal. Nonabusive and constructive coaching creates positive experiences that last a lifetime. Unfortunately, negative, abusive coaching experiences may also last a very long time. A woman seriously asked, "Isn't verbal abuse just part of sports?"[16] She is part of a growing number of people who believe that sports are about abuse at some level, as though it takes all kinds of abuse to win. However, sports are really about skill and, in many cases, teamwork. Within the exacting parameters of the rules of the game, men and women test their skills, balance, form, speed, strength, and endurance. They prepare themselves for the tests of life. Will they keep going when the going gets tough? And just as important, will they play fair? After all, if they don't play fair—follow the rules—they've failed the test. They've won a false victory. They've taken the coward's way. Isn't this what some corporate leaders have done? Did they grow up thinking abuse was just part of the game?

Good sportsmanship transferred to everyday life shows up as fairness, honesty, and respect for others. While it's true that many good coaches who are honest and fair pass these values on to their teams, some team players and some coaches, both in and out of the game, are less than sportsmanlike. Incidents of verbal and physical abuse perpetrated by coaches or players are making the news.

Abuse is a perverted way of "winning over" others. It's the opposite of good sportsmanship.

The most common form of unfair behavior is verbal abuse. When verbal abuse, temper tantrums, and outbursts of rage are tolerated in a coach or team member, the message is, "It's okay to launch personal attacks on others." Somehow, inflicting pain is considered justifiable, even a sign of strength.

If a coach is fired for abuse, no matter how able the coach is at his job, people of intelligence will realize that taking a stand against abuse is much more important than condoning it.

Teaching coaches to stop abuse both among team members and by coaches is essential if we are to live in a healthier world. See Appendix B for resources.[17]

In athletics, verbal abuse often takes the form of a gender slam. "Stupid" and "lazy" are not as common as, "Aren't you man enough for that?" or "You're being a girl" or, to the team, "Everyone has to hustle. Come on girls." When this is said to boys, it conveys that everything they were taught about name-calling, from nursery school through grammar school, is wrong. That name-calling is now a tool, and if you work harder than you've ever worked before, you might get the name-calling to stop. Here you might get acceptance, but only if you stop feeling.

The attitude of this coaching style is unkind, which may come from ignorance. The instructions are to grin and bear it. An eighteen-year-old boy said, "Don't complain; get bloody and get tired. That's the line, but gender slams don't make it easier."

Just as girls don't want to be called boys, boys don't want to be called girls. When one gender is used as a slam on another gender, both genders are put down.

For some coaches and some team members, name-calling is more than a tool of intimidation. It is also a way for those who have lost touch with their feelings to bond together against all the rules of mutual respect that they used to live by. *They bond together against respect because without empathy, they know no other way to connect.*

In teen sports, when a player misses a crucial play, he is doubly burdened if he has been told that he is not good enough. Everyone is counting on the one catch, the one goal, or the one home run. This monumental pressure from parents, coaches, teammates, and the school that is looking on is magnified by the knowledge that he will be accused of not being good enough, that he will be defined as a failure and left with guilt that should be borne by the abuser, who pretends that sports are not just games.

The belief that showering abuse on players leads to better players, that it makes winners, is a trend that permeates sports from kindergarten through college. It is only the tip of the iceberg of an abusive glacier of cold, ruthless, and toxic methodologies for coaching.

If a teen must function in the face of abuse, he may become part of the ruthless "jock hierarchy" students speak of, and intimidate others because he can't get back at the people who did this to him.

THE VERBALLY ABUSIVE COACH

Some people indulge in verbal abuse to gain control over you for many reasons. To make you, for instance, into the kind of pretend person they want, say a perfect athlete. A coach, for instance, who knows you want approval, may call you names to control you. Most teens will do almost anything to get approval from a coach, to get the name-calling to stop.

A pediatrician met with some coaches at a coaching conference. Amazingly, she learned that many of them believed that verbal abuse is a teaching/coaching methodology. This idea supports some coaches' need to have power and control over the players. Sure, some teens will do anything to avoid humiliation and intimidation. But does that make them better players and better people?

The verbally abusive coach may not only believe that being abusive is okay, but may also base his self-worth on being associated with the winning team, just like some teenagers get their value from being associated with the in-crowd. This gives a weak person a sense of control and ownership of the people being controlled. The coach who indulges in verbal abuse attempts to manipulate everyone under his or her control like puppets on a string.

Coaches set the tone of the team. What they say is accepted and acted out. Coaching practices influence the culture, just as the culture is influenced by these practices. At this time, because many people are uneducated and unaware of the power of verbal abuse to destroy self-esteem and self-perception, most people find it difficult to come to the aid of a child abused in a grocery store, much less on the sports field.

Bad coaching sets a negative tone of disrespect toward people. Bad coaching also teaches that speaking up against verbal abuse is weak. This is obviously backward thinking.[18] It perpetuates the power to abuse with impunity. I doubt that the coaches who live in, and through, the athletes realize that they have entered a destructive pretend world when they define them and their inner worlds.

Abusive coaching desensitizes young people. This is a dangerous strategy. Name-calling, for instance, defines people as objects, not people. Just as in war, objects are easier to shoot in anger than are real people.

Another danger of the desensitizing process is that if the coach succeeds in disparaging a player, he may lose touch with his feelings, in a sense, his humanity. No wonder some men have said that having feelings is a talent they don't have. These men honestly don't know what they feel. Consequently, they are incapable of knowing what others feel.

If a coach is motivated to maintain control at all costs, the abuse can escalate out of control. The coach, then, who is attempting to control the player, is, himself, out of control. One observer told me that he had seen this happen and almost called child protective services.

Not only have some coaches normalized verbal abuse, but also some spectators. People report observing intermediate and high school games in which the spectators stood by and watched children being verbally abused, harassed, accused, called names, and so forth, and they said nothing.

The mother of four boys, all athletes, said that their coaches and peers abused all the boys before they became big enough and strong enough to win the game or to threaten the kid who put them down.

Their father also indulged in verbal abuse, saying things like, "You're ruining the game"—accusing and criticizing if his son didn't win a certain play in what was *supposed to be* just a game. Some fine young men and women face this kind of disparagement and disapproval almost every day of their lives.

Some coaches set the opposite tone. They say, "Hey, no teasing. Hey, that's not okay. Don't say that to him. He's trying his best." These coaches help young people to see that disparagement is not okay. They wake them up to the reality of the world around them, helping them to become sensitive and aware of what is real and what is not.

The need for acceptance and inclusion is very powerful and cannot be overemphasized.

Not being an athlete, a fifteen-year-old boy endured abuse and a vicious beating in order to gain *acceptance* into a gang. "I knew this was going to hurt really bad, but I felt that if I could take it for just a couple of minutes, I'd be surrounded by people who loved me."[19]

Chapter VIII

Verbal Abuse at Home

IN SOME HOMES, THERE IS MUCH SUPPORT AND LOVE—CHILDREN have enough support to weather taunting, teasing, and all kinds of verbal abuse at school. In other homes, children are introduced to verbal abuse at an early age. Literally millions of people struggle to overcome the lifelong impact of verbal abuse.

We will look at homes now where children are not heard and seen, where they are not respected, where they do not have parents who have time for them, where they are criticized, and where parents try to shape them into the child they always hoped for, rather than to nurture the child that they have.

Vast numbers of teens and children of all ages come to school unable to focus and are restless, depressed, or angry because they experience verbal abuse at home, where it is supposed to be safe. At home, some teens witness it, and some are its target. Some may practice what they've experienced at home when they get to school. If not supported at home, if they are already troubled, teens and children will be much less able to cope with verbal abuse from their peers and others.

Verbal abuse in homes is usually a multigenerational problem, because most people who indulge in verbal abuse were themselves abused. However, all those who were abused do not necessarily become abusive to the next generation.

Three weeks before her mother's death, a young woman talked with her mother, who was dying of breast cancer and its complications. Her mother, knowing that death was imminent, called her daughter to her to share an important request and insight. Her words were etched in her daughter's mind: "Please," she said, "whatever you do, if you're ever married to a man who abuses your children, take them, and get out."

"But, Mom," the daughter said, "you didn't do that for us."

"I know. I thought that by praising you I could counteract all your dad's criticism of you," her mother said.

"But no, Mom. Dad's relentless verbal abuse, criticism, and derision over years shredded what little self-esteem I had. Mom, there's no way to shore up self-esteem when there's none left to work with."

Was this mother's early death precipitated by the constant stress of her own and her children's abuse? Since verbal abuse creates intense emotional pain and mental anguish, the immune system is compromised. Verbal abuse is one of the most exhausting and stressful experiences a person can endure over the years.

Countless teens have been and are abused in homes by a parent because the other parent didn't have the strength, the knowledge, or the means to rescue them.

We saw in the first chapter that Bobby and Danny were experiencing verbal abuse at home on a daily basis but were unaware that being called names was uncommon. When they were told that other dads didn't usually call their sons names, Bobby was shocked and Danny was unbelieving. Neither had known that it was abuse.

Likewise, many parents aren't quite sure what verbal abuse is, considering it a form of discipline (as misguided parents believe) or education (as some coaches believe). Many readers will, no doubt, have a good idea of what verbal abuse is and are probably careful to think about what they say. However, if one parent is verbally abusive, it is that parent who is least likely to want to read up on the subject.

Sometimes parents are in conflict about verbal abuse. One parent thinks that what the other parent says is verbally abusive to the child. The other parent says it's not abuse. If you know someone who won't read about it, yet you suspect he or she indulges in verbally abusive behaviors, then I recommend that you introduce the subject through the American Academy of Pediatrics. They have published an article about the mistreatment of children. The authors state, "Psychological maltreatment is a repeated pattern of damaging interactions between parent(s) and child that becomes typical of the relationship." I urge every reader to read the electronic article "The Psychological Maltreatment of Children—Technical Report" which you can find on the Web site *www.AAP.org*.[20]

Verbal abuse is one of the most prevalent of all forms of psychological maltreatment. The article points out that in a survey of teens about their experiences of verbal aggression at home, 50 percent experience severe aggression (belittling, degrading, cursing, threatening to send the child away, calling the child "dumb" or other such names).

According to the AAP, some of the behaviors that constitute psychological maltreatment are:

> *Acts that put down the child:* "Spurning (belittling, degrading, shaming, or ridiculing a child; singling out a

child to criticize or punish; and humiliating a child in
public.)"

Withholding love and affection: "Denying emotional responsiveness (ignoring a child or failing to express affection,
caring, and love for a child) . . . Rejecting (avoiding or
pushing away)."

We'll now look at the problem of verbal abuse in the home
from the perspective of a fourteen-year-old girl, Mary.

Mary had heard the words "verbal abuse" and, thinking
that that might have been what was happening to her, looked for
information on the Internet. She found me. Her statement
is heart wrenching and symbolic of the kind of abuse that can
go on in a home. While Mary's story is most likely not indica-
tive of what takes place in your home, since only a small percentage of mothers call their daughters vile names, I think it is
important to know that it does happen. By being alert to it, you
may spot the problem in a neighbor's child or in one of your
teen's friends.

Having someone to listen and be a "mom" to a girl like
Mary can make all the difference in her overcoming a childhood
of torment. Mary sent me this story before her mother cut off
Mary's communications with me.

MARY'S STORY

"Hi, my name's Mary. I'm fourteen years old and for as long as
I can remember, my mother has yelled at me, called me names,
anything you can think of, anytime I do even the smallest thing
wrong. When she's finished, she always expects me to apologize,
and then when I do, she'll apologize a few days later for yelling
at me. For a while, I just accepted that and let it go, but as years
go on, something builds inside you and you just can't keep it in

anymore. She acts as if just her saying, 'Oh, I really don't mean it' will take it away.

"Being a teenage girl, normal doubts are supposed to arise since you're changing so much, but I've noticed that now I believe that everything she said about me is true and it's led me to hate myself even more. Just today, what possessed me to find out more about this, and ask for help from somebody, anybody, was that she got the maddest I have ever seen her!

"For the first time, she told me repeatedly what a bitch I was, and was degrading me to things so much less than what I know I am deep down. She degrades me from being a person, she wouldn't even give me that much. She told me she wanted to hit me and keep hitting me until she didn't have to deal with me anymore.

"What caused all this?

"I wouldn't explain to her the personal life of my best friend, whose parents are getting divorced. She told me, how dare I treat her like that, and not tell her about those things. But I thought it best to keep my best friend's problems to myself. I know she wouldn't want me telling anybody else, even my mom, who is like her second mom.

"I'm scared she'll come upstairs and see me writing. She's been doing that at random times (coming upstairs) to yell at me more. I can't stop crying and I can't stop actually thinking I'm less than a person and everything else she said about me. I don't know what to do. I don't want to just sit there and listen to her abuse me anymore. I don't want to put up with this anymore. Please help me.

"You can use my story if you would like. I really want other people to understand that things like this happen. And I want a lot of other people who put up with it, not to have to anymore and to understand that it's verbal abuse, and not just how parents punish their children. Then people think it's all right, and normal when it's not."

I changed this girl's name to "Mary," but that's all I changed. There are other young people who could have written this account of being abused. There is no way any mother could figure out for certain if her daughter sent it—though possibly some mothers would be inclined to ask their daughter if she wrote it.

I am saddened by Mary's story, and I am also grateful that we have someone like Mary here on planet Earth—that after millions of years of growing and becoming, the human race has brought forth a person who, at fourteen, knows that many children think abuse is "normal when it's not."

And Mary has cared enough about people to want to help others know the truth. She is truly a commendable human being.

Children like Mary who are verbally abused at home, may not have the inner strength to reach out to others for support. A child who can reach out, tell a friend, and talk to a counselor may find enough support to survive without lasting damage.

On the other hand, a child who hears nothing but platitudes, who is *not told* that verbal abuse is *not* okay, may very well think he or she is to blame. Teens who are verbally abused at home may not realize that other children are abused, too. They may think, "Maybe something is wrong with me or the way I come across." Such children, if they don't themselves become abusive, can become the target of an abuser. They are not likely to have the skills and knowledge that would allow them to recognize a potentially verbally abusive person. Nor would they know that the best course is to try not to be friends with abusive personalities. Although some verbally abusive people are virtually impossible to spot early on, and have fooled even some psychologists, some can be sensed from across the room.

Reflecting on her teen years, we hear from a young woman, Laral, who also experienced verbal abuse at home and a half-dozen years later is still dealing with the impact.

"I was tormented at home during my teen years. I even had to leave and live in my car for a while. Anyway, school was a great retreat for me. I got very busy and participated in many activities that gave me a sense of accomplishment.

"But, I was very insecure and lonely. Looking back, I was never really in my own skin. It was like I was this person just trying to get away and I could never stop. I was always trying to not let the two worlds, home and school, come together. The confusion, sadness, loneliness, fear, and hopelessness are not something teenagers like to talk about."

While Laral, like Mary, was tormented most by her own mother, I hear from many mothers who observe their children's torment and fear for their well-being. These mothers, like Bobby's and Danny's mother, are searching for answers and ways to protect their children. A child will cry, "Mommy, please drive me," "Don't make me go with Daddy," or "Mommy, please don't let Daddy baby-sit me; he's always mad."

A mother recently said, "How can I help my three-year-old? When his dad walked out, he told him, 'I'm not coming back because you won't behave.' Now whenever Dad walks out the door, my child is in terror that his dad won't come back."

The father has defined his child's future, telling him what he "won't" do (won't behave); threatened the child with abandonment (not coming back); and blamed the child for his leaving ("because you . . ."). Defining, threatening, and blaming are verbally abusive and can begin long before a child is three years old.

Although this child is not a teen, the impact of the abuse may very well show up most when he is in his teens, when he confronts the many developmental challenges of becoming independent and truly self-defining.

If this father, abusing his baby, can get him not to feel anything, he may create another abuser, certainly someone tough enough and mean enough to verbally abuse his own child, if he becomes a father. This child will also be one of the teens no one can understand: seemingly not aware of others' feelings, unable to feel much himself, but in touch with his rage, stored from the time he was three.

In another instance, a man said, "My whole childhood was my mother yelling at me and me yelling back at my mother. All I ever wanted was a real person to talk to. Not the mother mask she hid behind. No matter how I approached her, all she turned to me was her mother mask. She showed her real self to everyone else."

The mother mask, to this man, was the critical, angry, ever-complaining person for whom he was never, ever good enough.

Withholding is a category of verbal abuse and shows up most as the silent treatment. Some parents use subtle forms of disapproval and withdrawal of love and responsiveness in order to try to draw their child away from his or her natural, innate personality and interests and turn him or her into whomever they dreamed of and envisioned and were surprised not to get. There are some parents who make the mistake of thinking that a child is like an empty computer for the parent to program.

Parents have the responsibility of raising their children to become responsible adults, to be able to make good choices, and to take care of themselves. Children can best do this if they are allowed to develop their own talents and style. Otherwise, the child suffers untold oppression and lasting trauma, knowing he or she was unacceptable in the eyes of a parent, as was, for instance, the teen who was *supposed* to be a ballerina but was born a very different person with a style of her own.

I believe one of the best ways to support teens in reaching their developmental goals is to make sure that they know the difference between what is real and what is not. And that teens know that every time someone makes up something about them, that person is not only pretending to know something about their inner reality, which no one can know, but he or she is also intruding into their inner space, and that is not okay. Some examples of the kinds of verbally abusive statements that are hurtfully intrusive are listed below.

VERBAL ABUSE IS PRETEND TALK

You're not listening.

You're just trying to show up _____.

You made me yell at you.

You like to hear yourself complain.

You think you're smarter than anyone.

You're talking back.

You're trying to have the last word.

Nobody asked you. (So shut up.)

Nobody cares what you think.

No one likes you.

You're good for nothing.

You'll never amount to anything.

You can't do anything right.

You're trying to get out of it.

You're a screwup.

You don't take anything seriously.

You're looking for trouble.

You're to be seen and not heard.

Get your _____ over here!

You've got nothing to cry about.

I'll give you something to cry about.

You're not hurt; you're just trying to get attention.

You're really not trying.

You shouldn't have to ask me that.

You already know the answer.

You're a troublemaker.

You think you're so smart.

What's wrong with you?
You'll do anything for attention.
You're a wuss (wimp, nerd, jerk, dummy, retard, bitch, idiot,
    etc.).

Name-calling changes over time. New names and adapted names pop up like weeds, and they spread like wildfire. A wuss, according to my clients, can't handle anything, even something only slightly unsettling. Disapproval and nonacceptance resonate with this phrase. I had never heard it before the mid 1990s. The first time I heard, "Don't be a wuss," it was from clients telling me what they heard their husbands say to their sons. One of these sons was just two years old. He was at the beginning of his training to take abuse without even the relief of tears. He was without recourse.

Home should be a safe place, but, unfortunately, it is where verbal abuse is often normalized. I have heard stories of very young children, especially baby boys, being called names for expressing their pain. "Don't be a wimp," is a common example. If children hear themselves called names, their sense of self and their self-esteem is damaged. If they live in a threatening atmosphere, the enormous stress over time is extremely damaging. If no one speaks up, the abuse is normalized.

The verbally abusive comments listed earlier tell people how they feel, think, what they know, what they are trying to do, and so on. It's all pretend talk and all rejecting of the real person. It's silly stuff, because no one knows any of these things about another person. No one can rationally define anyone in this way. Sadly, many teens have heard this verbal abuse and many other kinds of verbal abuse as well.

If parents are limited in their understanding of themselves, they may devalue the gifts and qualities their children possess. If they are ignorant, untalented, or expect their child to be a pretend child, they may not see their real child at all. Hence, they reject the real child.

At home, teens need to feel that their family is on their team, on their side, and really values them. Sometimes one parent will hear the other parent verbally abusing the child, that is, calling the child names and defining him or her.

Sometimes, verbal abuse of a child doesn't start until the adolescent becomes a sexual being. Girls may be put down for their weight, for the size of their breasts, even for their height. This is when the teen may not match a pretend teen in the mind of a parent or may not match an ideal teen in the mind of class-mates. In either case, for some teens, this is when their abuse begins.

Boys may be harassed, taunted, or ridiculed for the size of their muscles or for their height and strength. And just as girls may not match a parent's picture of how they should be, boys also may not meet a parent's expectations.

Some parents like children only when they are young and more easily controlled. Some resent the life and freedom their teens enjoy. Some parents are jealous of their children, who rep-resent their own lost youth, beauty, or strength.

Much verbal abuse in homes occurs when a parent is under the influence of alcohol or drugs. It is not okay to stand by and see a child being verbally abused without speaking up, without saying at least, "Hey, that's not okay."

Unfortunately, when a parent is intolerant toward a child, long before his or her teen years, the parent has already conveyed to the child that he or she is a bother, an aggravation, and a nui-sance, and therefore worthy of denigration. Usually any tendency to indulge in verbal abuse, especially criticism, will increase as the child makes choices that are more independent. If you are a teen reading this, and this is your experience, you must bring up the issue to a trusted family member, a school counselor, or a teacher. Groups like Alateen may also be helpful. See Appendix B for resources.

Sometimes one parent is verbally abusive to the other. It is important to avoid appearing victimized, no matter what. Even saying something as mild as, "That kind of talk is not okay" is important because a teen who hears a parent put down will not know what to do if he or she ends up in a similar situation. A young adult said that her mother was criticized and put down and so forth, and because she did not know how to respond appropriately, the daughter grew up with impaired coping skills. These skills are best learned in the home, with parents being good role models by not verbally abusing each other and by stopping verbal abuse when they hear it.

Actively model behaviors that deflect and neutralize any verbal abuse your child hears. If you are verbally abused, be firm and clear in your response. "What did you say? That sounded like verbal abuse; did you mean it that way?"

An eighteen-year-old says, "I told my mother many times that she was crazy, but I never really believed it. If I had I would have left much sooner."

A woman recalls her teen years at home and how even from childhood, she endured verbal abuse from an entire family who she said were spellbound, and, more than anyone else, her mother was at the extreme. *But, no one knew.*

These stories give testimony to the lasting impact of verbal abuse and to the fact that when verbal abuse occurs in homes, the child's welfare becomes the responsibility of the extended family and the community. This is a wake-up call to listen to teens.

When the verbally abused teen has also been a verbally abused child, she or he will take in what is heard just like any child will take in any parental warning, just *to survive.* Paradoxically, such abuse threatens survival. The spell—the illusions that lead a person to believe that he or she can know the inner reality of another person without asking—is deadly.

Why should all this have happened to me? people ask.

It is not to say that bad things don't happen to other people; it is that this thing, the spell, attempts with the sword of verbal abuse to cut out the minds of its victims while they are told by those who stand by, that it is to be borne stoically.

"To what purpose was this?" a client asked the other day. We talked and came to this discovery. This story is here to help all teens and former teens who were verbally abused at home. It came to me after many conversations with this client.

TO GIVE IT MEANING

All creation of one mind, determined to bring to planet Earth a being who had *all* gifts. The gifts she would be given would be, in every way, inner jewels, brilliant and powerful. But, with these jewels, she would also be given a task, and the task would be the most difficult of all such tasks because she would be given so many gifts.

If she came to planet Earth, she would be born in a modern age. She would be born into a home so backward, it would be as if it were not much more than the hut of a Neanderthal family. But, *worse than even that,* to the entire world, it would appear to fit in with modern times and with a good neighborhood.

Like in a Neanderthal's home, no one would speak many words. But, *worse than even that,* all the words that would be spoken to her, would be lies told to her, about her. ("You are worthless," "You are nothing.")

Like in a Neanderthal's home, there would be tremendous work to be done, every day, just to survive. But, *worse than even that,* all the work of all the people in the home would be given to her, and she would do it, just to survive.

Like in a Neanderthal's home, there would be only a few good things to wear. But, *worse than even that,* her clothes would be castoffs that she would have to make look good, to fit in with modern times and with a good neighborhood.

Like in a Neanderthal's home, the people in it would understand almost nothing. But, *worse than even that,* she would understand that something wasn't right.

But, *worse than even that,* she would have no one to tell.

But, *worse than even that,* she would not know what she would tell, if she knew whom to tell it to.

She came to planet Earth anyway.

She grew tall and strong.

She was so extraordinarily gifted, she could read and write, almost without effort, by the time she went to school. When she was still a child, she could hear music and see the notes in her mind. Someone from the neighborhood heard her play a piano. Almost automatically, she ended up being the only child playing in the symphony. But her parents told her it was nothing. She shouldn't. Then she didn't.

She found some things and, almost automatically, she made some art. She was so extraordinarily gifted, someone bought her art, but her parents said it was nothing and she gave away her money, to make someone feel better.

She went to school, a tall, shy, quiet, and awkward girl, head down to hide, in old clothes with her pants gathered around the waist, worn at the knees from scrubbing floors by hand. And she was shunned. The other kids laughed at her, and at her clothes, and she hardly spoke at all.

But even worse than if she had known nothing, she knew she didn't fit in. Something was wrong with her, and so *her parents were right.*

Almost automatically, she knew science and so she spent lots of time at schools and libraries working and working. She had been working so long at home, work was all she knew. And besides, it seemed better to be at school. At least it wasn't usually like a Neanderthal's home. When she studied, she didn't have to talk to anyone.

She met and married a man and made a home, but not knowing the difference, she had married a Neanderthal-like man. He was as familiar as people at home, but this one had said, "I love you."

Every minute of every day, she struggled to make her home *real* and not at all like a Neanderthal home.

The Neanderthal-like man she married hated everything about her because she seemed so real and so different from a Neanderthal. Her children, who loved her and were very tall and strong because they were born with her gifts, never heard her play a note. They never saw a bit of her art, forgot even that she had, almost automatically, earned a Ph.D. when she had spent so much time in schools and libraries. She, too, forgot.

In the midst of millions of dollars in income, she couldn't always buy food because all the income was hidden, all the checking accounts were empty, and all the credit cards were closed. She continued to work day and night. She washed and cooked and shopped and scrubbed and cleaned and carpooled and homeschooled and mothered her two boys and three girls and heard lies told to her, about her. "You have done nothing. You're nothing."

Then one day she called, and, in time, I heard her story, and she asked, "Why should all this have happened to me?"

At the time, a clear picture came to me with this answer.

Why, you're an angel. The angels all got together and said, "Let's send one of us to Earth with every gift." They all agreed that the fine gifts would be like jewels; they would never wear out nor lose their power. She came with the gifts of an athlete, strong and tall and slim; the gift of music to be a child prodigy; the gift of vision to make art; the gift of health to have fine children; and the gift of intelligence to become anything. Then the last angel said, "Let us give the gift of consciousness. And she must have a task. Her task will be this: To own every jewel she must recognize it no matter what anyone says."

Can you see how I might see that the purpose and meaning of your life is to gather your jewels and own them, then use them to see that you are priceless, no matter what anyone says?

It is important to know that no matter what you have been told about yourself, if you use your abilities, always doing your best, you will discover through experience who you are and of what you are capable. It may take great faith in yourself to persist when you are filled with doubt, but that is what trusting yourself is all about. By doing so, you can overcome the impact of verbal abuse.

COPING WITH VERBAL ABUSE AT HOME

People often cope with ongoing verbal abuse in several different ways, by giving up protestations and so remaining silent; by becoming numb, as if in a constant state of shock; or by becoming invisible to avoid being targeted in the future.

A woman I'll call Merig called on the day her teenage son, Del, sat down with her at the kitchen table, and told her, "Mom, I *hate* Dad." I learned that Merig had been so deeply under the spell of her spellbound husband, that she had taken only one tiny step to rescue her son and herself from verbal abuse. That was, that she called me.

Living in an upscale New England area, she had all the information that might save her but could only try to stand up for her son in moderate protests when his dad raged at him and threatened him with death. "I'll smash you on the wall. Your blood will be everywhere," Dad said. And sometimes the wrath was turned on her. They had endured every kind of threat and verbally abusive attack one might imagine.

One might think that they were terrible people and that their son, Del, was on drugs and supported his habit stealing cars. In fact, Del was a very gentle young teen.

What had they done to have such rage vented on them so often? They simply existed. Maybe one or the other of them looked to the left when pretend son or pretend wife looked to the right. That can really shake up a pretender's picture of how things are (in his mind), and so Dad felt frequently attacked by this "change" in "reality" itself. It was as if, to him, their existence attacked him.

Del's sister, Lana, had learned to avoid all of it. She made herself invisible. She disappeared from sight most of the time. She never mentioned a friend's name in her father's presence, nor a book, a class, an aspiration, or an opinion. Silently she felt it all.

What did Merig know? Unlike many women who find their relationship becoming gradually more and more difficult but can't put a name to what is happening, she had read my books on verbal abuse several times each. She knew she was abused, and she knew it wasn't her fault. She had tried to stop it. But still she was caught in something that immobilized her. She knew that a local women's abuse counselor, with whom she had met only once, was thinking of reporting her son's experiences to child protective services. For months since their meeting, she lived in fear that her son would be taken away from her.

Almost exactly like the woman mentioned earlier, who on her deathbed revealed that she had thought she could balance things out, this woman said the same thing.

She did nice things for her son, and she hoped that her kindnesses to him would "balance things out," and at the same time, she saw suddenly that nothing would. Her despair and feelings of helplessness grew as she saw her son increasingly abused. Her anguish only added to her paralysis. She felt she could bear being verbally abused herself but could not bear her son's abuse. Besides that, she knew that he had witnessed the verbal assaults she had endured. She knew he felt them, too. She knew that, for her son, witnessing abuse is like experiencing it.

Even as she hoped things would get better, even while wanting help, she knew it wouldn't come. It's such severe abuse, she thought. People would call her crazy. Even as her husband called her every *a, b, c, d,* and *f* word anyone could think of, she tried once again to get him to understand. Even as she sought relief, she knew no one would really believe it. Her husband was a well-recognized mental health professional. Finally, she began calling for help. Her burning desire was to know why she hadn't been able to act, why she was paralyzed, unable until maybe now to rescue herself and her son.

She spoke in a very quiet, gentle way. She couldn't understand why, until now, she hadn't reached out for more help. But her son had spoken. She faced the truth, at the kitchen table. Still, alone, she felt the old paralysis.

As we talked, I told her that she seemed to be suffering from the Stockholm syndrome. This syndrome is named for a group of people who were abducted and who, after being rescued, sided with their captors, refused to testify, helped them, and so on.

The Stockholm syndrome describes a group of symptoms. The person so afflicted has an emotional bond to the abuser that leaves the victim wanting the abuser to be happy. (How can you leave an abuser and make him *unhappy* when the syndrome drives you to make him happy?) This syndrome can be established in a few days but can last for many, many years. Most people, once away from the abuser, recover from it rather quickly. Hostage survivors, cult survivors, and domestic abuse survivors frequently have suffered from it.

- Victims perceive that the abuser could kill them.
- Victims notice that the abuser has decided not to kill them.
- Victims are grateful for having been saved from death.
- Victims are isolated.
- Victims perceive intermittent kindness from the abuser.[21]

Somehow, that he or she has not died, that he or she has been "preserved from death" by the perpetrator, leaves the victim feeling that he or she would need the abuser's permission to leave. After all, he has saved her life. But to get permission, she would need to get him to understand that what he was doing wasn't okay.

She went on to get local outside help. Her case points to the tremendous impact of verbal abuse, more horrifying than being hit and leaving thousands praying they would be hit so someone would believe them.

I think that in Merig's case, her son became the reality check she needed. And he had the strength and goodness within at thirteen years of age to tell his mother how he felt. She was able to make and implement a plan to leave with her son.

KIDS' COPING STRATEGIES

Verbal abuse, because of its tremendous impact on the minds and self-perceptions of teens, leaves them with various coping strategies. The longer the abuse goes on, the more severe it is, and the more authoritative the abuser is (such as a parent or teacher), the more extreme the outcome. Other variables apply, such as the inner nature and intelligence of the teen and the level of outside support. Here are some ways that teens try to cope with verbal abuse.

1. The teen tries to please and placate the person indulging in verbal abuse and to help other local victims; for instance, to "balance it out" as Merig did.
2. The teen becomes filled with rage and may hold it in as Del did, or may wait until he or she can direct it toward the abuser, or may act out anywhere in any way that looks like it will succeed. Or the teen breaks the code of silence and tells a parent the truth.
3. The teen tries to hide from and become invisible to the abuser, as Lana, Del's sister, did.
4. The teen attempts to escape temporarily in drugs and alcohol.
5. The teen escapes permanently in suicide.
6. The teen runs away, disappears.
7. The teen finds help and a way to avoid the abuser.
8. The teen numbs out, disconnects from self, and becomes an abuser in adult life.
9. The teen suffers through it, and then goes into therapy.

I've talked with thousands of people who experienced verbal abuse in their teens, and even though they seemed to manage their lives, there were some who eventually found that their ability to make good decisions, to make good judgments, or to cope in everyday relationships was jeopardized.

In summary, long-term or severe verbal abuse of teens and younger children impacts them so that they may have low self-esteem, be extremely accommodating, refuse to accommodate anyone, verbally abuse others, show unreasonable anger, feel depressed, become physically aggressive, or possibly become despairing enough to harm others or themselves.

Understanding how devastating it is to humanity and to the individual child, most people want to become part of the solution to the problem. They want to see it end as a "normalized" way of talking to others.

If you, as an individual reader, raise the awareness of even one other individual, you have become part of the solution. Verbal abuse is much too destructive to ignore. It is insidious and endemic. It is built in to our culture. But like any insidious problem, we can solve it, if we are determined.

Chapter IX

Verbal Abuse at School

WHILE TEACHERS ATTEMPT TO TEACH CHILDREN TO REASON, SOME stand by, observing unreasonable behavior yet not intervening. Possibly because they don't know how to intervene, they are afraid to intervene, or they don't recognize verbal abuse. In other cases, verbal abuse, bullying, and harassment may take place out of sight, and because of a code of silence, teachers and administrators are unaware of even serious problems.

When teachers do their best to implement strategies and admonish students who indulge in verbal abuse, their best cannot always counteract patterns learned at home and brought to school.

The school campus reflects the culture where verbal abuse is endemic and violence occasionally arises. The problem of verbal abuse is rarely addressed in classrooms, so we might have expected it to increase in intensity and frequency over time. It has. I make this assessment because verbal abuse, as a way of treating others, is like a system that is set in motion traveling through generations, to homes, parents, teachers, and children.

One of the most basic facts of how such systems work is that, if they are not recognized and stopped in some way, they increase in intensity and frequency over time.

The prime reason that people of all ages and backgrounds adopt verbally abusive lifestyles is that they are ignorant of what verbal abuse is and why indulging in it is, to some degree, an act of cowardice. Unfortunately, teachers have to deal with the outcome of verbal abuse that, in some instances, is glorified in the media and teen culture. However, the good news is that since verbal abuse is perpetuated out of ignorance, knowledge can go a long way toward eliminating it from classrooms and campuses.

In fact, schools have an excellent opportunity to virtually save the minds of millions from the devastating impact of verbal abuse. They can enlighten those who take it in, as well as those who attempt to fend it off while not even having a name for it. Certainly, those who don't know what is "wrong" with the verbal abuser can find out.

Children, who accept it as the way things are, can be taught to see it for what it is, an ignorant and often unconscious pursuit of illusory status, illusory connections, and an illusory world. In later chapters, we will explore ways to teach children about verbal abuse so they will all understand how cowardly behavior doesn't gain status, and how people who define others as a way of life do so because they lack the courage to stand alone.

As the world grows smaller, so to speak, more and more students encounter students from different cultures, with different values and belief systems, even different levels of maturity. Any teen who is developing a controlling personality and a fragile identity is likely to feel threatened by difference itself.

Different cultures, values, and beliefs are especially challenging to those teens who feel disconnected from themselves and who must, therefore, base all their certainty on an *idea* of what is right, who they are, and who other people should be. However, diversity can broaden and expand children's lives, enriching them and expanding their understanding of the world and themselves. Interestingly, the worst school I found, with regard to verbal abuse, has virtually *no* cultural diversity.

A girl in her senior year of high school talks about her experience of being verbally abused.

> *Kids always made fun of my clothes. "Why are your pants so short?" "Why don't you wear your pants below your belly button?"*
>
> *In the first couple of years of high school, kids pushed me, shoved me, tore up my books, called me a lesbian (because I had only one friend, I guess, another "loser" girl), and threw things at me. I suppose by their standards I was ugly, small, skinny, had brown hair (not blond!), and wore nontrendy clothes. I also had braces.*
>
> *However, later on in school, I "blossomed" and became popular and got a lot of attention from boys.*

Teens say that verbal abuse is pervasive in schools. Large surveys of students revealed that, "At some of our schools, nearly every student said he or she had been bullied or harassed at some point."[22]

Even though it is not possible to define another person's inner reality, attempts to do so are everywhere in schools. Are there any teens, teachers, or school administrators who haven't heard verbal abuse on their campus? How many parents have heard their children complain about someone putting them down, calling them names, excluding them from his or her group?

TEACHERS AND COUNSELORS MAKING A DIFFERENCE

Young people, looking back on their teen years, often refer to a teacher or counselor who reached out to them and were a support to them.

"I had many sessions with our school counselor to help me out with my outcast stigma."

Many teens say that the most important help they can get is having someone they can talk to who is always there for them.

Young Teens Spot Verbal Abuse

Preteens and young teens are old enough to know what verbal abuse is. As a gift of support to me, while I was writing this book, a friend of mine, "Sue," tried an experiment to see just what went on in school today. She explained to her niece, age eleven, and her nephew, age fourteen, that verbal abuse is pretend talk. When someone tells you about yourself, they are pretending that you are not who you really are. People often do this because you do not think, or act, or even look like they imagine you should think, act, or look.

People who verbally abuse you believe that you are (or should be) an imaginary person who compliments them, makes them look good, or acts like a person in their pretend world who makes everything turn out just the way they pretend/believe it will. This is like an abusive coach wanting you to score the winning touchdown so he can pretend he scored it and get the glory. But if you don't score it, he puts you down, because he is mad that his pretend world started to fall apart. To him, this "falling apart" feels like a personal attack on him.

Armed with the knowledge of what verbal abuse is, my friend's niece and nephew agreed to record comments they heard at school that sounded verbally abusive. Although they weren't both teenagers, they were good examples of how young students can recognize verbal abuse for what it is. Each day, they wrote down what they heard, and Sue carefully filled in a chart she made of what they told her. The following is exactly what they experienced in a nice school, in a suburban town in California.

SCHOOL VERBAL ABUSE CHART

Statement	Said By / Said To
You're such a blabbermouth.	Teacher / Student
You're so stupid.	Teacher / Student
You're such an idiot.	Teacher / Student
You're such a faggot.	Friend / Friend
You're so gay.	Friend / Friend
You're an idiot.	Brother / Sister
You never listen.	Teacher / Student
You're dumb.	Friend / Friend
You never pay attention.	Teacher / Student
Duh, why can't you get this?	Teacher / Students
You're so lame.	Friend / Friend
You're no fun.	Friend / Friend
You could never get an *A* in this class with your attitude.	Teacher / Student

Actually, even though I've heard thousands of accounts of verbal abuse, I was stunned by this disclosure. The students who were verbally abused were in training to be abusive. The students who were verbally abusive were *already* trained to abuse. The teacher, possibly exasperated because some student didn't match his perfect pretend-student picture, didn't seem to know that verbal abuse isn't justified. He didn't seem know he was demonstrating irrational behavior in class.

Even in his rational moments, the teacher didn't seem to intervene when students abused students, and these children were so very young.

I saw their handwritten notes and saw that they had compiled their list in just two weeks' time. One of the children who recorded some of the teacher-to-student comments said that they were mostly directed toward one student by his teacher—that this teacher picked on one particular boy and that the class saw it happen and never heard him apologize.

When an abusive teacher singles out one child in particular, the other children are also disturbed by the behavior. They live in fear, not knowing who might be next. The teacher is teaching them to blame others and teaching them how to find a scapegoat to protect themselves from abuse. He is also teaching them that it is okay to verbally abuse smaller, younger people and that, if you aren't a "winner" in the classroom, you get treated like the "loser" in a "dog-eat-dog" world.

One item on the student's list of abusive behaviors (mentioned earlier) was, "You're gay." Coincidentally, on a newscast, today, I heard a man say, "Millions of Americans don't believe being gay is okay." Of course, they can believe anything they want. But he was using "everybody does it, or believes it, so it must be okay" thinking to justify being against other people's sexual orientations.

It is important to teach children that people are what they are. And that the fear of not being okay or not being dominant prompts people to pass judgment on others.

These children could be taught how to respond to peers and authority figures. (See Stopping Verbal Abuse for information on how to respond to authority figures.) However, when a teacher has total control behind closed doors, a child who is abused by a teacher must have outside support. Making a chart like the one discussed and taking copies to parents, the principal, and the school board, simultaneously, may be the best course.

Some of the comments—"idiot" and "stupid"—that the teacher made to the student are the same as the statements made by the father to his sons in Bobby's story. Teachers who verbally abuse students—call them names, ridicule, and threaten them, like Bobby's father—normalize verbal abuse.

In some places, principals are powerless to remove a teacher because of teacher tenure laws.

If your educational system does not have the means to either educate and correct, or remove, an abusive teacher from the educational system, then I believe that the laws should be changed.

A woman said, "Funny, I have trouble remembering names of kids I went to school with, but I can tell you the name of every kid who tormented me from grade school on."

Teens suffer doubly if they are abused both at home and at school. A young girl I talked with wanted to help with my research, so shared some of her experiences with me. She exemplifies the anguish a teen faces who, though living at home, might just as well be homeless, with regard to the amount of emotional support that she gets.

Her story prompts me to envision an "Inclusion Club" in every school for each grade. She told me about how she is verbally abused and ostracized by the girls in her school. Here is some of our conversation with some of my thoughts following.

What do you want most outside of graduating from high school?

"I really just want to fit in."

Of course, that is the most natural desire in the world. Everyone needs to feel that he or she is socially accepted in his or her world. Teens do especially, because, for many, it is the only world they've got.

What do you think the kids are thinking about when they don't include you?

"I am not accepted by any group. I don't wear the same clothes as everyone else, and I don't act like them."

That must be hard. Do you think they have ideals that they want their friends to meet?

"Yeah, I weigh too much and I am too tall, not to mention I don't look at all like anyone else. I am an outcast basically."

It sounds like these kids are very immature and not able to think beyond the surface image of people. You sound really smart to me. Do you have anyone to talk to?

"I have one friend and she really doesn't care about anything I have to say. She has lots of friends so I kind of have to listen to what she tells me to do."

I guess it's good to have somebody not exclude you, but she sure doesn't sound like she's able to be the kind of friend you'd like, who would really listen to you.

"I am feeling so anxious and depressed. I guess I'm overreacting. It might be my fault that I have only one friend, but it just hurts to be alone."

I don't think that it has anything at all to do with you. I think you are in a world of teens who are caught up with trying to be popular and to be with the "right" people like they try to wear the "right brand" of clothing. It is very, very difficult to have to wait for friends till they get more mature and are feeling secure enough to include all kinds of people. For right now, I want you to know I think you're great, and fun to talk to, and that this time will pass.

This interview closed with my suggesting that she think about possibilities for herself. I asked her if there might be things that she could do just for herself to feel better, like maybe be a runner or a painter.

She decided to think about it.

A SECRET SETUP FOR VERBAL ABUSE

As a way of setting up students and teachers to face blame and accusations, some teens pester other teens in a relentless, almost sadistic, way. Then, when the victim tries to stop the abuser, the victim looks like they've started the fight.

A classroom assistant said she used to watch one student who would constantly shove his books over onto another student's desk specifically to annoy him. If called on it, the child would claim that he needed a little more room and didn't mean to make the other student mad. Or, he would subtly take his desk and tap it against the desk of another student, who was trying to write something. Or, as soon as the teacher stepped out of the classroom, he would turn around and take a student's notebook or pencil. She said, "I once witnessed a student get up, walk over a student's paper that had fallen on the floor, take both feet and pull the paper apart, and then keep walking."

When the victim complained, the boy acted like the victim, innocent of an accidental mishap, but would then verbally abuse the victim, telling him he was paranoid, too sensitive, or making a big deal out of nothing.

I wonder if he was wrongly accused in his childhood. In any case, since all these statements are verbally abusive, an alert teacher would call him on it. He would not get any satisfaction from having set up his classmate. A nonabuser would simply say he was sorry the paper was torn, but it was an accident. He wouldn't define the other child.

TEEN TORMENT

A young woman of twenty-five gives the following account of her high school years.

"When I was a teen, I was tormented a lot. I think a lot of that experience destroyed my self-esteem and left me very vulnerable. I was a 'not-rich' kid at a rich-kid school, so you can imagine how my clothes were ridiculed (my mom bought my clothes at thrift stores). I basically was called geek, loser, ugly girl, and things like that on a regular basis. Or just laughed at as I walked by, whispered about, excluded."

I am reminded of a woman treated this way in her preteens and teens. She looked back on her teen years and said she had felt completely excluded by her classmates. "Why," she asked, "does something like this have to happen to someone? It's like it's so abnormal, it makes life seem crazy."

I believe that verbally abusing others still is abnormal. I know there are millions of people who don't create pretend worlds or define other people or try to put themselves up by putting someone else down. There are millions who are not so afraid they might lose their perfect image that they shun all who don't have one.

CONFLICTS THAT MORPH INTO VERBAL ABUSE

Resolving conflicts is a skill children usually begin to learn in nursery school or kindergarten. There are healthy processes to resolve conflicts and solve problems. Usually both people involved in a conflict want to find a resolution. But teens, as well as the adults who are ignorant of these processes, have learned to rely on verbal abuse, intimidation, and threats to stop the process of negotiation.

Spellbound teens not only become abusive from observing and experiencing intimidation, but also they are attracted to it because abuse can quickly silence real people. Maintaining their pretend world is so important to some teens that they will abuse, and even pursue violence, so they will not have to endure discussion with real people. Once abuse begins, the interaction is no longer about a conflict. And it is no longer officially an argument. The interaction is about abuse and defense or protection from abuse.

Even when people are angry in the midst of a conflict, their intention is usually to solve it or to reach a compromise. But if one party is set on dominance and control, there is no way one can reach a compromise or resolution with him or her. Such a person is unwilling to come to the table with goodwill and wants to win at all costs. Winning through abuse by forcing the other to give up or walk away is a very sick kind of behavior that may cause the "winner" to lose all of his or her important relationships in the long run.

Even without conflict, when spellbound teens want to ensure that they can maintain their pretend position and pretend world, they may look for occasions to exert control and power over others. They may indulge in verbal abuse, attacking innocent bystanders just because they are there, acting like real people.

A mother of a young teen told me about her son's being constantly verbally abused by one other boy over a school year. The following year, she discovered that once again they would be in the same classroom.

She said, "I couldn't believe they had these two kids in the same class again, because the teachers knew about the problem. I went to the school to get him changed to another class and the secretary said, 'These lists are written in stone.'

"However, I persisted and explained my situation. Finally the principal got involved in planning which teacher would be the best to handle my son, and the secretary agreed to make the changes.

"Eventually, we moved to a new school district and that school was so much better. The teachers talked to my son in a gentle manner and he began to thrive. I can easily see how kids can shoot up a school. Sending a child to be abused at school every day is in itself an abuse. No one can take it for long."

While researching, talking to students, teachers, high school counselors, child therapists, mediators, and parents of teens, I saw how very different schools were. Not only are there major differences between schools based on each state's educational requirements, but also between schools in the same area based on the choices that the principal and staff make in running the school, establishing rules, and enforcing them.

THE WORST, BEST, AND MOST PUNITIVE SCHOOLS

THE WORST SCHOOL I FOUND

The school I describe here is the worst I found, as far as verbal abuse goes, although there may be, and most probably are, worse. This school is in a rural area. The surroundings are hilly, beautiful, and forested. Most parents, both fathers and mothers, have not gone beyond a high school education. There are good and loving people here, and there is also extreme oppression. The people are isolated. There is no public transportation. Violence in the school is high, both in the junior high school and the high school. Most fights break out over taunting and relationships.

A parent and a seventeen-year-old student who attended the school offered the following information.

"Verbal abuse is mostly name-calling and threats. They call it cracking on kids, dissing them, putting them down, and slamming them.

"Name-calling toward boys is often focused on gay bashing. The kids here are focused on gay bashing. Skinny kids get the most gay attacks. If a boy is thin or small, he is called anything that could mean he was homosexual. If the boys don't like a kid as young as ten, they will start in on him. It sets off fights. It's like putting out the message, 'If I don't like your face, or the way you act, I'm going to beat you up.'"

Prejudice against gays and lesbians is so prolific in teen culture that not only are preteens and teens, gay or not gay, harassed unmercifully in many schools, but also the word "gay" is considered to be derogatory.

Why would some boys care about another boy's sexual orientation? Why would they try to define another boy's sexual orientation as if they lived within him? I asked.

"Gays are a threat to the dominant male straight society. Any alternative to male dominance is a threat to the men here. It takes away their sense of the order of things. Their idea of order is that they are dominant, so about 50 percent of the women who live here are battered.

"The other big thing is insulting their mothers. 'Your mother's fat, ugly, a bitch, a whore.'

"There are three groups: the athletes, the juvenile delinquents, and the group that is picked on. The ones they call nerds are the studious, quiet ones. Both the athletes and the delinquents slam them.

"Athletics are very, very big. If you're not an athlete, God help you. The girls and boys both fight over relationships. They are intense; think they *own* their boyfriend or girlfriend. They are possessions. They believe in romantic property, so they have a sense of ownership. It's something they learn at home.

"Love is the be all and end all. They will do anything to retain the object of their desire; they will lash out at anyone who threatens that.

"The main difference between here and the big cities is women here don't know it's against the law for their husbands to beat them. They can't use a phone; he takes it along with the car. They are sitting ducks with no car, no money, and without a satellite they can't get TV.

"Certain groups of girls run around together. They torment someone outside of the group and they do it as a group—like a tag team. Girls get violent; it works for the boys, so should work for them, they think. But the girls are never violent and aggressive with their boyfriends. They don't want to lose him.

"They are as violent as the boys when it comes to fighting over their boyfriends. Some girls pushed another girl down the stairs.

"They stalked another girl because they saw her talking to one of their friend's boyfriends. It wasn't even one of *their* boyfriends. They decided the girl was trying to take him away from their friend. 'We're gonna follow you. We'll catch you alone somewhere. You can't have someone with you all the time. We'll get you again.' They threatened her life. 'We'll kill you.'

"She became hysterical at the thought of going to school, so her mother home-schooled her.

"Teachers are afraid of the abusers who are also physically violent. In an area where they know where you live, they can find you and attack you.

"There is no cultural diversity here. The school is supposed to be one-half a percent African-American. But everyone is white, so I don't know who the half percent is attributed to."

It seems clear that wherever people are defined as objects, some to keep and some to get rid of, there will be violence.

Further research is suggested to find any correlation between household tyrannies, the verbal abuse that is used to maintain them, and verbal abuse and violence in schools.

THE BEST SCHOOL I FOUND

In contrast to the worst school I found, as far as verbal abuse goes, I present here a school that represents one of the best. This school, like the worst school, is also somewhat rural. The surroundings are hilly, beautiful, and forested.

In contrast to the "worst" high school, this school is within an hour of a major airport, a large city, and two distinguished universities. The average income is a bit above the average in the state. The high school has a little over a thousand students. Most parents have graduated from college. Some have higher degrees. Women have careers. They often adapt their work schedules or take leaves from work so one parent can be home when the children are home.

A fifteen-year-old student who attended this high school offered the following about it.

"There are around twenty-five students per teacher.

"Kids who color their hair green, orange, blue, and so on are having fun, getting more attention from their friends.

"If a kid starts letting his or her grades slide, the teacher will pull the kid aside, will ask, 'what's the matter?' The teacher will try to reach out, like, 'If you want to talk about it, I'm here.'

"I think the kids here are more trustful of teachers and adults than at some schools. I've never heard a teacher yelling and putting a kid down."

What about bullying?

"I don't see bullying in school. I think that if there is any, it's outside of school and school hours. The teachers don't let stuff go! If someone has problems and acts out, they are suspended. The codes are strict."

What about kids who are different?

"We're pretty accepting of different people because there is a special school connected to ours that is for kids with mental disabilities."

What about name-calling?

"If someone calls someone a name like 'retard,' the teacher talks about it with the kid and whoever is around, reminding them that they can't put down kids who have disabilities.

"So, I'm very comfortable in school. The teachers have personal connections to the students, personal friendships. The teachers make a point of at least knowing all the kids' names even if they haven't had them in class. I feel safe. It's like a home. It's fun.

"Some of the teachers have taught the previous class the year before, so when you have the same teacher twice, it's easier to be friends.

"Seniors make an 'exit portfolio.' It's a collection of projects and photos that highlight their interests and achievements. They pick a mentor and there is a lot of teacher/student connection around that.

"I think if there's verbal abuse, it's mostly the sophomore guys that pick on the freshman group.

"It didn't happen to me.

"The campus is open for kids who drive to go out for lunch. And the school is very community oriented. They make a big effort to involve the community. We have lots of events that involve the community.

"There are a few loners and a few kids who hang together who dress with boots and leathers, well, scary I guess. They dress to try to look scary. Our groups have labels. We know who the jocks are and who the party kids are."

This teen and others have not experienced verbal abuse at home or in school. Although labeling occurs, children are not put down for having or not having an interest in sports or partying.

THE MOST PUNITIVE SCHOOL I FOUND

We have looked at the best and the worst schools considering the degree to which verbal abuse has taken over the students. Now, let us look at a school with the worst environment I found, an environment that is, itself, abusive, and an environment that automatically fosters verbal abuse.

A punitive environment is one that is ugly, rigid, cold, and has a prisonlike atmosphere. Just as we would expect in such an environment, the students are most definitely negatively impacted. If teens who come from deprivation feel rage at the injustice of their lives, how much more rage will they feel in a prisonlike atmosphere? The school's lack of warmth, its austerity, constraints to freedom, lack of activities, and damaging disciplines all make it stand out as the most punitive school I could find. It is a real public school. It does exist.

Juniors and seniors don't head out to the local sandwich shop to get lunch as they do in the best school I found. They don't sit or stretch out on grass under trees, either. In this four-year high school, during lunch break, teens stand in a prisonlike yard.

A teacher shared the following.

> There is nothing fun in this punitive high school, nor is there fun in the adjacent middle school. There are no balls, no basketball hoops, no hopscotch lines, no jump ropes, no jungle gyms, no "toys," no dominos games or chess games, no fun groups like there are in the best school where drama club and ski teams meet in their spare lunch time. In this school, nothing is allowed. Every door is locked but those necessary to be open for a known purpose.
>
> But, they do have an opportunity to push and shove each other in the schoolyard after lunch, to taunt smaller kids, to gang up with sometimes twenty against one or two. There is little else to do and their rage and frustration grow over time. They try to transfer their pain.

There is little contact with the community, and often students can't attend a school-sponsored event like a game. All grades, attendance and conduct records, and personal data are computerized and available at the touch of a button. Even though you are doing better than you usually do, if you don't have the expected academic grade, you are restricted from school-related functions in the community. The principal determines this. So even kids who are trying to do better are excluded. These students are outsiders already in their own community even by middle school.

The students who have fallen behind suffer, because the teachers couldn't teach them competency. They have no skill and never learned their times tables, so they can't do division, or pre-algebra. They stay back, go to summer school, and are so discouraged by sixteen that many leave. We have an extraordinarily high drop-out rate.

These kids are deprived. They are punished and deprived for just being kids. They are punished for our failure to teach and are abused at home and then at school.

An FBI study of the commonalities that exist among students who have acted out violently includes an "inflexible culture" or the development of an "unfair disciplinary structure."

While I do not believe in labeling any teens as potentially violent, I make the point that rigidity and a punitive atmosphere do not help to heal preteens and teens who come from disrupted homes. These teens come from working single-parent families. They get themselves up in the morning, take themselves to school, and come home to an empty house. They don't have a supportive, considerate, and caring family, nor do they have nurturing conversations with a parent. They don't have anyone checking on what they're watching and what they're doing. They are teens who hide from a raging alcoholic parent when they would otherwise be doing homework.

The schools I found didn't necessarily start out being the worst, best, and harshest. But they ended up becoming so, partly because they came to reflect many of their students' family and community environments. Some are healthy. Some are not. The schools are described here so that definitive characteristics will stand out. The extremes give us insights into the problem of verbal abuse in schools, homes, and communities.

Some schools may offer more than the "best" that I found, in terms of activities, awards, diversity, and so forth. Some schools may be worse than the worst, in terms of abuse, harassment, and violence. Some may be even less friendly than the most prisonlike school. But, the best, worst, and most punitive schools simply represent extremely different mini cultures where humanity flourishes or languishes, all depending on how enlightened the adults are.

School as a Haven from Abuse

Although this chapter covered verbal abuse in school, it would not be complete if it did not also note that high school could be the redeeming part of a teenager's life, if he or she is verbally abused at home. When a school provides a good balance of work and play in terms of counseling, conflict resolution, activities, community, and supportive teachers, it can be a haven away from home.

I interviewed a young woman about her teen years. They had been rough at home.

How was school for you in your teens?
"It was a place where I could be me. The only problem was I did not know who I was."

Most teens are still developing their sense of self, their iden-tity, in their teens. How did you manage?

"I had to fight to make it all look normal. I did everything well enough to keep the secrets at bay and my sanity in check. I think people thought I was troubled, but my looks and popularity and abilities kept the truth of it all away. You ask people now, and no one can understand why I am not a successful and happy person. 'You looked so good in high school,' people would say. 'All the other girls were jealous of you.'"

Without support at home, a supportive atmosphere at school can't meet all your needs. Verbal abuse undermines your sense of self.

"It is such a hard thing to explain that one just has to go on but that does not mean that all is well, that you are not being torn apart every day at home. No bruises, no scars, so all must be well. It was and is such a lonely place."

Schools are not the cause of verbal abuse, and teachers can't solve all the problems of verbal abuse taking place in secret or just off campus.

However, what would happen if an entire grade had training to learn what verbal abuse is? How it is pretend talk; how it is about pretending that there is a pretend world; that in the pretend world, putting someone down is supposed to put the other person up; that healthy people may occasionally indulge in verbal abuse when they're angry about something, but as soon as they say something abusive, and realize what they have said, they apolo-gize for the mistake. But some people become chronically abusive because they are trying to make their pretend world real. What if everyone knew that people who are verbally abusive or who bully are afraid, and that there are ways to respond to verbal abuse that attack the verbal abuse, *not* the person who indulges in it.

Ignorance plays a role in perpetuating verbal abuse. We can, therefore, take a major step toward creating a more peaceful and mutually beneficial world by bringing awareness to children and their parents. They can come to understand the illusions that deny people their rights, their freedom, and their personhood itself.

Chapter X

The Teen Who Verbally Abuses

W<small>HY DO SOME TEENS BECOME VERBALLY ABUSIVE TO OTHERS</small>? Do teens feel important or tough when they put someone down? Do they feel that they are retaliating against a real or imagined attack? Why do some teens gang up with others against a person who is different from them?

This chapter presents some answers to these questions and explores who these teens are and why verbal abuse has seemingly overridden their kinder nature.

I especially want those of you who are put down or excluded by your peers or others to understand the kind of pretend world these teens live in, so you will fully understand that the abuse has nothing to do with you, although it may still be hurtful and toxic.

I hope that any teen able to read at high school level will read this book, and that those who aren't so able will hear this chapter read to them by a parent, possibly a little at a time, leaving time for discussion.

WHO ARE THE TEEN ABUSERS?

Teens who indulge in verbal abuse can come from wealthy homes, middle-class homes, or poverty-ridden homes. Generally, they are subject to verbal abuse in some way during childhood or have been neglected and have seen abuse all around them, at home, at school, and in the media.

Often, teens who indulge in verbal abuse have no support at home. Caretakers raise some. They learn to be manipulative and abusive to baby-sitters. Their attitude is, "I can do what I want." They learn to threaten to get their way. They say they'll tell their mom things that they make up about their caretakers. They threaten them with the loss of their jobs. They become the boss of their caretaker.

Some go to public school and some go to private schools. Some of the private schools get a lot of money from parents, so they overlook the teens' behaviors. The teens, who have learned how to manipulate their caretakers, go on to manipulate in school. They can be abusive, and they are skilled in getting away with a lot. These teens aren't used to consequences. By cheating, they make their way. Life is about winning and getting away with everything, winning at all costs, and never being a loser.

In school, one of the ways some teens try to meet their developmental goal of independence from family is by building a secret teen world played out through games in which winning and wiping out the opposition are everything.

Most of the teens who end up being verbally abusive, whether from rich or poor economic circumstances, have parents who aren't invested enough in parenting to be involved when they are home. They don't know what goes on in their kids' lives. Even kids who are given everything materially can be neglected emotionally and suffer like kids who have nothing.

HOW DOES A TEEN BECOME CHRONICALLY VERBALLY ABUSIVE?

Although some children try out some of the abusive words they've heard, most don't turn into teenage verbal abusers. Most often, teens who do become chronically abusive were verbally abused in their early childhoods by someone older. Usually they felt in some way unacceptable. Possibly, they were not allowed to cry, to perceive their pain, or to trust their own experience. Possibly, no one was around to tell them that what happened to them was not okay. In other words, no one said to their abuser, "What you said sounds like verbal abuse. Did you mean it that way?" They were not protected in the *presence* of the abuser.

Teens don't start out life with the intent to become abusers. But, verbal abusers usually hear verbal abuse early in their childhood. They believe what they're told when they are abused, like, "You're never going to amount to anything." They learn to accept these lies about themselves, and every time they do, the lie takes the place of the truth about them. Some very smart people have gone through life thinking that they were not very valuable or worthy, because they believed the lies they heard about themselves. But, not all become verbally abusive.

The repetitive blows of verbal abuse can be so shocking to youngsters that they may eventually lose all awareness of their inner worlds. They may become desensitized, eventually losing touch with their feelings. They may eventually become, in a sense, disconnected from themselves. Gradually, they become less aware of the world around them, less responsive, perceptive, insightful, and empathetic. These are the children who are most likely to become abusive.

YOU'RE NOT HURT

While name-calling is a blatant assault, one that most teens recognize as abusive, in some ways, more subtle assaults can be more
damaging, because they are hard to recognize for the kinds of violations that they are.

Thoughtless and erroneous comments, like the platitudes
discussed earlier, can damage children, reverse their reality, and
even turn them into abusers, if other circumstances are present.
In effect, they can be trained to lose touch with themselves. For
example, a child hurt from falling down hears, "You're not hurt.
You have nothing to cry about. You're just causing a scene and
trying to get attention."

The child gets the message that she or he has no feelings, no
pain, and is basically "bad," as in the example given, for "trying
to get attention." Most teens who became abusive were given this
kind of message in thousands of ways. *This type of abuse erases
the child's inner reality, leaves the child prone to disconnect from
him- or herself and to create a pretend world.* [23]

If teens hear themselves defined by a person they trust from
an early age, they come to believe that what they are told about
themselves is true. Most children know that name-calling and
swearing is verbal abuse, but many do not understand the many
other kinds of coercive and destructive forms verbal abuse
takes, nor do they understand what is wrong with a person who
defines their inner reality in annihilating, denigrating, or dominating ways.

Children who are verbally abused by adults are taught to
believe that their personal truths, and even their own reality, are
outside of themselves, as if someone else knows better than they
whether they're hurt. *Teens who were abused and didn't know that
they were abused, or, knowing, never healed from it, end up with a
great need to feel superior to others, just to balance out how horrible they feel.*

Additionally, some children have become abusive because they have been severely traumatized by sexual and other abuse. But please note: Not all these children become abusive. Many heal.

Generally, abusers feel that their real self was rejected if a parent or sibling put them down, called them names, tried to shape them into someone else, or simply did not accept them; and so, they became angry, fearful, and disconnected.

CREATING A PRETEND WORLD

Without realizing it, these wounded children, who don't feel connected and okay, imagine a version of the world in which they are superior and where everything goes the way they want. It is a pretend world, and they come to believe it is real. Their pretend world is made up just the way they want, and in their minds, other people are not real. They are more like pretend people.

These wounded teens expect everyone to be as they envision them. They can be very angry when people and events don't meet their expectations, *in even the smallest ways*. They can feel enraged if a weather forecaster is off a few degrees or if the car is low on gas. They live in an illusory version of reality. Teens who become chronically abusive get angry and abusive when people don't act like they think they should act. From their view, there are only two life positions: winners and losers.

The world and the people in it must be as they want, or they feel assaulted. This is why winning is so important. Establishing superiority and rightness is essential to maintaining their "world."

To them, real people oppose, thwart, or get in the way of their having everything the way they want it to be. When victims back off or actually become frightened of their abusers, the abusers feel as if they have won and that their abusive behavior works. They feel more secure about their world. They become increasingly chronically abusive, and their pretend world seems increasingly right and real.

Another way to see this is that when teens are disconnected from their feelings and, consequently, from themselves, they end up trying to get a grip on reality by being *in* someone else's space, so to speak, telling them what they are and how they should be. Verbal abuse is always, in some way, defining of another person, because abusers are constantly trying to turn people into their pretend people, or trying to push down and get rid of the real people who inhabit their bodies.

These teens don't usually see themselves as abusive, because their pretend world seems so real to them. To them it is real. It is the way everything and everyone should be, and that is why they are described as being spellbound or under a spell.

Growing up, teens see verbal abuse all around them and so it seems normal. They can be so focused on maintaining their pretend world, where they are superior, that they have no idea of their impact on others.

Verbal abuse can become an automatic approach and response to others. For instance, teens feel important not only by criticizing and judging others, but they also use verbal abuse as a tool to manage their pretend world, that is, to shape people into what they envision them to be, or to discard the ones who don't have the qualities they want to be identified with. Young teens may never have heard that "bad-mouthing" someone is not okay. And they are rewarded with attention from peers who look on their judgments as valid.

Finally, sometimes teens and younger children hear one parent verbally abuse the other. It is hard for the child to comprehend that a parent is doing something wrong and is actually abusive. The child deals with it by deciding that the parent who is being put down must deserve it. That parent must have done something wrong. Therefore, the child comes to the erroneous belief that verbal abuse is okay, because, to the child's mind, it can be justified.

EXCLUDING OTHERS

Preadolescence, around third grade, is classically when verbal abuse begins in school. This is when preteens place higher and lower values on certain attributes, and then deride, or exclude, those who don't match their criteria. This is when they begin to construct a transitional world and look for a place in it. This is when teens who are not connected to themselves, their feelings, and their inner world look outside of themselves for reality. Appearances are everything. *How everyone looks and the image he or she projects are all there is.*

Consequently, these teens who indulge in verbal abuse and exclusionary behaviors look outside themselves for their identity. *No matter what, they do not want to be identified in any way with what they believe they are "not." And, they don't want to be identified with any characteristic that they don't desire. This is one of the primary reasons that teens exclude peers who are different.*

As insecure teens are pulled into the pretend world where appearances are everything, they feel an ever-increasing need to exclude those teens that they don't want to be identified with. They experience a desperate desire to be part of the perceived in-group that, in turn, intensifies their need to exclude and diminish all who don't embody their ideas of what is desirable and what is popular.

They will target people because of their race, ethnicity, disability, religion, appearance, clothing, brand of shoes, height, weight, accent, number of friends, parental income, interests, hair color, or any characteristic that they do not want to have themselves.

Another reason spellbound teens are exclusionary is that they need to keep their pretend world in existence. They must avoid talking to real people as if they were real. Doing so would disturb their pretend world. *Their pretend world is a world of appearances.* There isn't much that is real about it.

If they verbally attack a "victim" and he or she confronts them on their abusive behavior, they will do everything possible to avoid discussion with the real person. In these circumstances, instead of apologizing, spellbound teens often claim that the victim was to blame for what happened. Sometimes they feel so frightened seeing their pretend world and their assumed "superiority" threatened, that they actually do believe someone else is to blame for their behavior. Or if they have to admit to their behavior, they'll say that the person they abused deserved it.

Abusers sometimes defend themselves from responsibility by saying, "you made me . . . " as if you, not them, were responsible for their behavior. This can be confusing to victims: teens, children, and adults alike. They do not always realize that accusing and blaming are actually forms of verbally abusive denial. Naturally, abusers will say anything to avoid accountability for their behavior, because they are getting something out of it. They are maintaining their pretend world.

Not wanting to talk to the victim, and not wanting to step out of their pretend world, they simply deny the abuse as being abusive. Denial was described earlier as a terrible kind of verbal abuse that assaults people's minds.

It is essential to know that blaming denial has nothing to do with the real issue and nothing to do with truth. The abuser is in a pretend world and doesn't see the "victim's" reality at all.

Many young teens are extremely unsure of how acceptable they are to classmates. They may feel alone and abandoned when they aren't at the center of attention. They feel threatened when classmates treat peers who are different as their equals. They want to exclude them. Their identity is so fragile and so bolstered by a superior image of themselves that they cannot conceive of others as being different *and* equal. Their thinking-feeling is, "I have made myself up right, so there must be something wrong with you if you aren't like me."

YOUNG TEEN MADE BRUNT OF JOKE

A young woman, whom I'll call Dela, said that, as she looked at her high school years, the whole experience was colored by cruel behavior she experienced at the hands of several other girls.

"A girl I barely knew in the 'popular crowd' once gave me a note after class, that the girl said her friend, Ned, gave to her. In the note, he (Ned) said that Hal had a crush on me, but didn't know me and was too shy to talk to me.

"She said that I should go up and talk to him once in a while, like after class, and ask him what the homework was, or things like that, to get to know him. She suggested that I call him what his friends called him, Sal. So, I was really excited, thinking 'Wow, someone has noticed me and maybe I will get popular now!' So, I spoke to him a few times, nothing overt, just casually. A few days later, he passed me a note on the bus; I was really excited! I opened it up and it said, 'Marcy just gave you that note as a joke on me. I don't like you and I *never will*!'

"I was crushed and couldn't understand why someone who didn't even know me would play such a cruel trick on me. I was horribly embarrassed and several times after this incident, I caught them and their friends laughing at me."

I have no doubt that the girls in the popular crowd wanted to be the center of attention and felt threatened when classmates treated a less popular girl as their equal. They set up the whole scenario to both humiliate and exclude Dela, and they had the added bonus of being bonded together against someone, to feel connected and not so adrift.

Teens who are trying to develop a strong identity, and teens who are trying to enter a different world from their parents', fall easy prey to the spell. It can be very alluring to a teen who is unsure of him- or herself and isn't particularly popular to want to make a quick connection to other teens by joining with them against someone who is different. If teens don't feel that they are powerful and dominant and able to make their pretend world seem real, they may join with other pretenders both to feel connected and to dominate their targets.

ABUSERS SEEK CONTROL

Since spellbound teens have extra-shaky identities, which they've made up in their pretend world, they can't stand to see a real person acting real or being happy about something. Since they've lost touch with their feelings from abuse, trauma, or neglect, they aren't sure who they are. They want to control any real person who acts equal to them. They want to make him or her be like a pretend person in their pretend world, that is, someone subject to them. If they feel they are losing control, they will try to regain it by putting people down who are feeling good.

In boyfriend-girlfriend relationships, if they can put down the real person, they, metaphorically speaking, have more room within their friend's body for their pretend "dream" person, a slave maybe.

As young people pass from early teens to late teens, if they are overcome by the spell, they usually become more secretive and subtle in the ways they abuse. They are less random in their attacks and more selective about the targets they choose to dominate. They gain a kind of security when they keep their victims from feeling free to express themselves spontaneously. After all, if the people they target are silent, abusers don't have to risk seeing them as real people.

Abusers don't want to be confronted, nor do they want to lose their cool image. Picking smaller, less protected targets seems safer as the target isn't so likely to fight back effectively. A guy who harasses girls, for instance, is not likely to select a target with two really big older brothers.

Teens who don't grow out of exclusionary and verbally abusive patterns as they reach adulthood narrow their focus considerably. A relationship can be a teen's entire target. A teen may form a relationship with someone who, to the teen's mind, "is" the whole pretend world. If this happens, the teen who makes a partner or date into his or her "whole world," will be enraged when the person doesn't match their picture of how it should be,

In these situations, abusers focus abuse on this one person, and if they marry (and some teenagers do), if children enter the picture, the children may be part of their "whole pretend world," so they will be abused. Why? Because no one can be a pretend person, adult or child. It is very important to know that, once abusers focus on their immediate family, and it becomes their *whole* pretend world, they can present a perfect image to the world.

We met Bobby's and Danny's father, James, earlier. James indulged in name-calling and was at the extreme in terms of verbally abusing his family, but he presented a perfect image to the world.

Verbal abusers seem to feel more secure when their victims are feeling uneasy, possibly because they can get in their space more readily—tell them who they are and so on. In general, all verbal abuse is intended to keep abusers in the one-up power positions, so no one can get them to stop pretending that they are superior and their pretend world is real. When they keep people off balance, abusers feel safe from confrontation, so they can make their pretend world be just what they want.

Practice Wins and Destroying Opposition

Because teens grow up in a world that embraces winning over others, rather than winning *with* others, they use verbal abuse to end opposition. The idea of discussing differences or making compromises feels like retreat and failure to the teen who has embraced this one-up philosophy. Very often, there is not even an issue to win, so a teen who uses verbal abuse as a weapon will simply attack someone to have a win. It's like practice wins. Of course, to the person attacked, it can be devastating, cruel, and damaging. Especially if others witness this kind of abuse and find it amusing.

Verbal abusers seek wins everywhere, and in their desire to win, they try to destroy with words anyone who challenges them. They have a strong tendency to feel opposed, even when no one opposes them. Anything that is not going exactly as they want is experienced as an attack. They strike out verbally and may escalate to physical abuse to have a win over others and to have power over others.

Sometimes they will try to get the person they've targeted to cry or lose control. They experience this as a win and may even feel that they've done the right thing. *It is important to realize that verbal abusers don't really care what an argument is about; it doesn't matter whether the issue gets solved or not, because the abuser's main goal is to win, and to prove the other person wrong by dominating or overpowering the other person.*

Teens who verbally abuse other teens or younger kids seek domination because they want the world to be as they have made it up to be. And, they want people to see them as superior. They need to feel superior because they have felt so powerless when stripped of their human rights to have feelings and to have an inner world.

ABUSERS WILL NOT APOLOGIZE

People who aren't in a pretend world where they must win—and hold it together—at all costs might get angry when they are unjustly accused of something and indulge in verbal abuse, because they can't think of any way to get their power back. But later they do try to patch things up.

Generally, after an argument, if someone says something that attacks another person, he or she will apologize, but the teen who is spellbound will not apologize for abusive behavior. Teen verbal abusers want to pretend that there is nothing to apologize for. It is such a job to hold the pretend world together, that the teen abuser will not back down or show even the smallest capitulation to others for fear of losing power. They need to feel superior and in a one-up position, to win at all costs.

They aren't willing to compromise or even let someone go by who looks weaker, smaller, or less popular, because this would mean missing the opportunity to test their ability to control and gain compliance. When they gain control or compliance, they feel more able to keep their pretend world alive. They are terrified of giving up even the tiniest bit of control because it would put a crack in their pretend world, and if the crack widened, their whole world would fall apart.

To let go of their pretend world would be like dying. In that respect, they can't let go of it. They have to have the power to hold it in their mind, as that is the only world they have. They feel they have to go on pretending that they have won and are superior. They never want to have a talk with the person they've abused to reconcile the hurt feelings. They don't want to see people as if they are real, with real feelings. In fact, for some, their pretend world seems so much more real that the act of recognizing others would shatter it.

Obviously, teens who pretend to live within others, to know their thoughts, feelings, their worth, and what they are (as they demonstrate with name-calling), are unable or afraid to stand on their own, separate from others. These teens repeatedly define others, demonstrating fear and weakness because they are disinclined to stay in their own space by themselves, alone.

Teens, children, and adults alike, if not called on their verbally abusive behavior may develop a pattern of abuse and continue through life making up who and what people are. Over time, chronic verbal abusers usually become more abusive and angry because real people just won't be the way they want them to be— like pretend people.

BENEATH THE IMAGE

Knowing about the confirmed teen verbal abuser's pretend world, looking at the situation from this perspective, it appears evident that the teens who verbally abuse others, who pick on smaller or less able peers, who crave power over others, mostly do so because they feel

- Anxious
- Weak
- Powerless
- Victimized
- Depressed
- Afraid
- Phony
- Unimportant
- Disconnected

They don't know how to get an identity, inner connection, sense of mastery, or satisfaction in any healthy way.

CREATING AND MAINTAINING A PRETEND WORLD
OVERVIEW

In overview, the teens who chronically indulge in verbal abuse, constantly strive to create and maintain a pretend world populated by pretend people. In this pretend world, they define and diminish others in an attempt to keep others from showing up as real people, thus the pretend world can be populated by "lesser beings" who do and say what they want.

Teens who live in this pretend world feel okay because they can make it be just the way they want it to be. When real people appear, they can ignore and shun them, rage and threaten them, or taunt and diminish them, to "make them go away." Their pretend world seems real. They can feel as if the world is ending, and they are being attacked, when they can't find a way to make real people conform, or "disappear" in diminishment, or shut up. Teens who chronically verbally abuse and exclude others feel alone and adrift if their pretend world is threatened by reality. Consequently, they will increase the abuse and strive even harder to make real people wrong and responsible for their (the abuser's) behavior.

What we see is that a teen who frequently indulges in verbal abuse is doing so simply to keep a pretend world together. Keeping the pretend world and pretend people "alive" is what verbal abuse is most about. The angrier the teen becomes, the more the abuse seems to work. And generally, spellbound teens are angry when people appear as real people. They need the security of a pretend world because they usually cannot access their own inner-feeling world, so cannot build their own identity. Being the superior person in a pretend world meets that need. But it is a false identity, always threatened by people who are different. To them, different people can't be equal.

VERBAL ABUSE DOMINATES TEEN CULTURE

The ethic of looking out for the smaller or less able classmate has been reversed in some popular teen cultures. In many schools, the bigger, more able, more popular teens assume the right to tell other teens what to do. Some teens feel entitled to dominate smaller or less able teens, just because they are bigger. Even teens who would try to protect peers may face emotional and even physical attacks for doing so. Protected by the code of silence, abusers can become bullies attacking and harassing real students, making high school a hell on earth for their victims.

This problem is now at its zenith in the United States. Anything real about teens, such as their intelligence, their talents, their views, their individuality, is subject to abuse by another teen. Teens' preoccupation with how people look is many times greater than it was even twenty years ago.

AUTISTIC CHILD

There is a very small group of children who have neurological problems that make it very difficult for them to deal with the real world, no matter how good it is. Even with the most loving homes and supportive environments, they may show aggressive or unusual behaviors, sometimes at a very young age.

If you are wondering if your child may be out of sync with the world around him or her, then the book *The Out-of-Sync Child* should be helpful.[24]

Part Three

What Can We Do about It?

THIS LAST SECTION COVERS SOLUTIONS TO THE PROBLEM OF VERBAL abuse. Specific chapters address verbal abuse issues that confront parents, teachers, and teens. Each chapter presents insights, overall strategies, and specific techniques that are designed to assist adults who work with teens, and teens themselves, toward increasing maturity, consciousness, competency, and confidence.

"For Teens" presents ideas for discussion in homes and classrooms to assist teens in bringing the topic of verbal abuse into the open.

Chapter XI

Stopping Verbal Abuse

When very bad things happen
And you can't make sense of it,
When you feel as if you could die,
And no matter what you do,
You can't make anything be different,
There is one thing you can do
No matter how hard it is,
That is to know how you feel and resolve,
"I will never make another human being feel this bad,
Because I know how bad it feels."

If you make this agreement with yourself, you will be stopping verbal abuse. You will be transforming your pain and anger into a determination to end this malignancy called verbal abuse. If you do this *instead* of blowing it all off, pretending it didn't happen, shutting down your feelings so you space out and don't know what happened, you will be the representative of courage, strength, and integrity here on planet Earth. But if you try to pretend verbal abuse is okay, you will be entering a pretend world where there is nothing solid to stand on, a world that seeks its own destruction, because it will always, always encounter the real world.

If you find that you seem to be under the spell, living in a pretend world and regularly defining one or more people, just knowing what verbal abuse is, what you have felt, and how verbal abuse hurts others is a grand beginning for change.

A man said, "I have noticed that my kids' respect for adults waned as soon as they were in a school, where some of the adults did not respect the kids. The most effective policy seems to be where rules apply to adults and children alike . . . there has to be a role model to teach kids to respect each other."

STOPPING VERBAL ABUSE

Stopping verbal abuse (breaking the spell) takes on great significance when we consider the alternative—a world of pain and anguish, lost relationships, broken marriages, wounded and traumatized children, and the horrifying possibility that a person like Hitler, a cowardly abuser, could live for a time unrecognized. After all, he defined millions, and millions did not notice.

As we have seen, the impact of verbal abuse is tremendous. It is toxic and can create extreme emotional pain, mental anguish, and even illness because the target endures ongoing stress. Sadly, many young people endure it because they are simply unable to live in a better environment or attend a different school.

We also know that verbal abuse precedes other kinds of abuse. If a person is defined as not who they are, the person who is doing the defining can define them as anything.

A MULTIGENERATIONAL LEGACY

The impact of verbal abuse can last for years, and if the victim doesn't go through the process of recovery, he or she may pass on the legacy, becoming verbally abusive to the next generation. People who have learned to tolerate verbal abuse in childhood and through their teens are susceptible to it in adulthood. The tendency to be the recipient of verbal abuse is a multigenerational pattern. If a child's self-esteem is dragged down and she or he has no skill in standing up to verbal abuse, a difficult lifetime may be ahead. Even when victims know that what they were told as a child is not true, if they hear it again in adult life, they are much more inclined to doubt themselves.

Changing the pattern of verbal abuse is not an easy task. Be prepared for setbacks along the way. If you are the person who formerly gave the abuse, working for change is worth it!

If you were abused, it is important to know that you can't change the person who abused you. He or she must change him- or herself. I hope there will be change because the patterns of being either abusive or victimized can be perpetuated for generations.

TARGET VERBAL ABUSE

In stopping verbal abuse, the goal is not to target parents, teachers, or teens, but to target verbal abuse! If verbal abuse is recognized (both by those who indulge in it and those who are its target) and addressed for what it is—an illogical and toxic way of being with and behaving toward another person—and if parents, teachers, and teens know what it is, it can't hide out in the semi-conscious regions of our culture. When it is brought to light, we can see it for what it is. It is pretend talk that supports a pretend world filled with illusions; for example, that blaming someone makes your behavior his, or her, fault! Clearly, these illusions live in the minds of spellbound people.

Following are some topics that any adult, parent, or teacher can bring up for discussion with teens. Hopefully, many teens will want to read about verbal abuse, to understand the spell, and to become spell-breakers.

FOR DISCUSSION: VERBAL ABUSE IS PRETEND TALK

When people pretend superiority, importance, strength, and power over others, they do so because they are unable to perceive the separate reality of others, and, of course, because they feel weak. When they attempt to exert their imagined superiority, importance, strength, and power over others, they most often do so by defining them. When they define others, they are pretending to know their inner reality or pretending that they have the power to put themselves up by putting down others. It is all a fantasy that builds into a pretend world. People who enter that world, and believe in it, are spellbound.

Children, from preschool through high school, can learn that people who are pretending to know about others, that is, who and what they are, use verbal abuse. Verbal abuse seems to lurk around people who have expectations about how something is going to turn out, or how someone is going to perform, or even how someone might feel about someone or something.

Children can understand both, that it is hurtful, for example, to suddenly be called a name, and that the name-caller is making up something about someone. As hurtful as it is, it is pretend talk. People who indulge in verbal abuse are pretending to be more important because they feel so unimportant. They are pretending to be strong and powerful, but they are caught in the grip of tremendous feelings of powerlessness and fear.

FOR DISCUSSION: THE PRETEND WORLD

It is amazing to step into a pretend world where people pretend, for instance, that thinner people are superior to fatter people, and that taller people are more important than shorter people. It's also strange to hear people who pretend to be superior tell others what they are, for instance, "You're worthless," or "You're an idiot."

Only in a pretend world can people make up another person's value, or anything else about that person. It is hard to imagine that anyone would do this, but many people do because they don't realize that they are acting irrationally. *People who are spellbound almost always believe that they are rational.* People who make up things and say them behind other people's backs, really don't want to be confronted with their dishonesty. They just want to keep their pretend world going. Keeping the pretend world secret and keeping what goes on in it a secret helps to keep it going.

If a pretender has put you down, it may help a little bit to know about the pretend world. It is based on: bigger is better, difference is wrong, might makes right, looks are all that is important, and the surface or appearance of people is all that is real.

Silly, huh?

As silly as it is, if people become very deeply spellbound, it can also be dangerous. If that happens, and they are completely caught up in the pretend world, they can do really bad things because they no longer see people as real at all.

FOR DISCUSSION: TO BECOME A SPELL-BREAKER

You can break the spell and become a spell-breaker by:

1. Breaking the code of silence. People who want to dominate and control others made up the code of silence. For

instance, when people say or do something to a person that is not okay, they don't want victims to object. Usually, victims feel ashamed or that it is their fault somehow for being "picked" out for the abuse, or they feel too afraid to reveal the abuse, or they believe it was nothing to talk about, or they believe they were partly to blame for being abused, or they believe that revealing the abuse is a sign of weakness. The code of silence is ready to be broken.

2. Realizing that we are all a community. We can depend on each other. And, when someone verbally abuses you, he or she deepens the spell and that impacts you and everyone. Saying something like, "That sounds like verbal abuse. Is that what you meant?" is a way to wake up the person and break the spell. If the person doesn't stop and continues to harass you, talking about it to people who can help is very important.

3. Speaking up when you hear someone put someone down. Any time you see someone being verbally abused, if it is safe to do so, it is essential that you speak up in front of the abuser: "What did you say?" or "That's not okay." To accept what was said and to go along with a spellbound person are not okay. As a representative of the real world, real people are obligated to affirm what is real and what is not.

VERBAL ABUSE AND FEAR

People who chronically indulge in verbal abuse are afraid that others won't be as they imagine they should be. In other words, that they'll lose touch with their pretend world. For example, if a father has a pretend son, one who scores all the touchdowns, he might call his real son names because he didn't score a touchdown in some game.

People who chronically indulge in verbal abuse are afraid that they may be like, or identified with, people who are different from them. Their identity is shaky. Young teens have barely begun to realize who they are and are not expected to have a strong identity. Usually, once teens realize that they are being hurtful to classmates whom they put down for being different, they stop their abusive behaviors. However, some teens find it much more difficult to give up their pretend world. They are so wounded, that they would prefer to pretend that they are superior to those who are different.

VERBAL-ABUSE-SURVIVAL INSURANCE

One thing in particular allows verbal abuse to get a grip on teens. It is the code of silence. If they object to their own abuse, many victims have succumbed to the threat of being called names ("weak," "snitch"). Their belief, that other people's definitions of them are real, indicates that they are being caught in the spell.

Their unwritten agreement to stay "shut up" is called the code of silence. *This is great for the abusers, because the code of silence is like verbal-abuse-survival insurance.*

The code of silence tells teens that they are weak if they say no to verbal abuse. Many TV shows also teach the code of silence. They make it look okay to endure verbal abuse without speaking up. It is as if the room were filled with people who are mesmerized into unconsciousness, and so stand by, as if demeaning human beings is okay. Yet, it is likely that if they were not overtaken by the spell, and, for instance, saw a pet abused, they would say, "Hey, that's not okay."

If the code of silence doesn't get a grip in some teens' minds, and doesn't ensure silence, then sometimes abusers use the threat of violent retaliation. It is essential that every preteen and teen in the country know that the threat of violence against a person is the "assault" part of the crime of assault and battery, and that the police should be called immediately if such a threat is made, and also, of course, if the assault becomes battery.

EDUCATION CAN BREAK THE CODE OF SILENCE

Although many parents do teach their children not to call people names, and how to be respectful by saying, "please" and "thank you," many children grow up without being taught in school about verbal abuse. They don't have a health class or communications class or family-life class or citizenship class that includes information on what verbal abuse is and why it's not okay. Even more important, they don't know the best ways to cope with people who routinely indulge in verbal abuse.

Ignorance of verbal abuse not only harms children, but also opens the door to disastrous relationships. Since verbal abuse precedes violence, it is important that we know all we can about it.

I believe that the most effective way to end verbal abuse is to bring knowledge to everyone. For instance, once all the children in, say, seventh grade know that verbal abuse is pretend talk, they will have a better understanding of what to say when they hear it. Once they realize that those who regularly indulge in it are acting as if they are under a spell, they will be interested in breaking the spell. And, once teens who indulge in verbal abuse understand that others may see their behavior as cowardly, they may seek help.

Education can break the code of silence around verbal abuse. Irrational behavior that confuses teens and damages them, sometimes for the rest of their lives, can be discussed in the classroom. Teens can learn that to reveal verbal abuse and potential violence is a sign of strength.

THE OLD WAY OF STOPPING VERBAL ABUSE DIDN'T WORK

In the past, there were two primary ways people tried to deal with verbal abuse when they were its target.

1. People tried to explain themselves to get reconciliation. If the abuser said, for example, "You're looking for a fight,"

the victim said, "I'm not looking for a fight." This proved to be a futile way of dealing with verbal abuse. When people explain themselves, the abuser is glad to have been taken seriously. The abuser loves arguing or silencing the victim. And the victim forgets to tell the abuser, "Please stop pretending to know my motives."

2. People tried to get back at the person who verbally abused them. This, too, proved to be a futile way of dealing with verbal abuse.

The strategy of getting back at the abuser escalates the verbal abuse until it is all over the place.

SCHOOL/PARENT JOINT EDUCATION

There are two essential ways to stop the perpetration of verbal abuse. They are by (1) educating students, parents, and teachers about it and by (2) intervening appropriately when we witness it.

With training and administrative support, teachers and parents can work together to bring awareness about verbal abuse. Here are some suggestions.

1. Protect children by standing up to verbal abuse when it occurs at home.
2. Consider monthly parent discussion groups arranged with schools where parents of the children in each class meet to attend their own "class" to share their concerns and ideas.
3. Institute a teen team in each class, trained to spot verbal abuse and to support the abused student. This will be most effective if the whole class has training and all students have a turn on the team.

4. Hold school workshops that teach how to respond appropriately to verbal abuse and why kids indulge in it. This would enlighten the entire student body, so that the subject would be out in the open.

5. Have a monthly discussion at every grade level about why revealing verbal abuse, and asking for support from teachers, parents, and peers, is a good way to get verbal abuse out of your school so it can't hurt anyone anymore.

6. Any student who is threatened for breaking the code of silence around verbal abuse, or violence, needs security. Counseling and community agencies will need to intervene and supervise the troubled abuser to eliminate the fear of retaliation.

WHEN TO INTERVENE

Since people of all ages indulge in verbal abuse, so many, in fact, that it seems to be a part of our culture, knowing when and how to intervene is important.

Occasionally, you, whether teen or adult, as a representative of the real world may hear someone say something to another person that causes you to wonder if you are hearing verbal abuse. If you are not sure, you can ask one or both people how they feel about what was just said: "Are you feeling okay about that?"

If you are committed to stopping verbal abuse and you call it as you see it, or bring it up for discussion, you may encounter some people who think that you shouldn't be bothered by verbal abuse. They may say that if being assaulted with statements that define you bothers you, then you have a problem.

In general, these people are either pretending that assaults to your psyche, and the hostility they represent, are not harmful, wearing, and enervating, or they have lost touch with their own feelings. It is possible that they were abused and coped with the abuse by losing touch with themselves, particularly their feelings. If so, they would have a low emotional IQ.

BEING A SPELL-BREAKER

The most important thing to remember in confronting verbal abuse is to separate the behavior from the person. By that I mean that you address the behavior, "That's not okay," rather than accusing the person, "You're an abuser." Clearly, to attack the person rather than the behavior escalates the abuse, and accusing is a form of verbal abuse.

The following suggestions are meant to support you in whatever ways you are already taking a stand against verbal abuse.

SET LIMITS

The following list suggests ways to respond to verbal abuse, and to correct or limit it.

- Putting people down is not okay and I don't want to hear it again.
- You may ask nicely, but you may not give orders.
- There will be no name-calling in this house.
- You may not walk away while I am talking to you. Please excuse yourself.

Sometimes, especially with young children, simply saying that name-calling, for instance, is not allowed will put a stop to it. Children will try new things just to see how they work, and that includes verbal abuse.

THE SARCASM STORY

A young woman of eighteen told me the following:

"I remember when I was about eight years old, I heard a girl say something in a kind of exaggerated way. I asked another girl what she meant. She said, 'That girl's just being sarcastic.'

"I wondered why I hadn't learned how to be sarcastic. I kept my ears open and one day, I figured out how to do it. A couple of months later I tried it. A girl had gotten her coat muddy from falling down. I said something like, 'Oh, my, what a beautiful coat,' in a very sarcastic voice. Another girl said it wasn't nice. Then, I felt terrible, so I never tried to be sarcastic again. Until then, I didn't realize it wasn't okay. I felt like I'd gone to all this effort for nothing."

BE COMMITTED

Whether you recall being put down as a child, or being defined as an adult, or you just want to see positive change, your commitment is essential.

Your commitment to respond to verbal abuse whenever and wherever you see it, whenever it is safe to do so, bonds you with others who also make that commitment. Most important, it brings truth and light to untruthful and confusing interactions. Since a child may not ever have heard anyone stand up for him or her, your support will be essential. There might not be anyone else who will.

Even people who find that they, themselves, unthinkingly indulge in verbal abuse have the opportunity to bond with others against it and to enlist their support in pointing it out when it appears in an interaction.

KNOW YOU MAKE A DIFFERENCE

The problem of verbal abuse may seem so overwhelming that some people wonder if they should even bother to address it.

"Maybe the kids can fight it out for themselves," they might think. Well the kids might solve an argument by themselves, but when abuse is involved, you can make an important difference. This might be their first opportunity to learn what is, and is not, a fair fight.

Another issue that comes up for some people is that verbal abuse is so pervasive, bringing awareness can feel like walking against a huge tide. "Maybe this is just the way it is," they might think. Then it's important to remember that you don't have to take on the whole ocean, just the very local territory of home or school, or even right in the car with the latest car-pool riders!

SPEAK THE TRUTH

If you are respectful of other people and understand their separate inner reality, you cannot help but speak the truth to them. And the best part is, you are then modeling to young and old alike respectful communication.

RECOGNIZE VERBAL ABUSE

In order to take a stand against verbal abuse (not against the person), it is important to know exactly what verbal abuse is, as discussed in Chapter I. To be effective in fighting it, it is important to spot even its most subtle forms. For instance, sometimes a joke is not really a joke, because it defines someone. Sometimes a question is an accusation put in a "why" format.

With a lot of empathy, you can most easily spot verbal abuse by how it feels. Putting yourself in the teen's place, and knowing you wouldn't want to hear it, is enough to tell you what verbal abuse is. In any case, you do not have to memorize the categories of verbal abuse.

INTERVENE

Since verbal abuse can intrude anywhere, it is important to be not only alert to it, but also to step in to stop it when you hear it. It is not helpful to stand by and watch it move against someone. Seeing it wreck havoc on others and hoping it will be sated and disappear in a little while, will not put an end to it. It grows stronger as it feeds on people's energy.

First, assess the situation and determine if it is safe to intervene. Usually it is safe if you are dealing with one teen abusing another. But if you are in a public place and see someone verbally slamming a child, it may not be safe to intervene in the ways described below. If you feel compelled to rescue the child, simply say something that shows concern for the abuser, for example, "It looks like a rough day." That may divert the person enough to stop the verbal violence.

If you are its target, you may be stunned. Verbal abuse can move very quickly and catch one by surprise. If this happens to you, if you can recover from the shock, or "off balance" feeling, enough to even say, "What?" you will have taken a big step in fighting it off.

It is helpful to think of verbal abuse as an invasive toxic cloud that needs to be arrested instantly to preserve the well-being of the people who have been subjugated to it as well as the ones it is attempting to invade. If you think of it this way, it is easier to go against the abuse (the toxic cloud) and not the person who does its bidding.

CONFRONT THE SPEAKER AND NAME THE ABUSE

There are three parts to this step: (1) State what you heard that was not okay, (2) name it as sounding like verbal abuse, and (3) ask the speaker if he or she meant it that way. Here is an example: "When I heard you say _____ , it sounded like verbal abuse. Did you mean it that way?"

You have to name verbal abuse to stand up to it. Verbal abuse is deceit in disguise. It doesn't like to be called what it is. It likes to pretend it's something else—truth, for instance. If you recall, verbal abuse is the opposite of truth. Verbal abuse presents itself as truth when it takes over someone. "You're a wuss" is a lie that presents itself as truth. It is both silly and an assault. It says you are not who you are. But if you name it, it loses a lot of its power.

By asking offenders if they meant to be abusive, we don't judge or attack them. We simply correct them. And they have a chance to think about what they really mean. They have a chance to speak the truth.

ASK THE OFFENDER TO REPHRASE THEIR STATEMENTS

Can you think of a better way to say what you meant? Can you talk about the problem and not the person?

SUPPORT THE VICTIM OF VERBAL ABUSE

Supportive statements declare the positive about the victim. For example, "I sure don't see you that way. Can you see how I see you as very smart (strong, loyal, etc.)?"

TALK TO OTHERS ABOUT THE PROBLEM

By sharing your knowledge of verbal abuse, you can make a difference in many people's lives. It's very difficult to tell if someone you know is being verbally abused at home or on campus unless you witness it. People who chronically indulge in verbal abuse are usually very good at hiding it. They're so good at presenting a congenial image to the world, that some people have told me of visiting someone's home and staying a while, without knowing that one of the hosts was very verbally abusive to family members.

By bringing up the topic of verbal abuse, you might be helping others see it for what it is. A good introduction to verbal abuse is, "Did you know that when people define other people, they're being verbally abusive?"

Also, sharing information and asking a question or two can open up discussion of verbal abuse. For instance, "When people tell you what you are, what you think, or how you are, they are verbally abusive. Has anyone ever tried to tell you what you were doing, or saying, and it was just the opposite of the truth? How do you feel when that kind of thing happens?"

TEACH GOOD COMMUNICATION

Good communication approaches people within the context of curiosity.

Say	Rather than . . .
"What didn't you find funny about that?"	"You can't take a joke."
"Have you considered . . . ?"	"You don't know what you're talking about."
"How did you arrive at that conclusion?"	"You're jumping to conclusions."
"Why did you bring that up?"	"You're trying to start a fight."
"What bothered you about that?"	"You always have to have something to complain about."
"Can you tell me what I just said?"	"You're not listening."
"Are you feeling ill?"	"You just want to skip school."
"What kept you from doing your homework?"	"You're just trying to get out of it."

LET GO OF FALSE BELIEFS ABOUT VERBAL ABUSE

Following are some beliefs that condone or tolerate verbal abuse, one of the greatest assaults on humanity.

Hearing a teen verbally abuse another teen, one believes

- They'll work it out.
- Kids will be kids.
- It takes two.
- Verbal abuse never hurt anyone.
- You've got to give as good as you get.
- Taking verbal abuse toughens you up, so it is necessary.
- If you don't take it, you'll look weak.
- It's really just a joke.
- Older people have the right to define younger people.
- It happens to everyone, so it's not significant.
- There is nothing wrong as long as no one is hit.
- Ignoring it makes it go away.
- It's not my job to say anything.
- They're related, so it's domestic and I shouldn't say anything.
- I have to look impartial, no matter which one is abusive.
- The victim and the victimizer should both be punished.

EXTREME VERBAL ABUSERS DON'T CHANGE

Some people are very damaged from early childhood and have locked into a pattern of verbal abuse that is part of their way of being. They seem to live in a different world from the average person, and they want to impose that world on others. But others don't act and think like they imagine they should, so they are very frustrated. Usually they are almost constantly angry or ready to fly into a rage. Sometimes they are also completely closed off and unable to know their true feelings. They are unresponsive and

coldly cruel at times. It is very important to know that such a confirmed abuser may not be able to change, or may not want to
change, even when you confront him or her. If a person continues
to abuse you, even after you have addressed the issue, your best
strategy is to leave that person as soon as possible. He or she
might gain some insight in the future from someone else or might
not. The person just wasn't ready to hear about it from you. If
you've tried your best and the person doesn't show any insight,
don't allow yourself to stay, even if he or she says, "I love you."

PARENT-TEACHER GUIDELINE

Almost anyone can feel frustrated when overloaded with responsibilities. And so, almost anyone can say something that qualifies
as verbal abuse. The difference between confirmed abusers and
those who only occasionally indulge in it, is that they usually catch
themselves, or see a look on someone's face, or some other
response, that brings them back to themselves and the realization
of what they've said. These people are not locked into patterns of
verbal abuse and are ready to apologize or retract their comment
right away.

IF YOU HAVE INDULGED IN VERBAL ABUSE

If you realize that you may be indulging in verbal abuse yourself,
having this realization, and acknowledging it, is important. Here
are some suggestions: Look for help from a counselor you trust.
Read everything you can about verbal abuse. Ask the people
around you to please give you a signal if they hear something that
isn't okay with them. I recommend, "What?" as a universal
signal.

   If you seek help for yourself, you'll not only bring healing to
yourself but also to those whom you've affected. And, you will

eventually be in a good position to help others. Together with all who want a better, saner world, you can make a difference.

How to Acknowledge a Verbal Mistake

If you find you've said something that came across as abusive, here are ways to acknowledge the mistake and to set the stage for real communication. By acknowledging mistakes, you set a great example for others, and turn a negative into a positive.

- That didn't come out right. I meant to say . . .
- I'm sorry; I didn't mean that. I meant to say . . .
- I wasn't thinking when I said that. I meant to say . . .
- Let me rephrase that. It wasn't what I meant. I meant to say . . .
- Please forget that I said that; I didn't mean it. I meant to say . . .
- Let me put that another way. I meant to say . . .
- I can't believe what just came out of my mouth—I'm so sorry. I was completely out of it. What I meant to say was . . .

Tweaking Teen Talk

Here are a few handy corrections that parents, teachers, and observers can use when they hear kids indulging in verbal abuse at home or at school.

- *Name-calling:* "(person's name), guess what! We don't call people names here."
- *Accusing:* "(person's name), making up things about people is silly talk and is verbally abusive. Can you ask nicely?" (For instance, "Did you put that there?")

- *Angry yelling:* "(person's name), can you take a deep breath? Now can you tell me what's bothering you?"
- *Demanding/ordering:* "(person's name), did you know that if you ask for something with 'please,' people are more likely to hear you?"
- *Trivializing/discounting:* "(person's name), putting down what someone does (or says) doesn't make you better."
- *Threatening:* "(person's name), threatening people to get what you want doesn't work in the long run. Did you know that telling people you won't be their friend if they don't do what you want is verbally abusive?"
- *Denial:* "(person's name), did you know that pretending that you didn't say what we just heard you say, is a way of lying?"

I hope that you will take whatever steps you can to bring awareness to the lives of those who are under your influence. If you listen and respond empathetically, and clearly, if you set boundaries and express your needs, if you speak up against verbal abuse, you will be part of a growing number of people who are breaking the spell. If verbal abuse has impacted someone you know, he or she will need a touchstone—someone to help sort out what is real and what is not. Can you be that person? Lending a sympathetic ear can make all the difference.

Chapter XII

For Parents

JUST AS A BABY BIRD MUST BE BORN AND RAISED IN A PARTICULAR kind of nest, in a particular environment, to survive and thrive, so, too, must the baby human. The eagle cannot survive in a duck's nest. Nor can the hummingbird survive in the eagle's nest. But people can manage very diverse environments. They are extremely resilient. They can add parkas and protection for cold environments and sunscreen and shorts for hot environments. They can survive in the marshes and on the cliffs. They can adapt to many different physical environments.

While the bird must have the correct physical environment, the human must have this and also something else. As you've probably already guessed, just as humans must have a physically safe environment and be protected from physical damage, they must also have a psychologically safe environment and be protected from psychological damage in order to survive and thrive.

Children need to feel valued at home for their uniqueness, to be recognized, loved, and attended to. If they are, when they are in their teens, they will feel that their family is there for them and is on their side. There is no time more important than now for parents to renew their dedication to raising psychologically healthy children, because there have never been more influences on children from more places than there are now.

The report "Bruised Inside," mentioned earlier, says, "We endorse the primacy of the family but we also recognize that our schools are over-flowing with children who do not get the love, support, guidance and acceptance they need from their families."

For some very interesting reading and for an understanding of what teens face, I highly recommend that every parent read the report. It can be found online.[25] Being verbally abused, harassed, and bullied in school is a part of the problem our teens face. The other part is that many come to school already hurting.

PARENTING YOUR TEEN

Parents are called on not only to oversee their children's physical health but also their psychological health. Here are some of the ways parents do this.

Most parents are careful to see that their children are introduced to friends when they are young and, also, to meet their children's friends and families when their children are older. Most parents teach their children consequences and allow them to take responsibility for themselves as they mature. Many parents try to spend quality time with their children every day, taking an interest in them and their concerns. Beyond these very important parental tasks lies one of the most important, and that is to mirror reality to the child, and, thus, to protect the child's boundaries.

CROSSING BOUNDARIES

Most parents do their best, but even very well-meaning one may unthinkingly define their children and, thus, cross their boundaries.

When parents indulge in pretend talk, they violate their children's boundaries and so they weaken them. Pretend talk is talk that pretends to know something about someone without asking. It is defining another person, and so, even if it is well intentioned, it has an abusive quality to it.

Here is an example of verbal abuse that defines a child's motives.

When thirteen-year-old Joey (two years younger than his brother, Sam) showed his mom how well he cleaned his room, he was probably expecting some good attention and some praise for his good job. He heard pretend talk instead: "You're just trying to show up your brother." Joey had never even conceived of being able to "show up" his older brother, Sam, who seemed to know everything and do everything long before Joey.

Joey was in trouble, didn't know why, and wasn't allowed to explain himself. When he tried, saying that he just wanted to make the room look good for his dad, his dad said, "You're quibbling over words. 'Look good' and 'show up' are the same thing."

Here is an example of verbal abuse that defines a child's sense of self in terms of what she wants.

Judy always saw her daughter as a star cheerleader and beauty queen. In actuality, her daughter was a quiet artist who loved jeans and sweatshirts.

Coming into the kitchen on Saturday morning in her favorite outfit, she heard her mother say, "You don't want to wear that. It's not pretty." Judy told her daughter what she wanted! As bizarre as such a statement is, it is all too common.

Like all defining statements, it invades a child's inner being and attempts to erase her self-perception.

how parents could tell their children what
they want, but some parents don't even
...nealthy behavior. The girl whom we met ear-
...other insisted she be a ballerina, is a case in point.

When a parent or any adult pretends to know their child's inner reality, standing in their space, so to speak, the parent has crossed the child's psychic boundary and the child's inner reality is not mirrored. Instead, their inner reality is reflected back to them in a strangely distorted way.

This distortion is possibly the fastest way to destroy a child's emotional health; to leave him or her in self-doubt; to encourage future leanings toward drugs, unhealthy relationships, depression, and so on.

Since teens are almost wholly engaged in building a strong sense of themselves, their identity, who they will be when grown, and what they will do in their careers, clear mirroring is essential.

If you find you've crossed your child's boundary, an apology makes a vast difference. Suddenly the mirror is clear. The distortion is gone.

If, like Susan in Bobby's story, you have witnessed someone cross your child's boundary, you can best clear the distortion that was reflected to your child by speaking up in front of the perpetrator. For example, say, "What she [or he] said is not okay."

How parents reflect their children to themselves is very important. I don't believe there would be many gangs, wars, suicides, violent assaults, and social ills if all of our children throughout the world were well raised and well educated about verbal abuse.

An AAP journal article lists long-term consequences to children of psychological maltreatment. Among them are: low self-esteem, negative emotional or life view, anxiety symptoms, depression, suicide or suicidal thoughts, emotional instability, borderline personality, emotional unresponsiveness, impulse control problems, anger, physical self-abuse, eating disorders, substance abuse, low sympathy and empathy for others, self-isolation, noncompliance, sexual maladjustment, dependency, aggression or violence, delinquency or criminality, low academic achievement, learning impairments, impaired moral reasoning, and somatic complaints.[26]

If children's boundaries are weakened by incursions into their minds, they will have trouble developing a healthy sense of themselves and will be a more likely target for verbal abuse at school and in relationships, or they may become abusers. If children see a parent verbally abused by the other parent, they may see no way to stop these boundary violations from happening to them. For instance, a girl's mother is her model, but if she witnesses her mother being verbally abused, and her mother does not know how to deal with it, to stop it or leave the situation until it stops, there is no effective model for the daughter. If one parent verbally abuses the other, children are impacted by it. It doesn't matter which parent. If both parents are verbally abusive, the child is even more deeply affected.

One of the ways to avoid *inadvertently* or *unconsciously* responding to your teen as if she or he weren't really there, is to try to answer questions and set limits with your teen's perspective in mind. Your response should not be about your image, nor should it be about shaping your teen into a dream person.

In other words, if you must say no to a request, do so, but then explain why you can't go along with the request, making sure that your explanation is meaningful to the child. It should consider the teen's needs. For example, "You can't go there, because they won't look after you or properly supervise you," would be an appropriate answer. It is one a young teen would understand.

On the other hand, saying, "You can't go there, because what would the neighbors think of me [as a mother or father] if they knew I let you go there," is an inappropriate response and confuses the child. This kind of response is all about image, how one looks, and is not about the child.

Just as responses to teens that are all about parents' images would be confusing to them, so are responses that are directed toward shaping children into pretend children. For instance, the following comment is not about the real child. It's all about the pretend child. A parent says to a daughter, "You can't wear those jeans. You know you're my girl and you're too pretty to wear jeans. You need to wear pretty dresses to show everyone just how pretty you are."

If you know parents who talk this way to their teenagers, or even younger children, showing them this information may support them in understanding that their children are separate people with their own separate reality.

The following story is about a very unaware man, whom I'll call Bert, and his son, whom I'll call Rej. Bert liked sports immensely, loved to go duck hunting, and enjoyed a cigar after dinner, while discussing a business venture with his partners at his club. He thought Rej would probably follow in his footsteps. However, Rej enjoyed art, music, foreign languages, and philosophical discussion.

Every time Bert tried to involve his son in a hunting trip, or he had prime seats to a game, he would find that Rej was involved in something else. Bert felt so irritated that he began to criticize Rej for all the little things that he would have done differently, if he had been doing them himself. But all the criticism still didn't shape up Rej as Bert felt his son should be shaped up, or shaped into, that is, a chip off the old block. Not being able to make Rej be how he wanted him to be, the father became more irritable, angry, and sarcastically abusive. Rej felt increasingly rejected by his father, increasingly criticized, and increasingly unacceptable. Eventually, in despair and pain over never being acceptable, Rej tried out a quick self-medication, as he thought of it, a drug that was going around and was not too hard to get. This and other drugs weakened him, and eventually the son became ill, and before he was thirty he died of a rare disease.

When the parent's image, as well as the pretend child's image, is at stake, the parent is caught in a bind. The inner conflict between looking good and making the child look good can lead to a lot of crazy talk—a response that instills false guilt in a child and leads the child to worry needlessly about a portending calamity. This response tells the child that the parent is, or is about to be, a victim. For example, "Well, I guess you can go, but I'll probably have a heart attack earning the money to pay for it. But if you don't go, I know you'll never grow up to be a real man. Besides, if you don't go, I know you'll just be a pain to have around here."

Although no real child can be a pretend child, some parents verbally abuse their real children, unconsciously aiming to diminish them to such an extent that pretend children seemingly take their place. In other words, a real child is gone, and a pretend child has appeared like a puppet where a real child used to be.

WHEN ONE PARENT IS VERBALLY ABUSIVE

Many parents are not involved in preserving their image or creating a pretend child. But sometimes one parent is and the other isn't. In this case, the nonabusive parent doesn't usually know what to do. Both mothers and fathers have said to me, "I know I need to protect my child from verbal abuse, but my mate is abusive to our child and I'm never sure what to say, or when to say it."

Failure to stand up for a child can take place for many reasons.

Some parents are afraid to speak up, to take a stand against verbal abuse by one parent, because they are led to believe by authorities outside of the marriage, that they must always form a united front toward their child. They have been told to work out their disagreements about rules for the child in private, or with the assistance of a child psychologist.

After agreeing on the issue, they are then to present a decision to the child, showing that they cannot be manipulated or played one against the other.

This idea of standing together on issues can be an obstacle to protecting your child from verbal abuse. This idea can be taken to the extreme as the following real story shows.

I suggested to a psychologist who was married to a psychologist that she say, "Hold it, that's not okay" when her husband berated their son with abusive comments, including name-calling. She said, "I tried, but then he starts yelling, 'triangulation, triangulation,' so I've stopped."

"What does he mean?" I asked.

"He says we will harm or confuse our child by not standing united, and so a triangle forms between my son, me, and his father."

"Would you say anything if he poked your son with a pin?" I asked. "It will take your son longer to recover from the verbal abuse than the pinprick. And how would you feel if your spouse called you names in front of your aunt and she said nothing till later, when you were alone in your room, and she came in and said, 'He didn't really mean it.'"

The important point is that while it is true that parents must agree on, say, a bedtime for their children, and stand together on that so the child doesn't play one parent against the other for the favor of staying up late, it is never okay to stand by and see your child abused.

Often the child will model after the verbally abusive parent because the other parent seems so powerless. Generally, this powerlessness is perceived because the nonabusive parent says nothing in the presence of the abuser, though later may say something to comfort the child or placate the child.

The best thing for a child is to create a supportive, loving environment at home and never stand by when a family member, sibling, grandparent, or other relative is verbally abusive. Parents need to be protective and corrective.

IF YOUR TEEN IS BEING PUT DOWN

Guidelines

- *Open up communication:* "You're looking a little sad, what's happening?"
- *Show empathy:* "I can see that was hurtful. No one likes to be put down, or called names, or ____."
- *Validate your teen:* "Verbal abuse is not okay. It is pretend talk and it pretends something about you."
- *Emphasize that it's the abuser's responsibility:* "No one deserves abuse. That shouldn't have happened. What ____ said is not okay."
- *Point out that the abuser has the problem:* "Abusers pretend things about people because they are afraid. Sometimes they try to get people to be with them and against others because they don't know any other way to connect with people."

Here is how these guidelines could be combined into a supportive response to a teen who is being targeted with verbal abuse: "I can see that was hurtful. What she [or he] said is not okay, and it's making up pretend stuff about you. You certainly don't deserve it. It wouldn't be happening if they weren't so sick, afraid, or jealous."

When it comes to verbal abuse, one of the worst things a child can experience is abuse from one parent while the other parent looks on, utterly failing to take a stand against verbal abuse.

Following are some suggestions for dealing with this issue. Please, always ascertain that it is safe to speak up. If you are attacked by the abuser for interceding in front of your child, the child will also experience similar trauma. Assess the level of the abuse you are protecting your child from. If it is a casual negative comment, it should be dealt with at a lighter level than, say, an outright, blistering name-calling attack.

Your response to the abuse would be said with the intention that the abuser hears him- or herself, realizes what he or she said, and apologizes, for instance, "Oh, that came out wrong. I'm sorry; I should never have said that."

Parents aren't perfect. Knowing this, I recommend that they agree between themselves, that if one of them says something unkind or derogatory to their child, the other parent asks, "What?" so the offending parent can "wake up" and repair the damage.

TAKING A STAND AGAINST VERBAL ABUSE IN FRONT OF YOUR TEEN

- "(Adult's name), that sounds like verbal abuse; is that what you meant?"
- "Hey, that's not okay."
- "That's pretend talk."
- "That's silly talk."
- "That's nonsense."
- "It's not okay to talk like that. That isn't funny."
- "That's not okay. We don't call names, ever."

- "That's not okay. I don't want to ever hear that again."
- "What [Dad/Mom] just said isn't okay."
- "Please, leave the room until you can talk respectfully."

FOR PARENTS

Beyond stopping verbal abuse, parents also have a responsibility to affirm their children's intrinsic value. Sometimes life is so filled with demands, it is hard for parents to remember to give their teens positive strokes. Here are some examples of supportive statements.

- "I love you so much; you're a great kid."
- "You're such an important member of our family; we all count on your input."
- "I like you just the way you are."
- "I admire how you keep track of all your activities [finish your projects before you start new ones, keep such a good attendance record, operate the computer, sleep through commotion, look so up-to-date, keep up your determination, let go of things that don't work for you]."
- "You are part of a larger plan and have a place in the world."

CONVERSATIONS WITH YOUR TEEN

Some parents don't know how to initiate conversations with their teenage children because their own parents didn't spend time talking with them. One of the best ways to have conversations with a teenager is to have had them since he or she was little. But it is never too late to begin spending individual, quality time with each child every day. Some parents make time to do this. Others have never thought about it or put any plan into effect.

Although, at first, your teen may not have much to say about what is going on in his or her life, if you initiate daily conversations, it is likely that you will know if something occurs that upsets him or her.

If you haven't made a practice of spending some time with your teen every day, you may need to try a number of times before he or she opens up to you. Do keep in mind, that if your teen doesn't want to talk, you won't make it better by pressuring him or her. Instead, let your teen know that you are always there, and that if there is anything he or she wants to talk about, you will hear whatever it is without judgment. Be encouraging, bring up topics your child is interested in, and ask engaging questions.

ENGAGE YOUR CHILD

Almost universally, parents want to assist their teens as they grow through their adolescence. They want to see them reach a confident and happy adulthood, but many aren't sure where to begin or what to do. Having conversations is a good way to start. To engage teens, parents need to tune in to their behavior to see if they can tell their mood. They need to ask questions and to respond with empathy and enthusiasm as appropriate. In other words, parents, besides giving guidance, will need to talk with the openness and compassion one would talk with to a best friend.

Some teens have grown to adulthood never hearing engaging questions, or hearing them from only one parent. Some families, for instance, have structured their conversations around girls talking to their mothers and boys to their fathers. But interchanges between both parents are important.

If a child seems withdrawn or upset, you can open up dialogue with the child by asking, "Is anything bothering you?"

It may take some time and some assurance: "Whatever you tell me, I promise you won't get into trouble. I'm here to help you. I love you and there isn't anything you can tell me that will take that love away."

By engaging your teen, you can become closer to him or her. Following are some questions designed to engage your child. One or two at a time is enough. Otherwise, it would sound like an interrogation. The idea is to show your teen that you are interested. Another part of asking a question is responding with empathy. Since some parents have been very busy and have not quite realized how important conversations are, they sometimes aren't sure how to respond with empathy. Following this list of engaging questions, you will find a list of responses that show your teen you are listening and interested.

Engaging Questions for Your Teen

"How are you?"

"You look sad; can you tell me about it?"

"How are you feeling?"

"What do you think about . . . ?"

"Are you worried about . . . ?"

"Did you have a good day?"

"How did your test go?"

"What do you think of this?"

"Are you looking forward to . . .?"

"How is your friend . . .?"

"Do you have any ideas about what we can do about . . .?"

"Do you know about . . .?"

"What do you want to do?"

"What do you like most about . . .?"

"What do you like least about . . .?"

"What do you think is fair?"

"Have you been worried about something?"

"Have you had any bad dreams lately?"

"If you could have something be different, what would it be?"

LISTENING AND RESPONDING TO YOUR TEEN

Parents can help their teens by listening to them and attending to them. This isn't always easy to do because teens don't reveal everything to their parents. It is natural that teens, who are leaving the close ties of family and moving into the teen world, would want privacy. Teens are private and want to be separate from adults. But they are still at home and still in need of family support. So listening with your eyes as well as your ears is important. Teens can be suffering in silence.

The chapter "For Teens" suggests ways to introduce the topic of verbal abuse to your teens. Talking about it can break the silence around verbal abuse. This would include discussions not only of what verbal abuse is, that is, making up things about people, but also how some teens and even some adults exclude and define people who are different or who just don't have a quality the person wants to be identified with. A boy, for instance, who wants to be an athlete may try to befriend an athlete and to ignore a boy who isn't athletic.

Responses are as important as questions when you converse with your child. Following are some sample responses that, when used appropriately, show your interest as well as your empathy.

EMPATHETIC RESPONSES

"Mmm."

"Uh, huh."

"I see."

"Yeah."

"What a bummer."

"That's great."

"Oh, that's interesting."

"I didn't realize that."

"Wow, I'm glad to hear that."

"Oh, gosh, that's hard."

"How sad."

"I'm so sorry to hear that."

KEEPING TEENS SAFE

Good parenting by fathers and mothers is needed now more than at any other time in history, if for no other reason than that there are more people on planet Earth who can be harmed by the fallout from verbal abuse than there ever were before, and verbal abuse is a weapon that goes against life.

PARENTAL INFLUENCE

Fathers have a great influence on their children, particularly their sons. A kind and thoughtful father has an enormous positive influence on a child. An exemplary "good father" protects his children from many bad decisions by his acceptance and emotional support of his sons and daughters. Unfortunately, a dominating or controlling father also has a huge impact on how a child will develop. Almost all male verbal and physical abusers had absent, distant, or controlling fathers. While some had similar mothers, many did not.

The latest evidence is that even girls who become anorexic are more influenced by their father's, than by their mother's, diet concerns.

Mothers also have a great influence on their children. Emotionally healthy mothers usually have emotionally healthy daughters. Mothers who are verbally abusive usually had abusive mothers. Overall, the best odds at having an emotionally healthy child are present when the child has two emotionally healthy parents.

If your teen is not in a two-parent household, the parent who isn't present, if not abusive, should call daily to converse with him or her. If parents can afford a phone and separate line for their teen, I suggest getting one because there is much less chance of interruptions and problems between estranged parents.

If both parents treat their teens with high regard, respect, and clear boundaries, allowing for flexibility in their lives, they will be much more aware of any potentially verbally abusive relationship. Good parental models can go a long way toward helping teens choose good boyfriend-girlfriend relationships.

WILL YOUR TEEN HAVE A BAD BOYFRIEND-GIRLFRIEND RELATIONSHIP?

Some teens enter into relationships with pretenders who will never really see or hear them. A big clue is that the new person will avoid asking them any engaging questions. When these teens find themselves in long-term relationships, married, or parents themselves, they may suddenly notice that their significant other is verbally abusive, doesn't engage them in conversation, or doesn't show an interest in their thoughts and feelings.

One of the best ways to protect your teen from this kind of relationship is to inform him or her of this potential problem and help your teen know that an emotionally responsive person who can ask engaging questions is important. Go over the lists of engaging questions and empathetic responses so your teen knows what is normal and what is not.

The best insurance against bad relationships is growing up with good, empathetic connections to one's parents. By having good conversations with their parents, teens know much better what is normal and what is not. Ideally, both parents must be there for their sons and daughters.

How the Verbal/Physical Abuser Got That Way

This section very briefly summarizes how people have become verbally abusive. Very simply, abusers model themselves after the nonempathetic person; have lost touch with their own empathy through the pain of having a rejecting, nonempathetic parent; have built a safer, more accepting pretend world; and have populated that world with a family of pretend people. These pretend people are, in a way, split off parts of themselves. The abusers fly into rages or coldly put down their real family members when they don't act like their pretend people.

Some abusers don't include certain family members in this setup. They connect to these others in a different way. They bond with some family members against other family members. The bond is their connection.

Keeping Verbal Abuse out of Your Home

If your goal is to keep verbal abuse out of your home and to support your teenagers when they are abused, one way is to help them understand what is real and what is not. I suggest that parents invite their children to bond with them against verbal abuse and to let them know if it comes around.

I suggest that parents talk to their teens and younger children about what verbal abuse is. It is a way of pretending that destroys relationships and creates unfeeling people who harm thousands in their endless games of one-upmanship, winning over others, and so on.

I also suggest that parents talk to their teens about the media that they see, particularly television and videos. It is important that teens understand that shows in which people are harmed or disparaged are not good choices. Discuss the following question with your teens. Why would anyone feature the destruction of people's minds and bodies? The answer is, to make money.

Children who don't know yet how to negotiate differences or deal with problems may find it great to knock off the opposition, verbally or physically. Children who are bored may want excitement. Children who wonder what is going on in the grown-up world, may think *it* is on TV.

Parents might point out to their children that people destruction is not a good thing. And, they might say, please don't watch it.

Television and videos that show people making fun of people who don't win some particular event or contest are despicable. Discuss the following question with your teens. Why would anyone want to show people being derided, ridiculed, and humiliated? The answer is, there are people who take pleasure in other people's pain, and who also make money from other people's pain, and their sickness is called sadism.

Television and videos that show women as objects, not as real people, show gender defamation. This is not okay. Discuss the following questions with your teens. Why would anyone portray human beings as objects? The answer is, to make money. Why would people portray themselves as objects? The answer is, they have been abused.

APOLOGIZING

But what, if after all this, you are thinking, "I've been verbally abusive; I've given orders and yelled at my teen. I've even lost it a couple of times and said that she [or he] wasn't going to amount to anything or that I wished she [or he] was more like somebody else, et cetera, et cetera."

Then you have a wonderful opportunity. That is the opportunity to say, "I'm so very sorry I've said . . . or called you a . . ."

It's never too late to ask for forgiveness. However, apologizing isn't just about your getting forgiveness. *Apologizing is about giving reality back to your child.* It's about letting a child know that you fully accept him or her, as the person he or she is, separate from you.

I have talked to many people who have waited their whole life for an apology or a word of praise from a parent. One doctor's father went further toward seeing her as a real person at forty-seven years of age than he ever had in her whole life. Although he wouldn't apologize for his verbally abusive behavior, he no longer put her and her opinions down. He said that he agreed to disagree.

A woman of fifty told me today, that her mother had recently admitted to being rough on her for the first time in her life, but didn't apologize to her. The mother didn't take full responsibility for the abuse she had lashed out at her daughter. She said it was just that she felt angry inside, and it wasn't personal, her daughter "just happened to be there." But even with the small admission, the daughter felt some relief. Her mother at least acknowledged that what she had done wasn't okay.

In another case, a brilliant woman, who had been verbally abused by her father, had witnessed family members abused at home, and had heard verbal abuse from her classmates and her teachers in her teens, is healing and also forging a great life for herself in a beautiful part of Canada. I commented on her resilience and her still obvious pain. She said, "The ones that gave up are gone!" She was speaking of close family members who had both died, from extreme stress-related illness.

EMOTIONAL SUPPORT FOR YOUR TEEN

Emotional support is primarily the recognition of the feelings, interests, and concerns of one's child. Teens need to feel that their family is there for them and is on their side, that they form a team. With that kind of support, teens can better withstand the occasional verbal abuse that takes place in school.

BOARDING SCHOOL, YES OR NO

Some teens are eager to attend a special school that supports their academic or personal interests. Others, however, are exiled from their families and sent far away from home to a prisonlike environment where verbal abuse from peers and teachers is magnified exponentially.

One of the worst things that can happen to a child is to be sent to a boarding school, unless the child really wants to go to a certain school and it has a great reputation. Otherwise, it simply pulls family support from the child.

Some parents, believing that it is in the best interest of their child to help him or her prepare for college and to encourage his or her early independence, look to boarding school as the best solution. In fact, the experience of being ripped from one's entire support system truncates the child's floundering attempts to gain independence. Parents often unwittingly send their child to a "teen hell," according to a boarding school survivor. Facing torment in a teen world from which there is no escape, many teens have expressed their anguish over having been pulled away from their family life; of losing the support of cousins, aunts, uncles, friends, and neighbors; of having no refuge.

A young woman, Lina, talked about the virulent atmosphere she faced at boarding school, as did other girls who weren't regarded as the good students and good-looking popular ones. Even teachers, seemingly unaware, joined with the popular girls to reject the less popular ones.

As in most high schools, boarding school teens can be excluded and derided. Charming and brilliant young girls are treated like outcasts *if they are different.* Isolated from support, "Everything that could be wrong is exacerbated exponentially in a twenty-four hours a day, seven days a week world without relief," Lina said. "I was stuck, unwanted, and unwelcome in both places, at home and among peers. There was no caring person in my life. Occasionally, I could find only a moment's solace in the company of another unpopular outcast. The contrast to the life I had left was deeply shocking."

Another teen described the last days of her real childhood at boarding school. No kind mother cared for her. She faced, instead, an alcoholic housemother who came out of her room once every six weeks, in pink puffy slippers and a faded housedress, to give out a ration of love in the form of a piece of fudge. "That was the extent of any form of love I got," she said.

She was smaller and younger than her classmates by almost two years. So, being that smart, she *was* different. Being different, she was abused. Being abused, she let her studies slip. Being a low performer, she was called stupid. Until on the one-to-one verbal Wexler IQ test—as opposed to the mass-administered Stanford-Binet—she scored second highest in her entire school. But then she was brought into the headmaster's office and admonished for not having performed at a higher level.

Teens describe unsympathetic parents who will not listen as having turned a cold shoulder to them and as no longer loving.

"I thought if my parents loved me, they wouldn't send me here," said one young girl. They felt inexplicably and suddenly rejected by their own parents, then shockingly alone and rejected by exclusionary classmates and impatient and derisive teachers. And they had done nothing wrong.

Many parents don't understand that they might be placing their children in a strange and horrifying pretend world, a culture that is totally alien to them. The teens I talked to were good, smart children whose pleas were unheard and whose real selves were unseen. The boarding school experience left many children to go through life as social isolates with lifelong overlays of depression.

AVOIDING VERBAL ABUSE WITH CURIOSITY

One of the best ways to avoid inadvertently verbally abusing teens, or anyone else for that matter, is to approach them within the context of curiosity. By this, I mean that you are curious about their perceptions, feelings, thoughts, intentions, and so forth. If you are curious, you cannot make assumptions and you cannot define them. You instead allow them to be self-defining. This is so important because it is what being a *person* is all about.

Recall the story earlier about the daring, athletic girl, Vela, whose parents wanted her to be a ballerina. They defined her, yet she still became who she was meant to be. They didn't get exactly what they wanted, although she certainly became a compassionate and caring woman. And what did she get? Suffering. Because of the way she was raised, it was a very difficult struggle for her to become who she was meant to be. True to her inner nature, she became an entrepreneur and used the skill and daring and risk taking from competitive riding and skiing to amass a fortune in investments.

If, instead of defining her, Vela's parents had approached her within the context of curiosity, they would have asked her about herself, and she would have been able, early on, to exercise her human right of self-definition. If they had said, "What do you want to do? What do you like most about ballet? What do you like least about it?" They would have gotten to know their real daughter.

Since no one but Vela knew what she liked and what her interests were, Vela's parents would have had to accept her self-definition, if they had been curious about her. If you are curious about someone, you see him or her as a person, separate from you. A child is not "a chip off the old block," although many a father may believe his son is just that. I have heard many stories of men who were athletes in high school. They played football and made touchdowns, and married and became fathers, and one day faced a teenage son and couldn't believe he wasn't going to be a football legend.

A lot of verbal abuse occurs when people forget that their teens are unique individuals, separate from them. Name-calling can be directed at a real son because he isn't a pretend son, a star athlete for instance.

In an actual case, when a boy of fifteen failed to make a winning play in a game, his father, watching from the sidelines, promptly called him names: "You're a loser, a disgrace," he shouted. The father was behaving disgracefully and certainly was losing it, while he called his son a loser.

The verbal abuse that pops out of some people's mouths often describes them and not the person they are targeting. And, if it doesn't describe them, it may describe one of their fears, which they are negatively and unfairly projecting onto their child.

VERBAL ABUSE IS NOT DISCIPLINE

Some parents believe that discipline is about verbally abusing their teen. Nothing could be farther from the truth. *Verbal abuse shows a lack of discipline on the part of the person who indulges in it.* Verbal abuse in this case is about venting anger at not having a real teen be as good or as perfect as a pretend teen.

If you are a parent who believed that yelling and saying things like, "You'll never amount to anything" to teens was okay if they didn't obey, or didn't follow the rules they had agreed to, you were misguided and possibly abused in your own childhood.

Certainly, most parents are disappointed when their children disobey them, but some don't know that it is much better to say, "I am disappointed by your behavior. This is the consequence." Curfews or other restrictions may be the natural consequences of a broken agreement. Natural consequences that fit the offense teach cause and effect and self-discipline. Rigidity, too much discipline, no discipline, and verbal abuse defeat self-discipline.

Sometimes a father will remember being hit by his own dad when he broke a rule, and he may think that verbal abuse isn't as bad as being hit. Neither is okay. And neither helps the child.

SIGNS OF VERBAL ABUSE

If your teen says there is nothing wrong, but you think he or she is being verbally abused at school by another teen or an adult, the following signs can indicate that something is happening that deserves your concern: Your child is upset, has trouble sleeping, has nightmares, is suddenly much more withdrawn or seems much more angry and irritable, or appears anxious or afraid of going to school.

If any of these symptoms lasts more than a couple of days, then arrange for him or her to see an adolescent psychologist or licensed counselor trained and experienced in working with your child's age group.

If your child doesn't want to tell you what is going on, talk to your family doctor for referrals. Always do whatever can be done to keep your child away from the person who abuses. If it is a teacher or coach, try to change classes or activities, or, as some have done, change schools as a last resort. If your teen talks about someone being abusive, start with the teacher and the principal and ask for help.

So much has been written about good parenting and raising children, that I will just touch on a few points most relative to avoiding verbal abuse in the home. I highly recommend that parents read several books on parenting, talk with a pediatrician, or search the medical associations on the Internet for referrals.

For the most part, I believe that fathers and mothers try to do a good job of raising their children. On the other hand, strangely, with all that is written about children and parenting, I hear thousands of reports of verbal abuse. For instance, a mother told her older teen whom she had criticized her whole life, "I only criticize you because I love you." The depth of her unconsciousness is equal only to her daughter's pain at never being good enough in her mother's eyes.

We need look no further than the father described earlier who daily called his boys "stupid" and "idiot," to find a father equally unconscious and equally able to inflict pain.

I suspect that some readers will recall the home in which they were raised, and some of my teen readers will be wondering what father or mother I am talking about in the following notes on "The Loving Father" and "The Loving Mother."

THE LOVING FATHER

Children need kind, considerate, concerned, communicative, and respectful fathers. One of the most important people in a child's life is his or her father. The father's influence on a daughter is such that she will have the best chance of growing up to be a strong woman if he is supportive of her, speaks positively to her, sets clear limits for her, praises her, is protective of her, and is, above all, kind to her and her mother. Her relationships are more likely to be healthy if her father is empathetic toward her.

The father's influence on a son is such that he will most likely grow up with a strong sense of himself that will support good choices in relationships and work in the world if his father is able to be there for him in the following ways: He accepts his son, speaks positively to him, praises his successes, is protective of him, guides him toward taking responsibility for all his actions, shows him empathy for his difficulties and courage in adversity, honors his emotional life, is respectful to all people, and is, above all, kind to him and his mother.

If this is his way of being, when his son has children of his own, he will most likely be as good a father as his father was to him.

THE LOVING MOTHER

A loving mother is also kind, considerate, concerned, communicative, and respectful and is as adept as the father in expressing empathy, setting limits, and encouraging a sense of responsibility in her children.

A mother's influence lies in the stand she takes toward truth and the behaviors she models of courage and action in the face of adversity. She never stands by to see her children abused without speaking up in their presence. She does not "suffer in silence," as if being an adult female means one is powerless. If she gives and accepts only respect, her children will do likewise when they have families of their own.

TO TEACH YOUR CHILDREN

It is essential that children know that when someone defines them, they are pretending, and that when people pretend to know something about them, the pretenders are doing so because they are trying to make reality be other than it is.

Certainly, people survive verbal abuse, but no one needs it to become a good, responsible, and healthy human being. Putting down a person does not help him or her as much as affirming his or her positive qualities does. People can survive and get good jobs and be productive, but how much better might their lives be if they hadn't had to suffer the abuse? Wouldn't anyone be more successful as a human being if they were treated with respect so that they could grow to adulthood with confidence and trust in life?

PROTECTING YOUR CHILD FROM VERBAL ABUSE

I hear from thousands of people who don't know what to do when they hear their spouse verbally battering their child. Speaking up in the presence of the abuser and child is essential, as discussed earlier.

If this is an ongoing problem in your household, to help prevent future episodes of this extremely damaging behavior, ask your mate for an agreement in writing not to define your child.

If your mate breaks the agreement, and it is still an ongoing problem, pick up a tape recorder, put it on your belt or wear it some way, and after turning it on, tell your mate, "I want to be sure that I say things in the most constructive way to the kids and to you. I am monitoring my conversation on this tape, which is on now, so I can go back, listen to myself, and make sure I am speaking respectfully. I'll get you one if you want. Would you like one?"

Your mate may not be interested in taping his or her speech, but you can be sure your mate will be interested in preserving an impeccable image and so may stop abusing and may actually become a bit more aware. If verbal abuse ever escalates to physical abuse, call 911. I advise my clients to carry cell phones and to report death threats and physical assaults, as these are against the law.

Videotaping does not conflict with freedom of speech rights. Audiotaping does, unless the person is told that he or she is being tape-recorded. Many companies advise callers that they are being tape-recorded, with the following announcement: "This is being recorded for quality assurance purposes." For you, doing so may be an assurance of a good quality of life for your child.

Finally, if you know that your child may be subject to abuse, by all means, if you can afford to do so, have a "nanny device" installed. Check with an attorney to ascertain the laws in your state for any forms of taping. Some states are different from others.

Chapter XIII

For Teachers

I ADMIRE TEACHING OVER MOST PROFESSIONAL OCCUPATIONS. Some of my relatives are teachers. Like most teachers, they care about kids and have followed their calling in order to make a difference in young people's lives.

If I could wave a magic wand and make a dream world be real, I would give all the teachers in the country a gigantic raise in income. They have so much responsibility for the future.

Even though there are countless dedicated, wonderful, aware teachers in the country, there are some who are unaware of the impact of verbal abuse or who are untrained, or unable, to deal with it. And, there is a small percentage who have entered into the pretend world of the verbal abuser.

We saw one such example earlier. Two students had written down a teacher's and some students' abusive behaviors. Now we will look at a second teacher who is abusive, but not in the "putdown" way of the first teacher. This second teacher, instead of putting down her students, abuses with crazy rages.

She is a terrifying example of a person who, from my perspective, is at the extreme.

While most teachers do everything possible to support children emotionally, when one is abusive, we get a firsthand account of the impact of such abuse on children who witness it. The comments listed below are from children in the classroom adjacent to the one where the abuse took place. They overheard the abuse. Even though it wasn't directed at them personally, they *felt* as if it was.

I bring up this situation here because I believe that teachers and administrators are on the same team, working to educate our young, and yet, they do not seem to have the means to address the kinds of problems this teacher presents. They seem to be restrained from taking action by various agreements involving unions, teachers' contracts, tenures, and such, and by a lack of policies that would address the issue.

AN ABUSIVE TEACHER

In a magnet public school, one that draws children from all over the district for its special programs, there is a verbally abusive teacher who frequently rages. She yells at her students so loudly and so often in class, that the children in the *adjacent classroom* are distracted and disturbed.

When they hear her yelling, they begin spacing out, sitting still, staring straight ahead, and looking paralyzed. Observing this, their teacher invited them to write about how they felt. She was very careful not to say anything about her own feelings. She did give them a reality check. She said, "It's not healthy for you or me to hear that."

The children are very young. They deserve to be heard. Soon they will be teens, and they may read this book. One little girl wrote about her feelings as if she were writing a letter *to* the screaming teacher. Her plea, "Please stop with a cherry on top," touched my heart. Here is what they wrote, word for word. I took the liberty of correcting their spelling and calling their teacher "B."

The Children's Statements

1. "I feel bad because she screams. She screams too much she hurts our ears. And it hurts when she screams, so badly that I am sad for B's class."
2. "I feel really mad because if I were in her class I would never go to this school again. I would feel sad because of her yelling and punishing people for no reason."
3. "I feel bad for other kids in B's class. I will not like a teacher like that. They say that she didn't have enough love when she was small."
4. "When B screams I feel worried about the children because maybe one child got in trouble. I'm always worried when I hear the scream. It's good that I'm not in her class."
5. "I feel bad when B screams. So, so please stop."
6. "When B screams I lost my brain and I feel upset about it because it loses my concentration. And it cuts my time."
7. "When B screams I can't concentrate on my math. And my class needs it to be quiet. We need to concentrate."
8. "I feel uncomfortable and I can't concentrate when she screams."
9. "She hurts my ears and my friend in that class doesn't concentrate. Neither me. She screams very, very loudly and every time when the kids break something, she screams."
10. "When B screams I feel sorry for the students in her class. Sometimes I hear her screaming and then I cannot

concentrate. Now I want to say I wish she can stop screaming."

11. "When B screams it feels mad. Whenever we do something she screams. When she screams it makes me scary."

12. "I feel very disappointed and upset when B screams, because she makes me uncomfortable and I can't concentrate. When I think of something she make forget about it right away, so I have to write whatever I'm thinking of immediately!"

13. "I feel when B screams I feel mad. Whenever we do something she screams."

14. "I feel kind of mad when B screams because it breaks my concentration. It is so nice when she doesn't scream."

15. "When B screams it makes my ear hurt and it is making my brain hurt too. When we play, she comes and shouts then we have to work again until lunch. Every time she does that."

16. "I feel very bad when you scream. It really hurts my ears. I also think that it hurts everybody in the class and my teacher. I hope that you will please stop with a cherry on top. When you scream I can't concentrate. Love, ____ ps. I mean it please Stop."

The "Whistle-blower" (W) has told me that the principal has seen the children's notes and that "the principal requested that the school district provide some training for teachers on behavior (their own)." The school district has not yet responded as this book goes to print. W also told me that one of the rage attacks occurred when the children were taking "standardized tests."

Wow, I thought, *this really could impact so much. Not only the lives of the children, but also the test results, the school's rating, the kids' rankings, the curriculum plan. What if it happened during math? The scores would likely be low because the kids are traumatized. "Oh, let's teach more math," might be the response.*

On receiving the children's notes, and hearing the vice principal say, "Some people just have loud voices," W made sure that the administrator understood that "these were angry, scary, mean tones, not a 'loud voice.' The children sure knew that!"

She went on to say, "What is great here, although none of this should ever happen, is that the children were the judges, not me. It's not a matter of 'personalities clashing.'"

WHAT CAN BE DONE?

I suggest that teachers and parents discuss this situation in meetings throughout the country. Are there ways to monitor classrooms? Does your school have a fail-safe plan to deal with a teacher's craziness in the classroom? Do you have a school policy that forbids verbal abuse? Do you think a teacher-training program will make an extreme person well? Do teachers ever have psychological evaluations? Does your school have an 800 number for anonymous tips, or is there an anonymous tips box?

What would you do if you were in W's place?

I told W what I would do.

"I would copy the kids' notes. And, I would send each family their own child's note. Parents would then be aware of the situation and could determine what to do."

Several weeks later, students wrote of their feelings for the second time.

1. "I don't like how she screams. She distracts me while I'm doing a test. Even when I move another side she is so loud. And we get scared."

2. "When I was having a test I was disturbed by B. Next door, because she was yelling I felt sad for the kids that is in B's class because she yells to them."

3. "The lady next door named B during our test she disturbed us. The way she disturbed us is by screaming. At first when I heard her scream I was frightened. Then I got used to it but it still annoyed me. Now she always screams. It's annoying."

4. "When B yelled when I was taking the test I felt scared because if I were in that class I would be scared. I just wish she cared more about kids and stop yelling at them."

5. "When B screams she gives me a headache and I get dizzy and I can't concentrate and she screams only if they drop a pencil."

6. "When B screamed on Friday it was very disturbing for all of us. I feel bad for her class because she screams like a witch. I feel uncomfortable."

7. "When I was having a test. Next door, the teacher B was shouting and I don't like the shouting and I always lose my concentration and I have to mark the answer in the circle perfectly but I don't mark it good."

8. "When B screams it get me so upset I want to scream myself and sometimes I wonder why she screams so much when she can be nice and gentle and sometimes I really want to ask her why she screams but I'm always too shy!"

9. "I was comfortable because I didn't hear B shout and if I hear her then I wish she could put tape on her mouth."

10. "I don't like B distracting us because we do not like her screaming. Would she like us to be scramming all day? Or should we tell the president? What should we do?"

W will see to it that each child's parents will get a copy of his or her own statement. The principal is holding the originals. They have no policy about verbal abuse. Consequently, the head of their child abuse center has no means to act. And because there is no policy against verbal abuse, W plans to give each of the school board members a set of the children's handwritten statements. With this information, she will ask them to enact a policy against verbal abuse.

To help them formulate a policy, I gave her a model of a school policy, courtesy of Will Sinclair High School, in Alberta, Canada. You can find the policy on their Web site at *www.wrsd.ca/* and in Appendix A.

A No-Tolerance Policy on Verbal Abuse

The Will Sinclair High School policy includes the following:

"Under no circumstances will physical or verbal abuse towards anyone at the school be tolerated. For effective education to occur, school must be considered a safe place, and those who work towards destroying that 'safe' atmosphere will not be allowed to remain at the school."[27]

If the school district where W teaches had a policy like this, I believe that it would be able to correct, or remove, a seriously abusive person. W says that the principal has had complaints for several years and that a mother pulled her child out of W's class when she found out the abuser was next door. W learned from a colleague that the abuser had taught her child the previous year and she didn't want her child retraumatized.

I have felt much sadness for the children. Not only does trauma impact psychological development, but recent scientific studies tell us, "Because childhood abuse occurs during the critical formative time when the brain is being physically sculpted by experience, the impact of severe stress can leave an indelible imprint on its structure and function."[28] The report goes on to tell us that severe stress creates a greater impact before the child is eighteen years old, because the brain is still forming. Amazingly, the children know that their brain is being impacted: "It hurts when she screams," "It is making my brain hurt," "I lost my brain and I feel upset about it."

Regarding the incident, might the abusive teacher have created a pretend world of perfect children? Like any batterer, might she then fly into a rage when real children show up where her pretend children should be? Is she furious because her pretend world has fallen apart? Does she yell to get it back together again?

How can any school district expect to end violence, much less educate its children, if it doesn't even have a policy against violent verbal assaults, and if it doesn't notify parents of the children's experiences?

We know that verbal abuse precedes physical violence, whether it is a terrorist who defines us as infidels, or a molester who defines a child as a toy, or simply the fact that where there was extreme verbal abuse in families in childhood, subjects were much more physically aggressive as teens. And school substitutes for family for many hours of torture in this case.[29]

TEACHERS FACE ABUSE

Teachers and students alike have had to cope with the fallout that results when students routinely accept verbal abuse as a way of life. Students verbally abuse teachers; some won't stop talking, they disrupt the classroom, and they even threaten their teachers. It is estimated that every day, 5,000 teachers are threatened with physical assault.[30] Teachers need support, not only from the principal's office, but also from the community. Is there a program in your school that screens and trains volunteers to support the teachers?

In some schools, outbreaks of violence generate an atmosphere of fear. Schools emphasize the necessity of protecting students from student violence. They want their schools to be safe.

By knowing how to deal with verbal abuse, schools can most readily make their schools safer. Safety requires education and intervention at the beginning stages of violence; that is, of course, when verbal abuse shows up. Safety comes from knowing what verbal abuse is, and knowing why people engage in it. Safety comes from education that involves parents as well as teachers. Additional guidelines for educating about verbal abuse and intervening when it is heard are found in Chapter XI, "Stopping Verbal Abuse."

TEACHING ABOUT VERBAL ABUSE

Teens and everyone, for that matter, can live a better, happier life by knowing what verbal abuse is and by realizing that all different kinds of people may indulge in verbal abuse: a student, a boyfriend, a girlfriend, a teacher, a coach, a group or religious leader, a relative, or even a parent.

The necessity of addressing the problem and origins of verbal abuse has never been more urgent and important than it is now. We will explore ways to teach children about verbal abuse so they will all understand how abusive behaviors don't give status, and that people who regularly define others, do so because they lack the courage to stand alone.

Verbal abuse is not okay, because it defines people. It is especially defining of their nature, inner being, character, thoughts, feelings, and capabilities. Angry rages are likewise abusive because they also intrude on one's inner being.

Here are some important points about verbal abuse:

A. Many people get into a habit of verbally abusing and don't realize the impact.

B. Students as well as teachers can point it out, maybe just with a "What?" so that anyone can rephrase what she or he just said.

C. Some people are unable to keep themselves from intruding in someone else's mind, either by defining them or by raging at them.

D. Every person who has been around someone who verbally abused him or her and also physically abused him or her, when asked, said that the verbal abuse was worse. It takes longer to recover from the blows of verbal abuse than from the blows of physical abuse.

TACKLING VERBAL ABUSE IN THE CLASSROOM

If your goal is to end verbal abuse in your school, I suggest that you invite your whole class to be on the lookout for it.

Can you have an open brainstorming session with your class to make a list of what verbally abusive comments are? Opening up discussion in class can take the edge off verbal abuse when it rears its ugly head.

In moments of frustration, some teachers have been caught in the spell of verbal abuse and called students lazy, stupid, and so forth. Some have punished a whole class for one person's transgression. If you think you might have fallen under the shadow of verbal abuse, now is the time to resolve to teach respect.

A very good strategy is to invite your students to bond with you against verbal abuse. If you know you've never indulged in verbal abuse, all the better. If you have, your students may help you as you help them.

Can you enlist the cooperation of your class?

Can you ask them, up front, to help you kick verbal abuse out of the classroom, or off the campus?

Can you invite students to join with you in being against verbal abuse, not against people?

Can you talk to your principal and staff about the issue of verbal abuse? If verbal abuse is going on in your school, do they have ideas for improving the school atmosphere?

Can verbal abuse be discussed in language, physical education, and health classes?

Are teachers trained to know what to do when a child reports being verbally abused by another student, and what to do if they spot another teacher verbally abusing a student?

Can administrators set up training programs about verbal abuse—what it is and ways to respond that support victims, and teach abusers appropriate communications?

Can schools set up policies that encourage children to talk to teachers, administrators, parents, or other adults when they are verbally abused or harassed in any way?

Children have an unwritten code of silence around verbal abuse. Every effort must be expended to reverse the idea that telling about verbal abuse is not okay.

Teachers are underpaid and overworked in many schools. Teaching about verbal abuse may seem like just one more thing to put on the to-do list, but there is much that can be done in ordinary conversation with children.

The following suggestions for responding to children in the classroom are adapted from a joint project with Rick Lewis of the Safe Schools Program in Florida.[31]

HOW TO RESPOND TO VERBAL ABUSE IN THE CLASSROOM

1. Explain to your class about verbal abuse being silly talk that pretends all kinds of things about people. Sometimes it isn't only a way of venting a momentary frustration, but is a way of trying to keep a pretend world going. In

the pretend world, calling someone some derogatory name is supposed to make the name-caller be more important or better.

Explain to the class that if ever someone makes up something about them, like, "You're stupid, a wimp, don't know what you're talking about, trying to start a fight, etc.," they are pretending because they feel weak, lesser, or afraid and that nothing that is said to you this way is true.

That kind of pretend talk should be over when children are out of nursery school, but some children have come from such deprivation and trauma they just don't want to give up their pretend world. They need help.

For homework, can you ask your class if they would come up with ways to help the deprived abusers who are still playing "let's pretend"? Ask them to make a list of ideas to turn in the next day.

2. Be alert to it. To do that, you will have to recognize it. Name-calling is easy to recognize, but sarcasm, subtle putdowns, and abusive jokes aren't so easy to spot. Some comments, like, "you're a loser" are so common they can slip by. One way to check out what you hear is to say, "Excuse me, what did you say?" or "What?" Another way, if you aren't sure if a joke was in fun or not, is to say, "Are you okay with that? I don't think I'd like to hear that. Are you friends?"

3. Respond right away when you hear verbal abuse. Here are some responses to verbal abuse that recognize it, and also state very clearly that verbal abuse should not infiltrate a campus or classroom:

"Hey, that sounds like verbal abuse; is that what you meant? Can you say what you want respectfully?"

"Did verbal abuse take you over for a minute? Can you fend it off?"

"That's verbal abuse, and that kind of talk is not allowed."

"Verbal abuse is pretend talk and not okay here. We deal with reality at school."

"That is verbal abuse and not real. Please talk in a respectful way."

"Can you say it another way without pretending anything?"

"Would you try saying __ instead?"

Offer children a few responses that they can use if they are assaulted with verbal abuse—responses that don't escalate the situation.

"That's verbal abuse. Is that what you meant?"
"What?"
"I can't hear such nonsense."
"That's what *you* say."

4. *Model* self-correcting communications. The first time that you feel angry or frustrated by a student's behavior, you'll have an opportunity to show how respectful speech can accomplish your goals. If you miss the opportunity and say something you regret, you'll have another opportunity to model healthy communication by simply saying, "Oh, I really didn't mean to say that. What I want to say, is . . ."

5. Rephrase old abusive comments. Use constructive questioning substitutes.

"Did you hear me?" instead of, "You're not listening."
"Do you understand?" instead of, "You're not trying."

6. Support victims. Give positive messages. After a girl was put down, another girl said, "I need to bring her up." Well that's exactly what positive messages are about. They bring up the victim by showing support.

"That was verbal abuse, I don't believe it for a minute and I hope you don't."

"I really like you and I'm glad you're you."

7. Fear-based abusers are very real. Teens can understand that when people make up things about them (verbally abuse them), the abusers are really talking about themselves, either how they feel or what they're afraid of about themselves. Explain to teens that when people bond together against someone (like a group putting down or laughing at another person), they are joining in because they are afraid to stand alone, separate from the group. And this is fear-based behavior; at the extreme, it is the kind we see in hate groups that are bonded together against other whole groups of people. Not a courageous thing at all.

8. Having courage in correcting people who indulge in verbal abuse shows great strength. Explain that it takes great courage to stand up to verbal abuse in these ways, while not verbally abusing back.

9. Tell teens that the more open they are about verbal abuse, calling it as they see it, the less chance it has to take over a person or a class.

10. Present a positive alternative to verbal abuse.

"Did you mean to be verbally abusive?"

"Can you say what you feel or think and not what you pretend? What did you mean to say?"

"Can you speak without shouting so we can hear you? If you say, 'please,' I can hear you."

11. Support the victim. Teens don't want to ask for help, but if you know one is being picked on and want to be their support person, here is a way to ask them if that's okay with them.

"If you let me be your coach, and I hear something, I'll intervene, but not to get in your business. Are you okay with that?"

CREATING A SAFE ATMOSPHERE IN YOUR SCHOOL

1. Intervene. Invite all teachers and administrators to make correct and constructive intervention a priority wherever verbal abuse shows up on campus.
2. Create solutions. Make a priority of collaborating with your colleagues in creating solutions.
3. Teach responses. If all adults stand together against verbal abuse, and teach children how to take a stand against verbal abuse rather than against the abuser, they will make a positive difference, not only on campus but also in the greater society.
4. Build awareness. Teach children the difference between what is weak and what is strong, what is real and what is not, what is okay and what is not.
5. Get everyone's support. Ask for cooperation and inform your colleagues that there are ways to stop verbal abuse on campus. People can feel connected and united against verbal abuse because it is never okay to define another human being.
6. Have a counselor available and trained to support victims of verbal abuse. Having counseling available, at least at certain times, is important. Many teens talk about needing a refuge, someone to talk to. The boarding school teen told how the closed environment gave her no

refuge. The teen who had no home life described how there was no safe refuge.

TWEAKING TEACHER TALK

Rick Lewis points out that, very commonly, when someone wants someone to do something, instead of asking with a "please," he or she resorts to a two-step process of verbal abuse: (a) The victim's character is assaulted; then (b) an order is delivered. Here are some examples.

- "You aren't even trying! I can't believe you are so lazy! Now pay attention and get to work!" (Criticism and ordering)
- "If you weren't so busy being the social chairman of your table, you would have heard that the second time I said it! Why don't you try something new for a change and keep your mouth shut!" (Name-calling, accusing, insulting, ordering)
- "You're not listening. Why do you even bother coming to school? You're just taking up space and wasting my time! Listen up." (Accusing, criticizing)
- "Your attitude stinks. You'd better change it in a hurry, or else!" (Accusing, ordering, discounting, and threatening)
- "If you don't like it, that's tough. I don't care if you like it or not!" (Discounting)
- "You're so disorganized you'd lose your head if it wasn't attached. If that space isn't cleaned up in five minutes, I'm going to throw all that junk away." (Joking, discounting, and threatening)
- "You are pathetic. Stop your whining and get back to work or I'll really give you something to cry about!" (Putdowns, ordering, threats)

OUR WORLD IS CHANGING

Our society is increasingly aware of the value of all people and is therefore more sensitive to the disregard of human beings. Even in war, we now use smart bombs. We know that it's not okay to hurt innocent people. In the last century, carpet-bombing was not thought to be a wrong against humanity.

Years ago, society seemed to think it was the right of the boss to harass employees, particularly women. Now a more aware society has gotten the message that it's not okay. Though it still can happen, the abuser tries to hide it because it is no longer tolerated. This, at least, is an improvement.

SOME EXTRA STRATEGIES

Teens who have suffered in childhood can feel so abandoned and adrift that they sometimes form groups, gangs, and spur-of-the-moment collusions in order to feel connected to each other. However, they feel connected by bonding together against someone. This is when sexual harassment and sexist and racist remarks surface.

Here is where immediate responses are important.

Comment: "They're only good for . . ."
Response: "My experience has been a little different."

Comment: "They're all trash."
Response: "They aren't that different from us."

CLASS EXERCISES

1. Invite two students to enact the drama in Chapter XV and invite classroom discussion. What would you have

said? What would be an abusive response? Would the couple stay boyfriend/girlfriend if they weren't mutual?

2. Invite students to name contemporary songs or rap that put down people. Put titles on the board and discuss with class why the words are disparaging and what makes them pretend talk.

REACHING RESOLUTION

As schools have put into practice various ways to create greater safety, some teachers were instructed to step in if there were verbal jabs and verbal slams. Immediate punishment was the prescribed solution, but this was a solution without resolution. In many classes, teachers could no longer sit down with two children and say, "Let's talk about it until understanding and resolution are reached." Where this policy is in place, children no longer learn how to talk about the problem. Immediate punishment prevents negotiations and resolution.

A SMALL HIGH SCHOOL ENFORCES POLICY

In contrast to some schools where swearing is common in the halls and put downs proliferate along with gangs, a high school in Canada demands respect among students and toward administrators. This is the Will Sinclair High School, which provided a policy statement against verbal abuse, discussed previously.

I interviewed an administrator at the school while I was on hold waiting to talk to the principal. (I wanted to ask him if I could get permission to publish his school policy on verbal abuse.)

"What do you do if you hear a kid using the *f* word?" I asked.

"I heard one the other day," the administrator replied, "and I just said, 'If I hear that again you'll be suspended.' I really doubt I'll hear it again, at least from that student."

"What about bullying, where an older kid picks on a younger one. How do you handle it?"

"We did have an incident of bullying. We followed the kids a bit and when an assault took place, the RCMP [Royal Canadian Mounted Police] arrested them and charged them with assault."

Then I talked with the principal, Jimmy Clark. He sounded proud of the high school and has a right to be. The school band is the best in the country.

Since I had just heard from a student in Ohio about "jocks" and other students trying to put down band members, I asked Mr. Clark if that happened at his school in Alberta. He said that it didn't and that was because a number of the football players are in the band. They can be in the band because band practice is before school and football practice is after school.

If you've heard the phrase, "I take my hat off to you," you know that an old-fashioned sign of respect is shown by not wearing a hat indoors. No hats are worn in this Canadian high school (it's a school rule), so no one has a baseball cap to hide behind, but more importantly, the idea of respect for others is given more than a nod.

The school policy lets everyone know that verbal abuse is not okay. And, as we've seen, this school stands behind their code.

A MODEL CLASS

If we visualize something we want, we can develop a plan to bring it about. Let's envision a model class that breaks the spell of verbal abuse and the code of silence around it.

Imagine, if you will, a classroom or even an entire school where the spell is broken and everyone is on the lookout for verbal abuse. In this place, everyone is bonded together, not against each other or anyone, but against verbal abuse. What would such a classroom be like?

Possibly, there would be discussion about verbal abuse. About not letting it get a stranglehold in the school. Maybe it would be about how to help someone who is experiencing verbal abuse outside the school.

In the beginning, in order to break the spell, once a week the class would discuss what is real and what is not, what is pretend talk and what is not, what is inclusive and what is not.

The class would also discuss how teens are making their own teen world of changing styles, interests, fads, and so on. And some teens might be afraid to be associated with someone who is different.

They would discuss how teens, when they are figuring out their own identities, might be afraid that they will be labeled with an identity that isn't theirs.

They might discuss how teens who have money and clothes may be afraid they won't look perfect, like they "have it all," if they are friendly with teens who don't have money and the "right" clothes.

They might discuss how boys who don't yet know how tall or strong they'll be worry that they might not be tall or strong enough to meet a pretend world ideal.

They might discuss how teens and even some adults are sometimes afraid to stand on their own two feet and so they move into other people's space and tell people what they think and what they're trying to do.

They might discuss how teens who don't feel that they are very acceptable as human beings are afraid to be accepting of kids who don't seem to be a perfect fit for their transitional pretend world that is based on ideal models.

They might discuss how some kids enjoy sports and some enjoy playing music and some enjoy making Web sites, but how their interests don't make them better or worse than anyone else.

They might discuss how some kids try to harass and verbally abuse and put down kids because they have been totally caught up in a pretend world where saying it's so, makes it so. But, only in "let's pretend."

They might discuss how some kids think that sex is about proving that they are real men or real women because they are afraid that nature doesn't know how to grow them into real men and real women.

They might discuss how some kids need help in understanding that teasing and taunting are signs of the spell that they are afraid of being themselves alone without a pretend world.

They might discuss how some kids are afraid to accept kids who are different from them or to see them as equal to them, because they have made up a picture or idea of who they are and it has to be right, so they think no one else can be right, too, so the other kids must be lesser.

They might discuss how some kids have lost awareness of their own feelings or haven't given them time to unfold, so they think their girlfriend or boyfriend is their other half, a dream person.

Opportunities abound to make a difference in the lives of young people. To avail us of them, we must be alert to verbal abuse; we must know and teach that verbal abuse is always destructive; and we must demonstrate better alternatives, setting the best example possible.

As parents and teachers work together with teens to end verbally abusive patterns in all kinds of relationships—adult to teen, teen to adult, and teen to teen—I believe our world will truly be affected in a positive and lasting way. By making this a priority, this information will touch the homes our children create in their future. We really can make a difference.

Chapter XIV

For Teens

IF YOU ARE A TEEN, THIS CHAPTER IS SPECIFICALLY FOR YOU. Although I encourage you to read this book from cover to cover, this chapter summarizes and highlights information most pertinent to teen experience. It shows you how people who indulge in verbal abuse have, in a certain sense, forgotten themselves and their value, and out of ignorance and fear, pretend to know what someone else is, or something about them.

When teens pretend superiority to, or authority over, someone else's reality, they not only show their ignorance, but they sound pretty silly, especially when everyone knows what verbal abuse is about. I hope everyone in your school will learn what verbal abuse is. And, that you and your classmates can be bonded together against verbal abuse, but not against a person who indulges in it.

I encourage you as a teen to read and discuss this section together with your parents. Here are some ways to introduce the topic of verbal abuse to family members: Some kids just won't be friendly, no matter what anybody does. Have you noticed that? Do you know why? Some kids are into verbal abuse; do you know what could be done about it? Do you want to read about it?

RESOLVE TO SAY NO TO VERBAL ABUSE

When asked about youth violence, teens say that there is tremendous "peer pressure to fight back."[32]

But making more verbal abuse is no way to fight back against verbal abuse. The way to fight verbal abuse is to name it, to bring it out into the open, and to help the teens who chronically indulge in verbal abuse to get past the fears that drive them. Usually, abusive teens don't even know why bullies are called cowards.

Verbal abuse makes no sense and has no meaning, but one can transform the experience of it by determining never to do it. You have a choice: You may either perpetuate verbal abuse by passing it on to someone else, or you can stop verbal abuse by ending it right now. You can say no to verbal abuse by choosing not to pass it on. Then, you are more powerful than verbal abuse and it has no power over you. If you do choose not to indulge in verbal abuse, and you let others know that it is, at best, pretend talk, you will be breaking the spell of the pretend world where people pretend to be superior to other people.

There are some basic truths about your own reality, your own experience, and your own inner world.

The first truth: No one can define you.

When people tell you how, or who, you are, they are trying to define you. No one lives within you, so no one can actually define you, in terms of who you are, your character, value, potential, and so on.

The second truth: Verbal abuse is a lie.

People who indulge in verbal abuse are pretending. We can say that what they say is a lie, and, of course, it is. But they don't always know that they're making up things. They sometimes believe that if they say it is so, it is so. For that reason, it is easier to say that they are playing let's pretend. However, even though we know they are pretending, they are so unaware, they seem to be spellbound.

The third truth: When an abuse is named and brought out into the open, placed before the scrutiny of the world, it begins to wither and die, at least in the place where it occurred.

The fourth truth: Human beings are self-defining.

The only way to know what people mean, what they are doing, why they do what they do, what they are, how they are, how they feel, what they want, or anything else about their inner reality, is to ask them. When people say what they want, for instance, they are being self-defining.

Believing what people tell you about your inner self is a mistake. If someone is in a position of authority over you, is simply older than you, says they love you, or has seemed, until now, to be a friend, it may be difficult to really understand, that if this person defines you, he or she is verbally abusing you. Telling you what you are, or want, and so on, is always pretend talk. That a person could do it at all, means that, at least for the moment, he or she is spellbound. For instance, if you are trying to talk about a problem, and someone says, "You just want to start a fight," he or she is pretending to know what you *want*.

It is normal to feel sad when someone you care about, or want approval from, can't really see you or know you—when they actually tell you something about yourself, as if they were you and knew this thing about your inner reality. But, sadly, when people are caught in the spell of verbal abuse, it is as if a cloud has descended on them, blinding them to reality and shutting down their perceptions. It is as if the person you thought was there is gone, hidden in the cloud.

When people are "gone," so to speak, they are not there for you. When this happens, most people feel a sense of loss, and often they also feel inadequate or rejected. When people define you, they are rejecting the real you. For instance, as in the earlier example, the real you wants to talk about a problem. But someone says, "You *want* to start a fight."

Sometimes teens, and adults as well, will try not to feel the hurt of verbal abuse. In order not to have to feel the pain of rejection, and to get back the other person's acceptance, most people want to explain to the abuser that what he or she said isn't true. Explaining is a mistake. It won't wake up the abuser. In fact, the abuser may just argue against you, repeating what was said: "You just want to start a fight." When people are caught in the spell of verbal abuse, they can't hear you tell them that they are wrong. But, they might hear you say something like, "What did you say?" or "Aha, is that what *you* say!" or even "That's what *you* say!"

When abusers have to face the craziness of what they just said, they might wake up. They might for a moment have to go deep within, contact their true self, and ask themselves, "Is that what I really say, or is that pretend talk?" They hate to be responsible for what they say. If you hold up a tape recorder and say, "Please repeat that," they probably won't. In any case, they may be less inclined to try telling you what you want again.

It may not always be safe to respond to someone, especially on the streets, who is verbally abusive. For example, a girl is walking by a boy and hears him call her something she is not, "Hey . . . " It may be enough for her to know to the very depth of her being, both at an emotional level as well as an intellectual level, that a person who pretends to know what she is, as if he lived within her and had the power to define her, is afraid to stand on his own two feet. He can be pitied. He is, in a sense, occupying her space, demonstrating cowardly, not courageous, behavior.

It may not be safe for a boy to respond to a big and burly coach who calls him a "sissy," "wimp," or "girl." It may be enough for him to know, to the very depth of his being, both at an emotional level and an intellectual level, that when people fear losing control, or losing a game, they may show their fears by indulging in cowardly behavior. When a coach pretends to know what a team member is (a loser, for example), as if he lived within the player's space, he can be pitied. He is afraid to stand on his own two feet. And, he is playing let's pretend—trying to make his pretend world be real.

Teens usually know that they are growing and learning all the time. If you are a teen, it is important to know that there are two main developmental goals planted within you like seeds that will grow through time. One is the seed of identity. It grows into your own self-awareness, that is, your sense of self. The other is the seed of independence, of being separate from your family and eventually having a place in the adult world beyond your home.

Just as there are two main developmental goals within you, there are also two ways to move toward these goals. The first way is from your achievements, your successes, and even your failings. As you grow through your teens, you learn more about your talents and abilities. By trying out many things, you can discover your gifts. Some things are easy and natural for you. Others are difficult. For instance, math and art may both be fun and challenging, or you may have no interest in one or the other. As you learn more about yourself, your identity becomes stronger and your self-esteem grows. You become more self-aware, that is, more aware of how you feel and think about yourself and others. Thus, you develop from *within* and you have an increasing power to make your life satisfying and fulfilling. The more self-aware you are, the more you will know what you want to do in the world, and the more easily you will find acceptance in the world.

If you hear things said to you that are not true of you, it is good to remember that the people who are pretending that you are not okay, have tried to reach their goals of a strong identity, and of acceptance in the world, in a backward way. They have not developed from within but have created a kind of pretend world in their own minds, and they expect the rest of the world, or at least certain people, to conform to it.

A BROAD PERSPECTIVE

There is a much greater world and many more people in it than there are in your school. And, your school and the students and teachers in it are not necessarily representative of the world you will be living in for many, many years to come.

In the real world, beyond school, there are no nerds, geeks, band fags, jocks, retards, popular ones, insiders, or outsiders. These labels are given to people based on very superficial appearances and passing interests. Most adults know that labeling people is a kind of baby talk, or pretend talk, that has nothing to do with who people really are, and what they will do with their lives.

You may have a wonderful family and loving parents. You may be tall and strong. If you are a girl, you may be slim; if a boy, have lots of muscles. You may have many friends and know some of the things you want to do when you are grown. You may have cool clothes and have a lot of trust from your parents and get pretty good grades. If this is true for you, you may not have heard much verbal abuse. And, you may not have felt rejected and excluded. But, some kids do feel rejected and excluded.

BECOMING INCLUSIVE

Some teens may not fully realize that their classmates feel rejected by the teen world. But some do. If you care about these individuals who feel rejected, what can you do about it?

To become part of the adult world, to mature into a healthy person who can have a good life, you must interact with, and get to know, many different people throughout your life. It also requires that you know people who are not all interested in the same thing.

If you choose, you can practice how to be inclusive, not exclusive. You don't have to become best friends with people you don't feel very compatible with, but you can include others in conversations and in groups from which they would usually be excluded.

BECOMING INDEPENDENT

If you choose, you can stand strong for yourself, refusing to do anything just to be in step with others. It is not healthy and can be dangerous to go along with anything that you know isn't good for you, just to be accepted, or because you feel sorry for the person coercing you.

Some teens go along with others to be accepted, and so try drugs that could addict or kill them; drink that could harm them and, in quantity, kill them; and sex before they are old enough to support a family.

By moving toward a more real world and a less pretend world, you will be actively participating in your own maturation. Most of the really creative, productive, and accomplished people in the world were not part of an "in-group" in their teens. They had friends but not a party room—full. They were too busy pursuing their interests so that, by the time they were well into adulthood, they could make a blockbuster movie, design one of the most beautiful buildings in the world, open a veterinary clinic, or be an astronaut. Following your interests and saying no to verbal abuse, stepping out of the pretend world and into the real world, is well worth it.

IF YOU'VE INDULGED IN VERBAL ABUSE

If you realize you've been verbally abusive to someone, making a resolution to change, and asking your friends to let you know if you say something abusive, would be a great step toward mature and real relationships. As long as teens live in a pretend world, and pretend to be up when they put someone down, they lose out in the end because real people will give up on them. Similarly, if they try to have a win at any cost, it is highly likely that there will be a day when the cost will be more than they ever dreamt.

If you realize that you've gotten into a habit of indulging in verbal abuse, you are free to break the pattern and you have a responsibility to stop hurting others. If you find you are having trouble stopping or that you feel angry a lot for no reason, don't hesitate to find a counselor you like who can support you.

If someone points out verbal abuse that you've committed, all you need to do is say you're sorry, and then say what you meant, rephrasing what you need or want in a nonabusive way.

If you aren't sure if you are verbally abusive to people at home, it might be a good idea to keep a tape recorder on so you can listen to yourself and see if you are speaking respectfully, or if you are unconsciously saying things that are hurtful to others. Remember that it's important to find out the truth. If you define others, you are not being rational, and your thinking won't be as clear as it would be if you spoke in a real way rather than a pretend way.

People really admire the courage it takes to be honest and straightforward and the strength it takes to refrain from joining with others against some person. Mature people know that when people feel weak and are afraid of standing alone, they try to bolster themselves up and gain cohorts by joining others against people who are different.

IF YOU HEAR VERBAL ABUSE AT HOME

If people in your family indulge in verbal abuse, you can be proud of yourself for being the clear-thinking, honest person in your family that breaks the pattern of abuse. Criticizing, accusing, blaming, and abusive anger show up a lot in families that have verbal abuse in them. Remind yourself that experiencing verbal abuse isn't healthful. And it is even less healthful to shut down your feelings until you feel nothing.

To understand how to respond to verbal abuse and why people indulge in it, I suggest that you read all of this book, if you haven't already, and flag the parts that are most relevant to you. It may also be very helpful to talk with a counselor about the problem.

If you feel abused by a parent, please keep in mind that being a biological parent doesn't mean that a person automatically knows how to be a parent. Some parents don't know how to parent at all, and some are very damaged and are passing on the damage, as was Bobby's and Danny's father in Chapter I.

If you are subject to abuse, it is important to not take it in. You may not be able to leave a home where abuse takes place, but you can choose to affirm that you are okay, and that you don't deserve it. The person who abuses you is psychologically damaged. A teen told me how she chooses to be on her own side, rather than on the side of the abuser. "Even when I lose confidence, I stay on my own side. I may be shook up, but at the same time, I don't turn against myself. I don't take it in. I don't believe it."

Teens try to make sense of what they are told, especially by people they trust. But double messages ("I love you," "You're a dummy") don't make sense until you know that people who talk this way don't really see you. Generally, this is because they have an *idea* or vision of who you are. They love their *idea* and they *think* it is *you*. Consequently, they are angry when the *real* you appears.

Teens who are wounded because a parent cannot really see them, and because they face that parent's anger, suffer beyond almost anything imaginable. Many stop feeling. And unfortunately, they are then incapable of empathy. They make up a pretend world and start the cycle over again, not even seeing themselves as abusive.

People who verbally abuse you, do so when either their image of you, or their own image, is threatened. Verbal abuse is not about a particular issue like getting a book back to the library on time. Verbal abuse is never justified.

RESPONDING TO AUTHORITY FIGURES

Here are a few suggestions on ways to respond to authority figures. The responses can be adapted for teachers, parents, or bosses.

Someone says, "You'll never find it; you're so disorganized."
Response, "Mr. [Miss, Mrs., Ms.] _____, you're my teacher and you can grade my work, but you have no authority to attack my personality. Did you know that what you said sounds like verbal abuse? Did you mean it that way?"

Someone says, "Class has started. Get your fat butt over here."
Response, "Mr. [Miss, Mrs., Ms.] _____, you're my teacher, and I accept your telling me that class has started,

but I do not accept your denigrating my body and ordering me. Did you intend it to be verbally abusive?"

Someone says, "Wake up, stupid."
Response, "You're my parent, and I believe you are trying to ask me to wake up. Did you know that name-calling is verbally abusive and I do not accept being called names? Did you really want to verbally abuse me?"

TEENS WHO TORMENT

It might seem like teens who put down others are just mean, but it is mostly something else. They are trying hard to fit in, to have the "right" image, and to be accepted by other kids, and they are very uncertain of themselves. They don't yet know who they are. They are really afraid to seem connected to anyone who doesn't match their ideal, which is usually modeled on a movie star, celebrity, or star athlete.

Since they feel so unsure of themselves, they really want to be associated with kids who match their ideal. And, they put down kids who aren't like their ideal, or they exclude them. They might even get together with some kids to put down anyone who is different. In this way, they feel connected to each other, bonded against someone. But it isn't a real connection. Real connections are built on empathy.

Sometimes people do bond together to do something, like put up sandbags to keep a river flood away. But kids who get together to exclude another person or to harass another person, do it just to feel connected to each other. When they bond together against, say, all the people of a certain ethnicity, we call their groups "hate groups."

Since they can't see the undeveloped inner parts of themselves, their focus is on "what's out there," that is, how they look to others and how they come across to others. Since teens don't fit exclusively in either their parents' world or the adult world, they almost have to make a kind of transitory world. As they develop their teen world, some lose touch with themselves and see all of reality as outside of themselves. Then their transitory world becomes a pretend world that is so real to them they don't want to leave it or grow out of it. Even worse, if they are at the extreme, they begin to hate real people in the real world.

When they reach adulthood, they become, in some ways, like grownups who are still teens inside. They feel so out of touch with themselves that they are always in someone else's space, trying to shape them into what they want them to be. Often they have no concern for others, and sometimes they get to positions of power where they betray or harm thousands of people, while they try to make their world be the way they want it to be.

GROWING UP AND OUT OF VERBAL ABUSE

Most teens grow out of their transitory teen world. Many teens find that when they are ready to go to college, or when they get to college, the whole experience of being with their peers changes. Most teens who are sixteen to eighteen have developed so much, they've stopped needing to be in their pretend teen world. Kids who felt so hurt, so out of it, and so rejected are much happier. Suddenly, their peers appreciate them. Instead of focusing on the appearance of people, mature teens are very focused on people's qualities, insights, talents, honesty, openness, and intelligence.

The transitional, or pretend, world has faded away. It doesn't matter anymore if their friends all wear the same style jeans, or wear their socks or hats a certain way, or any of the other current codes of the teen world.

TEENS WHO STAY SPELLBOUND

A fairly small percentage of teens fall into the category of not developing the parts of themselves that were meant to emerge through their teen maturation. We see them as adolescents in adult bodies, or even sometimes still toddlers in adult bodies. Many of them have developed great images, but there is nothing inside, so to speak. The saying, "Don't judge a book by its cover," came from people realizing that the image they saw of someone might not reflect the true person. This means that no one can be sure of how someone is, inside, until they've really gotten to know him or her over a long period of time.

Sometimes, it is possible to spot people who didn't develop, by the signs they show of still living in a pretend world. Unfortunately, they are adults who still call names, put down people, have temper tantrums, and try to shape people into their idea of who they should be. And, like some of the coaches discussed earlier, they think that spellbound behaviors are normal.

A BIT ABOUT BULLIES

Almost everyone has heard someone say that bullies are cowards. But many people, if they think about this, can't quite figure out what the bullies are afraid of. We now can say that when a person is verbally abusing someone, or even pushing or hitting them in a bullying way, they are trying to get in their space—getting in their mind, telling them how they think ("You're jumping to conclusions"), or even getting in their physical space, pushing them over. So people call bullying behavior cowardly because the person who bullies seems unable to stand on his or her own two feet. In fact, the person who bullies appears to be afraid of being separate and not in someone's space. Getting in people's space makes the bully feel safer, in control, and less afraid of being alone. Clearly, this is cowardly behavior.

Some kids want to make their pretend world be the real world *no matter what*. These kids bully real kids. They're generally bigger than the kids they verbally abuse. These kids may push, shove, or punch others weaker than themselves.

When kids who bully become old enough to drive a car, they are often aggressive drivers, trying to push the car in front of them. They want to be in the other person's space. One of the other ways that some bullies try to get in someone else's space is by playing music so loudly, that it is in everyone else's space.

I've heard that years ago, people knew a lot more about bullies and they were embarrassed to be caught bullying. They didn't want the rest of the neighborhood to think of them as bullies and, therefore, as fearful.

It is a fact that people who verbally abuse people on a regular basis are afraid *not* to be in someone's space. They are afraid to stay in their own space, alone.

Some Teens Don't Hear Abuse

Some teens, but not many, pay almost no attention to the transitional teen world. They know deep down that it is transitory. They know that "who is friends with whom" makes no real difference in the long run. They know that putdowns don't actually make anyone less valuable, nor do they put up the person who says them. It seems silly to think it does.

Possibly the teens who hardly noticed the groups and labels of the teen transitional world had a strong family of siblings and relatives and, of course, parents, who gave them great emotional support, who taught them all about the teen world, and who showed them much more interesting worlds.

Possibly the teens who didn't care who befriended them were born into the world with some great gift that launched them into a separate world. Usually these teens are practicing for the

Olympics; or showing art in real galleries; or are writing music, immersed in a world of symphonies, concerts, and friends with like interests.

Other gifted teens may be rejected by their peers because they are very real. Without enough support from their family, they may suffer through the teen years, not knowing why they are rejected. But later they may make not only their place in the world, but also their mark upon it.

GETTING HELP FOR HARASSMENT

If you encounter a person who terrorizes you, go to your parents, your teachers, your school counselor, or your school principal. If you have gone to everyone and you are still harassed, and school authorities cannot protect you, and if, behind closed doors or on the way home from school, you are still threatened; then write your story with details of what you've heard and experienced, and by whom, with as many names and dates and descriptions as you can recall, as well as the efforts you've made to stay safe and get help. If you have any witnesses, ask them to sign it. Then, send a copy to your teacher, principal, school board, school paper, city newspaper, local police departments, and, of course, your parents.

SPELLBOUND PEOPLE DON'T WANT THE SPELL TO BE BROKEN

The spell can be so deep that spellbound people are terrified of being responsible for their own actions, of telling the truth, and, most of all, of losing their grip on their pretend world and on the people who inhabit it.

An example of a spellbound person is the teacher, mentioned earlier, who told a teen, "Don't be a snitch." Some spellbound

people learned to pretend that if no one talked about abuse, it wasn't happening and it would be okay. In another example, Danny and Bobby (found in Chapter I) were under the influence of their spellbound father, and were learning to be spellbound. If no one told them that name-calling is not okay, they could have come to believe, as the teacher did, that they should suffer in silence, or that name-calling is okay, or even that they should not feel badly when they were called names by their own father.

Spellbound people deny reality. They seem to exist in a pretend world where they can't lose, where telling people what they are is commonplace, and where saying something didn't happen changes the past.

People who are deeply immersed in the spell, have said that they want to stay spellbound because their pretend world is so safe. They want to "keep it together," even though they do become frustrated and sometimes very angry maintaining it. They feel they can make it be like they want if they just keep defining everyone and putting them in their place, like characters on a stage.

As spellbound pretenders, they don't want to give up their seemingly magical power.

Obviously, deeply spellbound people want to silence spell-breakers. They want to shut up real people, and to get them to hide what is going on. When people point out verbal abuse, abusers call them all kinds of things, like, "snitch," "weak," or "tattletale," or "fink."

Healthy adults don't denigrate spell-breakers; they call spell-breakers "Whistle blowers," likening them to referees who blow a whistle to call a foul. Spellbound people want to punish whistle blowers. Other people want to reward them.

This makes a certain kind of sense. Spellbound people don't want to give up their pretend worlds. Consequently, they don't want to listen to spell-breakers. They want to walk away from them, even while they are talking; or call them names, yell at them, or accuse them of things, to silence them. Words are their usual weapons. Name-calling is one of their biggest weapons.

It is very important to know that if teens think that saying it's so, makes it so; that being called weak, makes them weak; that being called a snitch, makes them a snitch, they can be silenced. That would be a terrible thing. Imagine children at younger and younger ages being defined, demeaned, and denigrated, unable to speak out because they might be called a snitch! The main point is, don't believe in the names you are called, and know that the name-caller is spellbound.

Taking a Stand and Breaking the Spell

If you do not let anything stand between you and the truth, and if you make every effort to speak the truth, and if you seek always to know the truth, you will not be a purveyor of verbal abuse. This doesn't mean that you won't at some time forget yourself and speak rashly. But, an apology will keep you from falling under the spell.

It is truly courageous to take a stand against verbal abuse. When you hear it, even though you may have seen adults stand by as if powerless, refusing to accept it can lessen its grip on the world. Here are some ways to stand up to verbal abuse: "That sounds like verbal abuse; is that what you meant?" or "I don't appreciate that," or "Don't call me names and I won't call you names. Is that fair?"

A truly great person, woman or man, girl or boy, is recognized by his or her inner strength, and that strength most often appears when the person is aligned with truth.

If You Forget Yourself

It takes vigilance to keep verbal abuse away. If you've said something verbally abusive, here are some more ways to stop the spell from descending on you. By retracting the irrational thing you said, you can then say what is true.

RETRACTING COMMENTS

"That came out wrong."

"I meant to say . . ."

"I'm sorry; I wasn't thinking."

"I don't know why I said that. I'm sorry."

"It seemed funny, but I can see it wasn't."

"I'm sorry; I didn't mean that at all."

"This is what I meant to say."

"I'm sorry; please forget I said that. I was mad about something and I took it out on you."

"I take that back. I know it was uncalled for."

COURAGE AND COWARDICE

An eighteen-year-old girl said, "It's easy to be compliant and submissive, and hurt, and wounded, and to sneak away. It's bolder and braver to take a stand. It's really courageous."

We know now that people who feel weak try to bolster themselves up by verbally abusing others. But, it's important to know that verbal abuse is never justified. It's not okay.

But here's what you can do:

- Courageously stand up for the truth by standing up for others:

    "I like Marcie; she has a great sense of humor."

    "They're not so different from us."

    "That's just gossip. I don't want to hear it."

- Stand up for yourself when you hear verbal abuse; for instance, "That's what YOU say. What is your name? How do you spell it?" This suggests that you hold the abuser accountable for his or her behavior.

- Watch out for danger. Sometimes it is dangerous to stand up for yourself. Sometimes the best strategy is to walk away.

EXCLUSION AND WHERE IT LEADS

Recall the fifteen-year-old boy who said that in school he talks like he is dumb so he won't be called a nerd, because nerds don't have many friends and aren't invited to parties. Many teens feel the pain of rejection because they are excluded from some group. Ultimately, the kids who do the excluding will miss out.

A STORY ABOUT EXCLUSION

A group of people is trying to survive in a sinking lifeboat. They are a half mile from an island. There are five people in the life raft, but it has a slow leak. It won't support everyone. The strongest person believes that "might makes right" and the less strong should be excluded. He throws everyone overboard.

The woman who knew what plants to eat on the island is gone, overboard. The man who makes boats from trees is gone, overboard. The boy who knew how to navigate by the stars is gone, overboard. The girl who could make fire from sticks is gone, overboard.

The strongest man reaches the island alone and realizes he has no food, no boat, no navigator, and no heat.

Then he thinks, "If we had all hung on, and worked together, we might have pushed and kicked the raft to shore and all survived. Alone, I probably won't survive."

The teen world and the greater world we all live in certainly need protections and exclusions, but I would hope that every teen who reads this book, would, in the next few days, reach out to be inclusive of someone. And, hopefully, this will become a lifelong pattern.

Chapter XV

Boyfriends and Girlfriends

TEENS OFTEN HAVE A ROMANTIC AND IDEALIZED VISION OF THE WORLD, and of love and marriage as well. This is natural. There are two main reasons for this. First, they don't have much real-life experience to help them gain a more realistic view. And second, the culture of music, movies, and TV usually romanticizes real life. Of course, that's what makes the music and stories so appealing. But, this romantic view can lead to difficult relationships.

Teen music and culture play a big role in modeling obsessive love as the ideal in teen relationships. This is the kind of love that tells teens that love is about possession and needs that are so intense, one would die for love. This message is very unhealthy because it is more about pretend, dream people, than it is about real love. Real love is about seeing and hearing the real person, and it isn't possessive.

The popular, idealized, and romantic version of love is extreme and illusory, clouding and confusing abuse issues. By that, I mean, if you were led to believe that possessive love is real love, then you might think jealous rages are not abusive! Likewise, if you think you must give up everything to make your significant other happy, you may give up your most treasured values and ideals. If you think you will die if your significant other likes someone else, you may have been led to believe that this fatalistic, all-or-nothing picture of relationships is real love.

Dramatic and romantic declarations of love may either deny your reality or be used to try to manipulate you by making you responsible for another person's happiness, as if you were not a separate person, free to choose for yourself. It's not healthy to give up your own view and personal reality, just to get along with someone or to keep someone around.

Dramatic views of relationships depict dependency and powerlessness as normal. For instance, statements such as, "I can't live without you," "You're my whole life," "You're my very breath," "You're a part of me," "No one could love you as I do," "I'll never let you go," have not only been spoken in many heartrending scenes and songs, but have also been spoken by most batterers and stalkers. Such declarations even lurk behind many homicide-suicides.

Although people have said these same dramatic statements in moments when they are carried away by emotions that they want to emphasize, it is important to know that in real life, anyone who says that you are a part of them may not be healthy for you. They may experience you as a dream person, not a real person. So, they may demand more and more from you, and be angrier and angrier because you are a real person.

If you are with someone who makes dramatic claims of their love, and demands dramatic declarations of your love, this is a sign that your relationship may not be healthy at all.

Someone who looks like a dream can become a nightmare.

It may seem to you, if you are a teen, that if these songs are part of your culture, they must be describing what real love is. But that is not true at all. What is prevalent in teen culture is not always in anyone's own best interests, because drama and dreams *sell* well. They are out there mostly because they serve the best interests of the *economy,* not you.

Many teens are verbally abused on dates. Some girls believe that they must gain the "acceptance" of their abuser by being more likable or submissive, instead of seeing that the only solution is not to date an abusive boy. And, unfortunately, some teenage girls think it's okay for a boyfriend to put down a girlfriend.

Although some girls may verbally abuse boys, especially in their early teens, even in the "worst school I found," girls who would verbally abuse other girls and even hit them were not known to batter their boyfriends. It is therefore *less common* for girls to be abusive in boyfriend/girlfriend relationships; however, some are. When girls are abusive to their boyfriends, they are either very young and immature or they are usually suffering from a personality disorder, an alcohol or drug problem, or some other emotional disturbance. This has proved to be true in more than ten years of research.

We've seen how people create pretend worlds; pretend students, sons, daughters, and so forth. An even more difficult problem can occur when boys and girls build boyfriend-girlfriend relationships. Usually teens go out on dates to movies, parties; go bicycling, walking, inline skating, swimming, and so forth to get to know each other. They both want to have a special friend in their life who cares about them and shares the ups and downs of their days with them.

I have talked with many people who didn't know what was wrong with their relationships. They felt bad in them. They thought they should feel better. They wanted their date to be happier with them. They thought they just weren't able to get across what they meant so their date would understand. They could never quite figure out why they weren't happier. Some of their friends told them they were lucky to have such a great person in their life. But these unhappy teens didn't know exactly what they were experiencing. They had never been validated. They didn't have a name for verbal abuse.

VERBAL ABUSE IN A RELATIONSHIP

When you are dating, your date will not necessarily be the person everyone else sees. Some people are just the same around everyone, but some people are very different when they are alone with a date. For that reason, it is important that you decide for yourself if your date is right for you. You cannot count on your friends' opinions. However, if all your friends have met your date, and most say that there is a problem and that they don't think this person is good for you, then you have reason to be concerned. If your friends and parents think that your date is not right for you, ask them how they formed their opinions.

When there is verbal abuse in a relationship, it is much more likely that the person who is abused will point out the problem or want to end the relationship. However, sometimes it's the other way around. The person who indulges in verbal abuse ends the relationship. This is because the abuser gives up trying to turn a real person (you) into a pretend person (an all-need-meeting dream person).

Spellbound behavior shows up most often in boyfriend-girl-friend relationships. If you recall in the chapter "Verbal Abuse at School," there was a story about the worst school I found. Both boys and girls would threaten and even physically assault any boys or girls who they thought were interested in their boyfriend or girlfriend. This happened because, in a spellbound way, they believed they owned their love interests. They couldn't see them as real people. They saw them as possessions that they owned, like objects to fight over. It is very demeaning to have someone fight over you, as if he or she had the right to decide whom you could be with, as if you had no mind of your own.

Most of the troubles in the world come from this idea that people are objects, and that other people can make their decisions for them. That is one of the reasons that it is so important that you understand how verbal abuse can gradually take over a relationship.

Verbal abuse can run rampant in couple relationships when the abuser doesn't see the other person as a real person. Instead, the abuser sees the other person as a dream person. For that reason, he or she will put down the real person, indulging in any kind of verbal abuse when the real person shows up where the dream person is supposed to be. This is the same reason that some people batter a person who is close to them. No one wants a relationship that might become verbally or physically abusive.

When teens don't understand about the spell, and don't realize that their date is really trying to erase them and fill their body, so to speak, with a dream person, they don't break off the relationship. About one-third of teens experience physical violence in dating relationships.

People who indulge in verbal abuse are under a spell, believing in a pretend world, and so they expect their partners to look, act, talk, and think like they want, as if they were, indeed, pretend people. They believe in their pretend world. They want to make it happen, and they want to rule it. In a relationship, their whole pretend world may be their date.

Since many models of dating relationships come from movies, some teens think their date is supposed to look like and act like a dream person; for instance, a glamorous singer instead of a real person.

Although spellbound people indulge in verbal abuse at times with other people, they usually are most abusive in their dating relationships. They really do act as if they lived within their significant others. They may tell them where they should go, what they should wear, how much they should weigh, what they need, what their problem is, what their sense of humor is like, or even what they are trying to do.

One of the most common arguments that comes up in dating relationships is the following: The partner says something about a particular behavior that really bothered her or him. The abuser says, "You're trying to start a fight."

Even though one person is seeking resolution, the other, being truly spellbound, pretends to know the other's motives. This, of course, is not rational behavior.

It is so important to know all you can about verbal abuse because sometimes it is very subtle, and only gets worse after a dating relationship becomes an exclusive commitment or engagement or marriage.

Your date's thinking of you as a dream person, may, at first, sound flattering, but a dream person is really only an idea of you. And if you do not think, talk, act, or be like the dream person, your date may get very angry, define you, call you names, accuse you of all kinds of things, and even hit you.

News reports of assaults on dates and on spouses are misleading if they are called "disputes" or arguments, because they are almost always attacks on real people who don't show up as dream people.

Deeply spellbound people many not accept anything that is real about you. They may be so frustrated when you don't act like their pretend dream person, that they are angry with you all the time. Of course, no one can be, or ever will be, a pretend person, a dream girl or dream boy. No one can be. A dream person is an ever-changing figment of the abuser's imagination.

Stalking a person by following them, or by phone, can happen when the abuser wants to know where the "body" is that harbors the dream person. Some girls carry a cell phone or pager so their boyfriend can keep track of them. If they don't, in some cases, their boyfriend will threaten them or assault them. In some places, girls often come to school with black eyes.

When teens are with a spellbound person for quite a while, they feel terrible, because they can't have a thought of their own, and they feel imprisoned and hated, even when hearing, "I love you."

One of the reasons some teens continue to date people who verbally abuse them, is that they begin to lose confidence from the abuse. They begin to think, "No one else would want to go out with me." The longer they stay in the relationship, the worse they feel, and the worse they feel, the more they think no one else would be there for them. It takes strength to break off a bad relationship.

Girls can put down boys just as boys can put down girls. But in boyfriend-girlfriend relationships, girls rarely batter their boyfriends. It can happen, but it is so out of context with what girls' culture is that it may be severe and dangerous. Sometimes a girl will hit back if she is hit. Anyone who is battered, or who is threatened with bodily harm, should call for help, because battering and this type of threat are against the law. And parents should also be told, even if it means giving up a verbally abusive relationship. A verbally abusive relationship is not worth having. When people are verbally abusive while in the beginning, or courting stage, of a relationship, it is a sign that the relationship will become much worse over time.

RESPONDING TO VERBAL ABUSE ON A DATE

If you experience verbal abuse on a date, it is very important that you respond immediately. You can say, "I like you, but I don't like that behavior and I will leave if it continues." If your date puts you down, defines you, gives you orders, or in any other way verbally abuses you, then it is best to date other people and not to continue dating the abusive person.

VERBAL ABUSE AND SEX

Boys may believe that their friends won't respect them as real males if they don't have sex with a girl. They may feel pressured by their friends to try to have sex before they are ready. They may be called all kinds of names that assault their sexuality if they don't have sex when they are still very young. Some twelve-year-old boys start getting this pressure from other boys.

Sometimes a boy may feel pressured by a girl who believes having sex will make her a real woman. Pressuring is done by verbal abuse. It is filled with threats, "You'll never grow up," or "I'll kill myself if you don't give in"; taunts, "Still a baby"; accusations, "Need to ask Momma first"; and name-calling, "You're a wimp." If anyone tries to coerce you to have sex before it is really right for you, he or she is being verbally abusive and that is not okay. Anyone doing this most likely grew up hearing verbal abuse and thinking it was normal. And, the verbal abuser probably thought it was okay to tell you what to do, as if he or she was you and knew what you should do and how you felt.

It is best to have the idea that since sex is never 100 percent safe from possible pregnancy, it is best to wait until you are mature enough to handle the responsibilities and the level of commitment mature sex demands.

ABOUT BOYS AND VERBAL ABUSE

Some boys may try to be tough to impress other boys in order to gain their acceptance and approval. They might grow up to think that treating girlfriends as if they were nothing, or as if they were possessions, will make them look powerful and in control, but, actually, after a while, girls usually leave verbally abusive relationships.

If you are a boy who has thought it was a good idea to impress your friends this way, please keep in mind that boys who didn't have enough loving acceptance from their fathers often feel it is very important to impress their male friends. They may seek male acceptance and approval because they didn't get it from their father.

If you meet a girl who yells at you, ridicules you, or tries to put you down, don't date her. This is not in any way culturally condoned, so when a girl is abusive, she usually has a pretty serious personality problem. It may go very deep, and you can't rescue her.

Rick Lewis of the Safe Schools Program in West Palm Beach, Florida, offers this tip for getting along with a date. Try the "Empathy Bridge." Here is how it works. When you have a different opinion or want to make a different choice than your date wants to make, for instance, where to eat dinner out, be sure to acknowledge your date's feelings and thoughts first. To do this correctly, it's a good idea to say something like, "Yes, that is a beautiful place, and the music is good." Wait two pauses: pause, pause. Then, after your pause, say, "I am concerned about the . . . (price, noise, long line, or whatever)"— absolutely do *not* say "but." This will help you to see your date as a separate person with separate views and feelings. And, it will help you to speak respectfully, instead of giving orders, "We're not eating there"; or countering, "That's a lousy place"; or discounting, "Who asked you?" Please don't forget that ordering, countering, and discounting are forms of verbal abuse.

About Girls and Verbal Abuse

There are some girls who think that boys are normally hurtful or mean or should be allowed to think they are in control of their girlfriends. This is not true. Healthy people understand mutuality and the give-and-take of relationships.

Some girls may try to please their boyfriends and to figure out what will make them happy. If these girls are put down, they may think that they need to be more pleasing. If they are abused and pushed around, they may think that they can find the key to end the abuse and gain the love they want, by just being different. Like trying different keys, they try different ways of acting.

If their boyfriends criticize them, instead of thinking, "It's nobody's business but my own what I wear, or how I do something," they think, "This is the thing I have to change so he will be happy." Some girls think that a jealous boyfriend loves them. The kind of jealousy that checks up on you and your whereabouts is a sickness. *It is not a sign of love.* It is a sign that your boyfriend can't see you as a person, and so isn't happy for your freedom and your friendships.

If you have been thinking this way, please keep in mind that girls who didn't get enough time and good attention from their fathers may feel it is important to get the approval of their boyfriends. If they saw their mothers accept demands or abuse, they may feel that they, too, must be accepting, and that it is normal to be treated as inferior.

Looking back on her teen years, a young woman talked to me about them. She said that every time she even glanced at another boy, her abusive boyfriend verbally abused her in a tyrannical rage. She thought, "He really just wants me all to himself." Now, however, she realizes that she was afraid of him and just *wanted* to believe he loved her. After she left him, she realized how much kinder and more attractive other dates were.

A boy who indulges in verbal abuse is generally so disconnected from himself that he's out there in someone's space, telling her who and what she is, as if he were she. All the while, he may think he is tough, but, to those who know what verbal abuse is about, he comes across as a coward, afraid to stand on his own two feet. He is always in his girlfriend's space, as if he lived there and knew who and what she was and how she should be and what she should do.

Some girls, looking for acceptance from boys, who don't know what verbal abuse is about, try to be "one of the boys," that is, to be like the ones who seem tough and in control. This prevents a good relationship from ever beginning.

Some girls believe that a girl is more valuable if she has a boyfriend, so even when verbally abused, most girls don't tell anyone. They don't understand why anyone would try to control them, so they blame themselves. It is very rare for a girl to reveal this, to come out and say, "He's trying to control me." It takes a lot of self-esteem to know that the abuse has nothing to do with you, that you don't deserve it, and that it is nothing to be ashamed of. It is the abuser's shame.

The famous singer Brandy told her story in *O, The Oprah Magazine* in the July 2002 issue. She set an example for girls and women. She knew that a bad relationship lowered her self-esteem, and she told the world how she didn't need that kind of thing in her life. Any teen or young woman who finds herself in a bad relationship, would be wise to get some support and move on. Most people say, "Why didn't I break that off sooner?"

If you are put down in your relationship, it is almost certain that it won't get better.

A survey of teenage girls from the ninth grade through high school revealed that one in five teen girls where the survey was conducted was assaulted by a date. Girls who were interviewed for this study said that although they were pushed at times and witnessed demonstrations of violence, like wall smashing, and were concerned that they might be hit or be sexually abused on dates, *they were most often verbally abused*. One girl who was out of high school said that she witnessed girls verbally abused in her high school, and she wondered what it was like for these girls in private if this is what they endured in public.

A fifteen-year-old girl said, "They swear at us. They don't hit us yet."[33]

COMMON QUESTIONS ABOUT BOYFRIEND-GIRLFRIEND RELATIONSHIPS

In this list, I shall call the boyfriend or girlfriend your "date."

Q. *I'm not sure if I am verbally abused or taking it wrong. How can I tell the difference?*

A. Most of the time people want to see the very best in their date and feel embarrassed and hurt to think that maybe they are hearing verbal abuse. The easiest way to tell is to notice if usually no one else is around when you hear something that makes you feel hurt. Or, if there are people around, they snicker or look uncomfortable. Next, notice if this happens when you've just expressed an opinion about something or are just feeling great, so you don't expect to hear the abuse, so you're taken by surprise.

Also, since sometimes people say things without thinking, notice if your date is quick to apologize when you say something about what you heard.

Lastly, if, for instance, you say something like, "Wouldn't it be fun to go to Blackies for pizza?" and your date says something like, "You sure try to boss me around," or "You always want things your way," then yes, you are being defined and told what you are doing. That certainly is abusive!

Q. *How can I tell if my date just had a really horrible day, didn't mean to be abusive, and never, ever will be abusive again?*

A. To answer that question and to further our example, let's suppose that you think something like, *Maybe my date is filled with worry about failing a class and is so cranky I'm not being heard right.* Now, let's say you try to explain yourself so the problem will be resolved, "Hey, I'm not trying to tell you what to do. I'm just asking if you want to go to Blackies for pizza." If your date gets mad or sullen and argues against you and tells you, "That's not what you said. Now you're trying to start a fight," and if you try to explain that you *aren't* trying to start a fight, and then you try to explain what you wanted to know in the beginning, "I want to know if you think it would be fun to go to Blackies for pizza," and your date says, "With you trying to pick a fight, why should I?" and, if by now you feel sad but you try again, explaining that you aren't trying to pick a fight, and your date counters your explanation with another accusation, you *are* in a verbally abusive relationship.

Q. *My date lets me pick places to eat but questions me about who I talk to and where I go, so I sometimes feel like my life isn't my own. Is this verbal abuse?*

A. If you say, "I really don't want to talk about it. I don't like it when you question me," or you say, "It is my own business whom I talk to; please don't question me. I'll let you know if I like someone better. So please don't worry," but your date keeps questioning you, then your date can't really hear you and doesn't want to. This would be a verbally abusive relationship. Your date appears to be jealous of your own separate life. This kind of relationship can turn from what you may have thought was a dream relationship into a nightmare.

Q. *It's hard to remember how we get in these fights. Is there any other way to tell if I'm hearing verbal abuse from my date?*

A. If you feel hurt by what you hear or by the general approach your date takes toward you, ask yourself if you were defined by your date. Sometimes it is hard to remember what happened. Following are some statements that define a person. They are all abusive.

Do you always have to start a fight?
You want me to be the "bad guy."
You're too sensitive.
You just don't have a sense of humor.
If you loved me, you would . . .

Q. *What makes these comments abusive?*

A. They are abusive because they tell you about your inner self. No one on planet Earth can go within another person and tell him or her how he or she is, how he or she feels, how he or she is made, or what he or she is trying to do or should do, and so on.

Q. *I don't think my date says anything abusive unless he is really mad at something I probably did. Is that verbally abusive?*

A. Anger directed at you, even for a mistake, is usually abusive anger. If, when he is angry about something, he calls you names or makes accusations, he is still verbally abusing you, and he may have a real problem with his anger. Abusers often get angry when they can't have their way, when they think it will silence the people they target, or when they can't make their partners be the pretend people they want.

Q. *Why does my date seem angry when I have a different opinion?*

A. A person who sees a date as a dream person, can't bear for him or her to think or behave differently from their idea of that dream person. After all, a dream person is like part of them, the part that they never experienced or developed. They don't want to lose their dream person. For them it is like losing a part of themselves. A real person cannot live in the same body as a dream person.

Q. *Can this explain why abusers get so jealous?*

A. Yes, they don't want to lose the body that harbors their dream person. That is why some abusers stalk the partner who left.

Q. *Is that why my date puts me down?*

A. It is very likely that your date puts you down so you will kind of "disappear," and there will be more room in your body for his or her dream person.

Q. *Why does my date walk away when I'm talking?*

A. A dream person is never saying what you're saying. So, your date doesn't want to hear you. *Your opinions are going to be wrong no matter what, because they can't ever exactly match what your date has in mind.*

Q. *So what most should I watch for when I am with a new date?*

A. Notice most how you feel. Do you feel hurt or happy?

Q. *How did I get into a relationship with someone who is verbally abusive? Why didn't I see it?*

A. Sometimes people get into these relationships because the person doesn't act abusively early in the relationship, but after a while acts more and more abusively.

Q. *Is there a way to tell, like a red flag?*

A. If you are defined or put down at all by your date, it probably will get a lot worse. Teens and adults who grew up with very healthy, warm, loving parents, usually find it a lot easier to spot an unhealthy person. They don't try to find logical reasons for the behavior, like "a bad day." But there are no guarantees. Even psychologists have been fooled, but only for a while!

If you heard verbal abuse when you were young, subtle verbal abuse may not stand out as a warning signal. Sometimes friends don't see it, and they may tell you it's a good relationship. That could be an influence. It is always best to trust your own experience.

Q. *Why did I go back after I told my date I was through with the relationship?*

A. Your date may seem perfectly healthy at certain times and then act abusively again. This is what makes verbally abusive relationships so confusing. You might think the good behavior is going to last.

Q. *Why does my friend stay in a verbally abusive relationship?*

A. Maybe your friend isn't ready to give up hope that things will get better, and if your friend's date is acting nice some of the time, your friend could be confused by the changes.

QUESTIONS TO ASK YOURSELF

Here are questions for you to ask yourself to find out if you are experiencing verbal abuse, or if your date sees and hears you, and talks with you in a mutual way.

Does your date:

- Ask you how you feel about things now and then?

- Ask you what you think about things now and then?
- Seem enthusiastic about things now and then?

These statements, or ones like them, show you that your date is interested in getting to know the real you. On the other hand, does your date:

- Make promises and then break them?
- Accuse you of things?
- Tell you what to do?
- Give orders instead of asking nicely?
- Act jealously or question you about your own business?
- Say, "We're . . . " or "We need . . . " without asking you first?
- Say things that hurt, but when you mention them, tell you they are just jokes?
- Say things that hurt, but when you mention them, tell you you're imagining things or that the conversation never took place?
- Do you wonder if your date really sees and hears you?
- Do you wonder how to say things right so your date won't get mad?
- When you are with your date, do you sometimes feel like you are walking through a minefield, never knowing when the next explosion will occur?

The answers are obvious indicators of a good or bad relationship. If you are pleased with the answers, then you probably have a good relationship.

STILL WONDERING?

If, after reading this far, you are still wondering if your date is under the spell, living in a pretend world and afraid to really see the real you, ask yourself if he or she has asked you engaging questions. Spellbound teens don't ask engaging questions, because they live, at least in part, in a pretend world, with a pretend partner. Rather than break the illusion, *they simply avoid any sign that their partner is a real person.* For example, a real engaging question, like, "How do you feel about giving that talk in speech class this afternoon?" would elicit a real response. Any answer would show your date that you were really you, with your own feelings and thoughts.

Usually people who verbally abuse, as well as those with an extremely high potential to become abusive, don't ask real engaging questions of their dates. They may, however, ask questions about the business of what's happening, like, "Have you got a ride to . . . ?" or "Have you got that book I wanted?" or "Did you bring my stuff?"

Sometimes everything functions as if there was a real relationship because the business of what's happening is handled well. Everything functions in terms of getting to places, deciding where to eat, deciding who will drive, and so on. Since everything functions, some teens don't notice that their boyfriend or girlfriend isn't relating to them on a personal conversational level. This kind of relationship is potentially disastrous because the person who can't relate is, likely, living in an illusion.

SOME GUIDELINES FOR DATING

- Date in groups until you are in your late teens.
- Don't drink on your dates. Call for a ride home if your driver has been drinking.
- Don't date anyone who has angry outbursts.
- Don't date anyone who rages at the world, or you, or things.
- Don't date anyone who puts down the opposite sex.

- Don't date anyone who verbally abuses in any of the ways discussed in this book.

A teacher told the following story. It illustrates a young teen's misconception about adulthood and the way women are treated.

> *I had one thirteen-year-old student walk up to me with tears in her eyes and tell me that the boys were treating the girls like women. When I questioned her further, she explained that she had written a note to a boy that she liked. The note ended up being passed around, and laughed about, with a few abusive "jokes" made about it.*
>
> *The girl seemed to believe that, as a girl, she was likable and would be well treated, but that when she became an adult woman, she would be mistreated. She was surprised that she could be mistreated while still a girl!*

What Is Healthy in a Boyfriend-Girlfriend Relationship

Have you tried to talk about your wishes and to tell your date about what bothers you, being careful to talk about your feelings with "I" statements, but been told, "you're too sensitive," or that something else is wrong with you?

A healthy person would:

- Ask, "What bothers you about what I said? Oh, I'm sorry." Or, he or she would say, "I won't make those kinds of comments anymore."
- Ask, "How do you feel? What bothered you about . . . ?"
- Rarely, if ever, slip back into the same unacceptable behavior.

- Talk over anything bothering him or her instead of beginning abusive anger.
- Listen to you respectfully and would respond with empathy. If your date had a different opinion about something, instead of trying to override you, he or she would say something like, "That's interesting, but have you thought about this . . . ?"

If you answer "yes" to any of the following questions, you might be with someone who exhibits unhealthy behavior:

- Has your date pretended to know your inner reality, to tell you what you should feel and how you should be?
- Even after asking your date not to behave in a particular way, does your date persist in the same behavior anyway?
- Do you try to say things "right" because you never know when your date will get mad or unexpectedly have an angry outburst?
- Does your date ignore you when you try to talk about how you feel, or what you think, or your opinion on something? Or, does your date angrily override you and not listen to any reason?

A LIGHT PERSPECTIVE

THE BODY SNATCHER

The phrase "body snatcher" takes on a completely new meaning when someone starts telling you what you feel and think. Do they really think they know? If you are dating someone who talks like this, you may be with the Body Snatcher type. The Body Snatcher is a person who pretends to live inside you and know you better than you know yourself.

THE ALIEN FROM ANOTHER PLANET

If your date says, "You're a part of me," it may sound like you're really close, but this person may be the Alien from Another Planet (AFAP) type. The AFAP doesn't want to let you out of sight. After all, when you're gone, a part of him or her is gone, too. If you leave, this type is apt to pursue you to the point of stalking you. Because the AFAP may really feel that you are a part of him or her, he or she may go looking for that missing part— the part that he or she has anchored in you, so to speak.

THE CREATURE FROM THE BLACK LAGOON

If you hear, "You're my whole life," you might momentarily think you are very, very important to this person. But try having a life when it seems to belong to someone else. It can feel like you've met the Creature from the Black Lagoon—someone who smothers you, owning everything you do. Like, you tell a joke, and ten minutes later the Creature tells it, getting lots of points with friends. And you say, "Hey, that was my joke," and the Creature says, "No, it wasn't. I've heard it before." Eventually the Creature will try to own your life.

THE DEAD-RIGHT DEMON

"I can't live without you"—sounds like the most dramatic commitment in the world. But the Dead-Right Demon, who will pretend to die so easily, threatens self-destruction just to win. It sounds pretty desperate, doesn't it? Some terrorists go all the way and do self-destruct. Afraid to live and let live, they seek the coward's way out. "If you won't think what I think and do what I want, you are the enemy." Many homicide-suicides come from the same mind-set.

ENGAGING QUESTIONS

If you are a teenager who is reading this, it may be hard to imagine that some people have been in a relationship for thirty or forty years with a "significant other" who has never asked them about their views or feelings. Following are some examples of asking.

- "How do you see it?"
- "What are you trying to do?"
- "Did you do it?"
- "What do you want to tell me?"
- "What bothers you about this?"
- "What outcome do you want?"
- "Can you tell me why you're saying this?"
- "What do you mean?"
- "What is your intention?"
- "Did you intend that to sound like that?"
- "Do you recall what happened?"
- "What did you hear me say?"

PATTERNS IN RELATIONSHIPS

Verbal abuse often happens in intimate relationships. Many adults recall being "kept in their place" as kids by parents or teachers who thought they had full license to say whatever they wanted to about their character or heritage simply because they were adults talking to kids.

In some of the worst-case scenarios, children accepted that kind of abuse as normal and what they deserved. Even when they tried to escape it, when they grew up and formed other relationships, they either didn't recognize it or didn't know the subtle warning signs, because no one had told them what the signs meant. Without realizing it, some got themselves back into the same abusive situation with spouses, best friends, or boy-girlfriends. Some, who grew up with abuse, unconsciously perpetuated the problem, becoming abusive without fully realizing it. Thankfully, these patterns usually can be broken.

The sad part is that abusers often miss the joy of uncoerced love or affection. They have no insight into how destructive their way of being is for the people they want to be close to. They are often shocked and embittered when their relationships end.

A CHOICE TO TOLERATE VERBAL ABUSE

Some people choose to tolerate verbal abuse because there is some value in staying in the situation. Although they know that the abuser is really weak and living in a pretend world, and that they don't deserve to be abused, they put up with it when they are getting some other value and they know it's a temporary situation.

Fourteen-year-old Jimmy was getting good money helping the local grocer, Erwin, stock his shelves. Even though Erwin was very cranky, critical, and enjoyed making cutting comments at Jimmy's expense, Jimmy stayed on the job because he knew it would be over when summer vacation ended. He just wanted the money and decided to ignore the abuse. Mean comments, which weren't funny, didn't bother him quite as much as missing a paycheck did.

Suzie, fifteen, decided to stay with a verbally abusive gymnastics coach because her family was moving in a few months and she'd soon have a really great coach. She knew that she wouldn't have to put up with the abusive coach much longer, so she decided to tolerate it for a little while more. When she considered the positives and negatives of going or staying, she decided she didn't want to lose the progress she'd made by giving up practice.

Some people have very little choice at all. If a teen suffers verbal abuse from an abusive parent, or from someone in the family who is on drugs or who is alcoholic, for instance, finding alternatives can be very difficult. Options might be talking to the school counselor, talking to an understanding relative or the parents of a friend, or attending a teen Al-Anon meeting.

The need to feel that there is someone special in your life can also make it very difficult to leave an abusive girlfriend-boyfriend relationship.

A parent may stay to protect a child or teen from another parent's unsupervised access. Often, people wait to leave until a child is old enough to testify that a parent is not fit to parent.

There are other reasons that people stay in verbally abusive relationships. Sometimes they think it is normal or that there is no choice.

Sometimes, victims have no option. They are too old, or too young, or have no way to live away from the verbal abuser. Sadly, this is the way many teens are trapped.

DEALING WITH VERBAL ABUSE

If you hear verbal abuse, rather than explain yourself, point it out whenever the abuse happens. It's important to respond immediately, but without attacking the person. Always label the verbal abuse: "That sounds like verbal abuse." That way, the person who is doing it may realize that it is not normal conversation.

People who indulge in verbal abuse may want to change once they realize that they've been telling people what they are. For instance, most people don't want to come across as pretending to be their dates, but this is exactly what they are doing when they define their date's reality.

SAMPLE RESPONSES TO VERBAL ABUSE FROM A DATE

- "Don't take that book bag. You look like a nerd with it."
  Sample Response: "Were you asking me or giving me orders? I wonder if you realize that ordering and name-calling are both forms of verbal abuse."
- "Are those your mother's clothes or are you auditioning for bag lady?"
  Sample Response: "Did you know that your sarcasm is insulting and is a form of verbal abuse? I don't accept verbal abuse."
- "You're a pain in the you-know-what."
  Sample Response: "Verbal abuse is, too. I've decided not to verbally abuse anyone, and I will not accept verbal abuse from anyone."

TEENS TEACHING TEENS: DATING DRAMA

This drama can be put on by two students to show how a boy and girl resolve a conflict. It is a nonabusive interaction with positive resolution.[34]

Situation: Jim and Sue, who have been going together for six months, are discussing what to do on Friday night.

Sue: "I'd really like to go to a movie, just the two of us. We've gone out with your friends the past two weekends. I like them and all, but I'd really like to be alone with you on Friday."

Jim: "But Sue, I already told Bo and Darla that we'd go to Jake's Pizza with them on Friday."

Sue: "You set a date for both of us without asking me? Jim, I don't like that. Please don't do that anymore."

Jim: "I figured I'd surprise you. Besides, last week you said you'd like to go to Jake's sometime soon. I knew you wanted to go, otherwise I wouldn't have set the date without discussing it first."

Sue: "I do like the place, and usually it would be fine. I just wanted to be alone with you. When we're out with Bo and Darla, you usually end up talking with Bo most of the time. Darla's okay, but . . . it's just not the same when we go out with other people. You know what I mean?"

Jim: "Yeah, I get it. Listen, how about if we go out with Bo and Darla on Friday, then go to the movies by ourselves on Saturday?"

Sue: "I can't. I told you I have to work on Saturday."

Jim: "Oh, yeah. That's right. How about Sunday afternoon?"

Sue: "Oh, all right. Just do me a favor. From now on, would you ask me before you set plans for us on Friday night?"

Jim: "OK. That's a deal."

Endnotes

1. Patricia Evans, *Controlling People: How to Recognize, Understand, and Deal with People Who Try to Control You.* Adams Media Corporation, 2002.
2. "The Psychological Maltreatment of Children—Technical Report" by Steven W. Kairys, M.D., M.P.H.; Charles F. Johnson, M.D.; and the Committee on Child Abuse and Neglect. *Pediatrics,* Vol. 109, No. 4, April 2002, p. 68. Available online at *www.pediatrics.org/cgi/content/full/109/4/e68.* Accessed 24 April 2002.
3. M. A. Straus and C. Field, *Psychological Aggression by American Parents: National Data on Prevalence, Chronicity, and Severity.* Washington, D.C.: American Sociological Association, 2000.
4. See *The Verbally Abusive Relationship: How to Recognize It and How to Respond,* by Patricia Evans, Adams Media Corporation, 1992, 1996; and *Verbal Abuse Survivors Speak Out: On Relationship and Recovery,* by Patricia Evans, Adams Media Corporation, 1993.
5. Developed by the National School Safety Center. © 1998, Dr. Ronald D. Stephens, Executive Director.

6. "Bruised Inside: What Our Children Say about Youth Violence, What Causes It, and What We Need to Do about It." A report of the National Association of Attorneys General. April 2000.

7. NIMH—Suicide Facts. The National Institute of Mental Health, on the Web at *www.nimh.nih.gov/research/suifact.htm.*

8. The National Association of Anorexia Nervosa and Associated Disorders, on the Web at *www.anad.org.*

9. *Pediatrics,* Vol. 109, No. 4, April 2002.

10. Excerpt from press release July 27, 1999, by the American Academy of Pediatrics.

11. *Checklist of Characteristics of Youth Who Have Caused School-Associated Violent Deaths,* developed by the National School Safety Center. ©1998, Dr. Ronald D. Stephens, Executive Director.

12. "'Dog Eat Dog' has rough spots." *Contra Costa Times,* June 17, 2002, p. D1, by TV critic Chuck Barney.

13. "AAP Outlines Medical Concerns for Female Athletes." Press Release, Tuesday, September 5, 2000, from a policy statement published in the September issue of *Pediatrics.*

14. *Pediatrics,* Vol. 109, No. 4, April 2002.

15. Testimony of the American Academy of Pediatrics on Media Violence before the U.S. Senate Commerce Committee. Presented by Donald E. Cook, M.D., FAAP AAP President, September 13, 2000.

16. Adapted with permission from "Verbal Abuse and Sports," by Patricia Evans, at *www.VerbalAbuse.com.*

17. Adapted with permission from "Verbal Abuse and Sports," by Patricia Evans, at *www.VerbalAbuse.com.*

18. For more information on how people connect to people in a backward way, see *Controlling People,* by Patricia Evans, Adams Media Corporation, 2001.

19. "Bruised Inside: What Our Children Say about Youth Violence, What Causes It, and What We Need to Do about It." A report of the National Association of Attorneys General. April 2000, p. 25.

20. "The Psychological Maltreatment of Children— Technical Report" by Steven W. Kairys, M.D., M.P.H.; Charles F. Johnson, M.D.; and the Committee on Child Abuse and Neglect. Available at *www.AAP.org*, the Web site of the American Association of Pediatrics.

21. List adapted from *Domestic Violence Response Training Curriculum*, November 1991, by Jeri Martinez. For more information, visit *www.syntac.net/hoax/stock.php*.

22. "Bruised Inside: What Our Children Say about Youth Violence, What Causes It, and What We Need to Do about It." A report of the National Association of Attorneys General. April 2000, p. 25.

23. For in-depth information about the process of discon- nection and the pretend world, see *Controlling People*, by Patricia Evans, Adams Media Corporation, 2001.

24. *The Out-of-Sync Child: Recognizing and Coping with Sensory Integration Dysfunction*, by Carol Stock Kranowitz, Berkeley Publishing Group, a Division of Putnam, 1998.

25. "Bruised Inside: What Our Children Say about Youth Violence, What Causes It, and What We Need to Do about It." A report of the National Association of Attorneys General. April 2000.

26. "The Psychological Maltreatment of Children— Technical Report" by Steven W. Kairys, M.D., M.P.H.; Charles F. Johnson, M.D.; and the Committee on Child Abuse and Neglect. *Pediatrics*, Vol. 109, No. 4, April 2002.

27. Reprinted with permission of Will Sinclair High School.

28. "Scars That Won't Heal: The Neurobiology of Child Abuse," Martin H. Teicher, *Scientific American,* March 2002, pp. 69, 70.

29. "From Parent Verbal Abuse to Teenage Physical Aggression?" *Child and Adolescent Social Work* journal, 2000, Vol. 17, No. 6 (December), pp. 411–430.

30. The information for this fact sheet was excerpted from the following book that was developed by CSPV through a grant from the W. T. Grant Foundation: Lorion, R. P. (1998). *Exposure to Urban Violence: Contamination of the School Environment.* In D. S. Elliott, B. Hamburg, & K. R. Williams (Editors), *Violence in American Schools: A New Perspective* (pp. 293–311). New York, NY: Cambridge University Press.

31. Adapted with permission from a training program developed by Rick Lewis, Training Coordinator, Safe Schools Center, Palm Beach County School District, Florida.

32. "Bruised Inside: What Our Children Say about Youth Violence, What Causes It, and What We Need to Do about It." A report of the National Association of Attorneys General. April 2000.

33. "Study: One in Five Teen Girls in Mass. Assaulted by Dates," by Michael Lasalandra and Susan O'Neill, *Boston Herald,* Wednesday, August 1, 2001, p. 16.

34. Printed with permission from Rick Lewis, Training Coordinator, Safe Schools Center, Palm Beach County School District, Florida. From Teacher Training Program by Rick Lewis.

Sample School Harassment Policy

Wild Rose School Division Policies, Will Sinclair High School, has adopted a ZERO TOLERANCE policy for personal and sexual harassment. Students need to know that harassment violates human and civil rights. We take a serious stand on this issue and our community support in this regard is substantial. Violators will be dealt with properly and with consequences. The school policy is at *www.wrsd.ca.* Policy printed with permission of Will Sinclair High School.

SCHOOL POLICY

A student shall conduct him/herself so as to comply reasonably with the following code of conduct:

A. Be diligent in pursuing his/her studies.
B. Attend school regularly and punctually.
C. Cooperate fully with everyone authorized by the school board.
D. Comply with the rules of the school.
E. Be accountable for his/her own conduct.
F. Respect the rights of others.

As in any public place, there are expected rules of conduct at Will Sinclair High School. The underlying rule is one of respect; something all persons at the school should expect from others and should show to the people, the building, and the area around Will Sinclair High School. Following are the specific rules that everyone is expected to observe:

HARASSMENT POLICY

Here is how the Will Sinclair High School describes harassment. As you can see, it goes a long way toward preventing verbal abuse.

1. Harassment has an intent and/or effect of putting down, abusing or hurting someone, and this creates an intimidating, hostile, and offensive school and learning environment.
2. Personal Harassment is any behavior, verbal or non-verbal, that is hurtful or humiliating to another person.
3. Sexual Harassment is any unwanted verbal or non-verbal behavior that is sexual in nature.

These are types of behavior which constitute personal harassment:

a. Unwelcome remarks, jokes and innuendoes, re: age, national, or ethnic origin, gender, disability, appearance or race.
b. Gestures or staring of an intimidating nature.
c. Any other kind of intimidation.

These are types of behavior which constitute sexual harassment:

a. Unwelcome sexual remarks, jokes, or innuendoes, re: body, attire, or behavior.
b. Leering or gestures of a sexual nature.
c. Intimidation with sexual overtones.
d. Unnecessary physical contact such as: touching, pinching, fondling.

Action to be taken:

1. Tell the offender to stop. "Your behavior is offensive, stop doing it." (If the situation is not resolved or if you are unable to talk to the person harassing you, then go to step 2.)

2. Advise your teacher or counselor of the problem.
3. Administration is advised of the problem.
4. If the complaint is substantiated, appropriate action will be taken.

PHYSICAL OR VERBAL ABUSE

Under no circumstances will physical or verbal abuse towards anyone at the school be tolerated. For effective education to occur, school must be considered a safe place, and those who work towards destroying that "safe" atmosphere will not be allowed to remain at the school.

ALCOHOL, ILLEGAL DRUGS, AND SMOKING

As educators, we can only advise students as to the difficulties alcohol or drugs can create. However, we are able to demand that students committed to our school avoid the use of drugs or alcohol during the time school is in session or during school sponsored activities. Any student who challenges this demand, faces suspension and/or recommendation of expulsion from Will Sinclair High School. Where illegal acts occur it is the position of our school to inform the R.C.M.P. and follow through with charges where appropriate.

Smoking and use of smokeless tobacco is prohibited in Will Sinclair High School and is also barred from Will Sinclair High School grounds. Failure to abide by this rule may result in suspension from school.

DEFIANCE OF AN ADULT

When any adult at the school makes a reasonable request, a student has the responsibility to respond accordingly. Unreasonable requests should be discussed with the school administration. Outright defiance will be considered a major disciplinary situation.

PROFANITY

Will Sinclair High School, or any other public area, is not the place for profanity. All persons in the school must recognize the need for appropriate language. In short, no profanity is the order of the day (barring you hit your toe unexpectedly on the volleyball standard).

APPENDIX B

RESOURCES

ALCOHOL

AA (Alcoholics Anonymous)
Phone: Directory assistance or (888) 4AL-ANON
Web site: *www.alcoholics-anonymous.org*

Alateen
Web site: *www.al-anon.org/alateen.html*
Alateen is a fellowship of young Al-Anon members, usually teenagers, whose lives have been affected by someone else's drinking. If you or someone you know might have a problem related to overconsumption of alcohol, this is the place to start getting help.

Students Against Destructive Decisions (SADD)
Web site: *www.saddonline.com*
SADD's goal is to provide students with the best prevention and intervention tools possible to deal with the issues of underage drinking, other drug use, impaired driving, and other destructive decisions.

AUTISM

Autism Society of America
Phone: (800) 3AUTISM
Web site: *www.autism-society.org*

DOMESTIC VIOLENCE

The National Child Abuse Hotline
Phone: (800) 422-4453

National Domestic Violence Hotline
Phone: (800) 799-SAFE
Web site: *www.ndvh.org*

National Organization for Victim Assistance
Phone: (800) TRY-NOVA
Web site: *www.try-nova.org*

National Resource Center on Domestic Violence
Phone: (800) 537-2238

EATING DISORDERS

National Association of Anorexia Nervosa and Associated Disorders (ANAD)
Address: P.O. Box 7, Highland Park, IL 60035
Hotline: (847) 831-3438
Fax: (847) 433-4632
E-mail: *info@anad.org*
Web site: *www.anad.org*

If you or someone you know might have an eating disorder, this is the place to start. The National Association of Anorexia Nervosa and Associated Disorders—ANAD—is the first nonprofit educational and self-help organization in America dedicated to alleviating eating disorders of this type. There are also self-help groups for victims and parents, educational and early detection programs, and a listing of therapists and hospitals treating anorexics.

HYPERACTIVITY DISORDERS

CHADD (Children and Adults with Attention-Deficit/ Hyperactivity Disorder)
Phone: 1-800-233-4050 (Monday–Friday, 8:15 A.M.–5:15 P.M. Eastern time)
Web site: *www.CHAD.org*

A national nonprofit organization in response to the frustration and sense of isolation experienced by parents and their children with AD/HD.

RAPE

Rape, Abuse, and Incest National Network
Phone: (800) 656-HOPE
Web site: *www.feminist.com/rainn.htm*

SUICIDE

National Hopeline Network
Phone: (800) SUICIDE or (800) 784-2433
Web site: *www.hopeline.com*

VERBAL ABUSE

VerbalAbuse.com
Web site: *www.VerbalAbuse.com*
For more information about verbal abuse, resources, books, services, and a bulletin board for immediate support, check out this Web site.

YOUTH SPORTS

Positive Coaching Alliance helps players develop good sportsmanship habits through drills, discussion, and modeling sportsmanlike behavior. The organization offers training and publishes a newsletter. They state the following: "As a local Partner, your organization will continually receive tools and strategies that can dramatically reduce negative incidents and encourage a positive environment for all involved in the youth sports setting." Check out their Web site at *www.positivecoach.org* or e-mail them from the site for more information.

Athletes for a Better World provides a code for living for your school/team that you can download and use in your school/team's mission statement. Check it out at *www.aforbw.org/CodeForLiving/Index.html.*

Index

See also communication
silent treatment, 80, 108
South Park, 89–90, 94
spellbound people, 18–20
  and code of silence,
    47–51
  defending against,
    167–68
  exclusion by, 151–52,
    154
  failure to mature, 245
  reactions of, 32, 159
  refusals to apologize,
    157
  resistance to spell-
    breakers, 247–49
  in romantic relationships,
    256–59
  self-perceptions of, 150,
    167
  and verbal abuse at
    home, 112–13
  See also pretending;
    pretend worlds
spell-breakers, 167–68,
  173–79, 229–31, 247–50
sports, 42, 44, 90–91,
  96–100, 292–93
Springfield, Ore., 57
stalking, 259
Stockholm syndrome,
  118–19
Students Against

Destructive Decisions
  (SADD), 290
suicide, 66–67, 292
superiority, 30, 36
support, 177, 202, 224, 225
Survivor, 43, 89

T

taping, 209–10
targets, 154–55
teachers
  handling of verbal abuse,
    37–38, 123–25, 133,
    137–38
  prevention of verbal
    abuse, 215–17
  responses to, 242–43
  and stopping verbal
    abuse, 171–72, 220–25
  verbal abuse by, 127–29,
    180, 211–15, 226
  verbal abuse of, 218–19
  See also schools
teens
  culture, 160
  immunity to verbal
    abuse, 246–47
  motives for verbal abuse,
    243–44
  values of, 35
  worlds of, 35–46
television, 59, 87–95, 90,

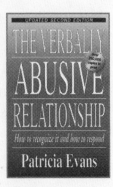

Verbal Abuse Survivors Speak Out
On Relationship and Recovery

Verbal Abuse Survivors Speak Out draws upon the experience of thousands who responded to Patricia Evans' first book, *The Verbally Abusive Relationship*. Their letters highlight Evans' in-depth exploration of verbal abuse issues and bring increasing clarity and insight to the reader. You will learn the stories of other women who have struggled against the fear and oppression engendered by verbal abuse, and have made the decision to insist on a change. Some of these women are just beginning to understand the problem, some are planning to leave their relationships, some have already left, and some, with their spouse, have made a commitment to change their relationship for the better. Their stories can give validation to suspicions and fears, and can provide courage, hope, and a road map for healing and recovery.

Trade paperback, 5½" x 8½", 224 pages, $10.95
ISBN: 1-55850-304-8

Available wherever books are sold.
For more information, or to order, call 800-872-5627
or visit *www.adamsmedia.com*
Adams Media Corporation, 57 Littlefield Street, Avon, MA 02322

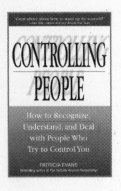